SUBMARINES

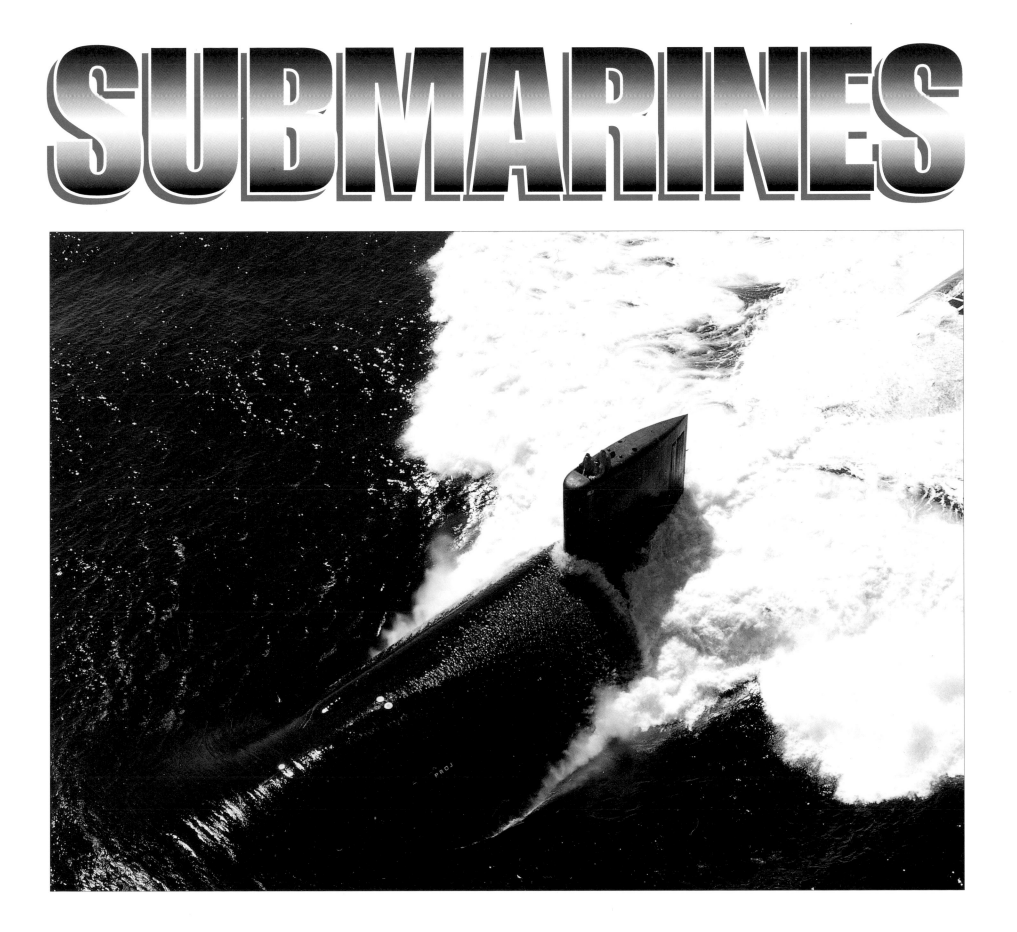

SUBMARINES

Leviathans of the Deep

T. L. Francis

MetroBooks

MetroBooks

An Imprint of Friedman/Fairfax Publishers

©2000, 1997 by Michael Friedman Publishing Group, Inc.

Library of Congress Cataloging-in-Publication Data Available Upon Request.

ISBN 1-56799-427-X

Editor: Sharyn Rosart
Art Director / Designer: Kevin Ullrich
Photography Editor: Kathryn Culley

Color separations by HBM Print Ltd.
Printed in Hong Kong by C & C Offset Printing Co., Ltd.

10 9 8 7 6 5 4 3 2

For bulk purchases and special sales, please contact:
Friedman/Fairfax Publishers
Attention: Sales Department
15 West 26th Street
New York, NY 10010
212/685-6610 FAX 212/685-1307

Visit our website:
www.metrobooks.com

Page 1: *Columbia* (SSN-771).

Page 2: Submarines *Salmon* (SS-182), Seal (SS-183), *Pickerel* (SS-177), *Plunger* (SS-179), *Snapper* (SS-185), and *Permit* (SS-178) in a nest at San Diego in 1940.

Page 3: Depth gauge from *Ling* (SS-297).

Page 4-5: Five S-class boats at Pearl Harbor some time in the 1930s.

Page 8-9: Six O-class submarines in the Central American-Caribbean area, circa 1923-24.

Page 10-11: *Robert E. Lee* (SSBN-601) at Newport News, Virginia, circa 1960.

Page 12-13: *Rhode Island* (SSBN-740).

DEDICATION

To my mother and father.

ACKNOWLEDGEMENTS

I have dedicated this book to my parents because I owe so much to their good influence on my life and work. Among the many things they taught me was an appreciation of learning, having a critical eye towards all things, and the benefits of reserving judgment until one has time to reflect on a subject. This book would not have been possible without them.

This work is the result of the contributions and support of a number of people, not all of whom can be named in the space available. Scott Price of the Coast Guard Historian's Office was particularly helpful. At the Naval Historical Center I must thank both Glenn E. Helm, a librarian and friend at the Navy Department Library, and Richard A. Russell, a historian in the Contemporary History Branch, for their friendly advice and assistance. My coworkers in the Ships' Histories Branch, C. Kevin Hurst, Raymond A. Mann, and John C. Reilly, Jr., are both friends and colleagues. I would also like to thank Mark L. Hayes and Gary E. Weir for their help with this project.

I should also thank Sharyn Rosart, Kevin Ullrich, and Kathryn Culley at Friedman Fairfax Publishers: they were at all times both enthusiastic and professional. For picture reference assistance, I thank John Donaldson, Public Affairs, U.S. Atlantic Fleet; and Lt. Cmdr. Hal Pittman and Lt. Edward Bucletin, Media Operations, Office of Information, Department of the Navy. Lt. N. Seguna, Media Liaison Office, Director General Public Affairs, National Defense HQ, Canada, also deserves mention.

Most of all I must thank my wife, Meredith E. Eriksen. It was her drive that overcame my temperamental nature, in this and other projects.

In conclusion, I hope this book serves as a partial introduction to the complexity and uncertainty inherent in all navies, and submarines in particular. All erroneous judgements and misinterpretations are mine alone.

Contents

Introduction 12

Chapter 1
The Limitations of Technology 14

Chapter 2
The Great War 32

Chapter 3
Interlude 1919–1939 48

Chapter 4
The Second World War: Submarines Triumphant 62

Chapter 5
The Search for a Strategy 92

Chapter 6
The Secret War 110

Chapter 7
The World Outside the Cold War 126

Bibliography 140

Index 142

Introduction

Can you draw out Leviathan with a fishhook,
or press down his tongue with a cord?
Can you put a rope in his nose,
or pierce his jaw with a hook? …
Can you fill his skin with harpoons,
or his head with fishing spears?
Lay hands on him;
think of the battle; you will not do it again!

Job 41: 1–2, 7–8

Sailors and shipwrights throughout time have savored the old and seductive idea of a boat that might dive beneath the sea, attack and sink enemy ships with impunity, and return to the surface. What we now call the submarine, an underwater boat hidden beneath the sea surface, has fascinated inventors for millennia. The first practical submarines did not appear until the late 1800s. Uniformly small, leaky, and dangerous, they were no match for surface warships. As technology improved over the years, however, and submariners gained experience during two world wars, the submarine soon matched its surface opponents in range and lethal capabilities. In the early 1960s, dramatic advances in nuclear propulsion and sea-launched intercontinental ballistic missiles elevated these once puny craft to the ranks of the most powerful warships in the world. They became true Leviathans of the deep.

The *Robert E. Lee* (SSBN-601) fitting out at Newport News, Virginia, sometime during 1960. The third nuclear-powered ballistic missile submarine to join the U.S. fleet, and the first to be built at Newport News, the *Robert E. Lee* joined the SSBN squadron at Holy Loch, Scotland, in 1961. The submarine conducted deterrent patrols in the Atlantic and Pacific until it was decommissioned on December 1, 1983.

Submersible or Submarine?

An interesting technical distinction exists between "submersible" and "submarine." Although both are called "boats," a slang term from the days when submarines were little different from torpedo boats, a submersible is designed for surface operations but has the capability to submerge for short periods of time. The famous diesel-electric submarines of the world wars, for example, were actually submersibles.

A true submarine, on the other hand, is specifically designed to cruise underwater. Only nuclear-powered submarines fit this definition, since, with virtually unlimited fuel, they can remained submerged for months without breaking the surface. Since common usage has come to refer to all underwater warships as submarines, that is the convention used in these pages.

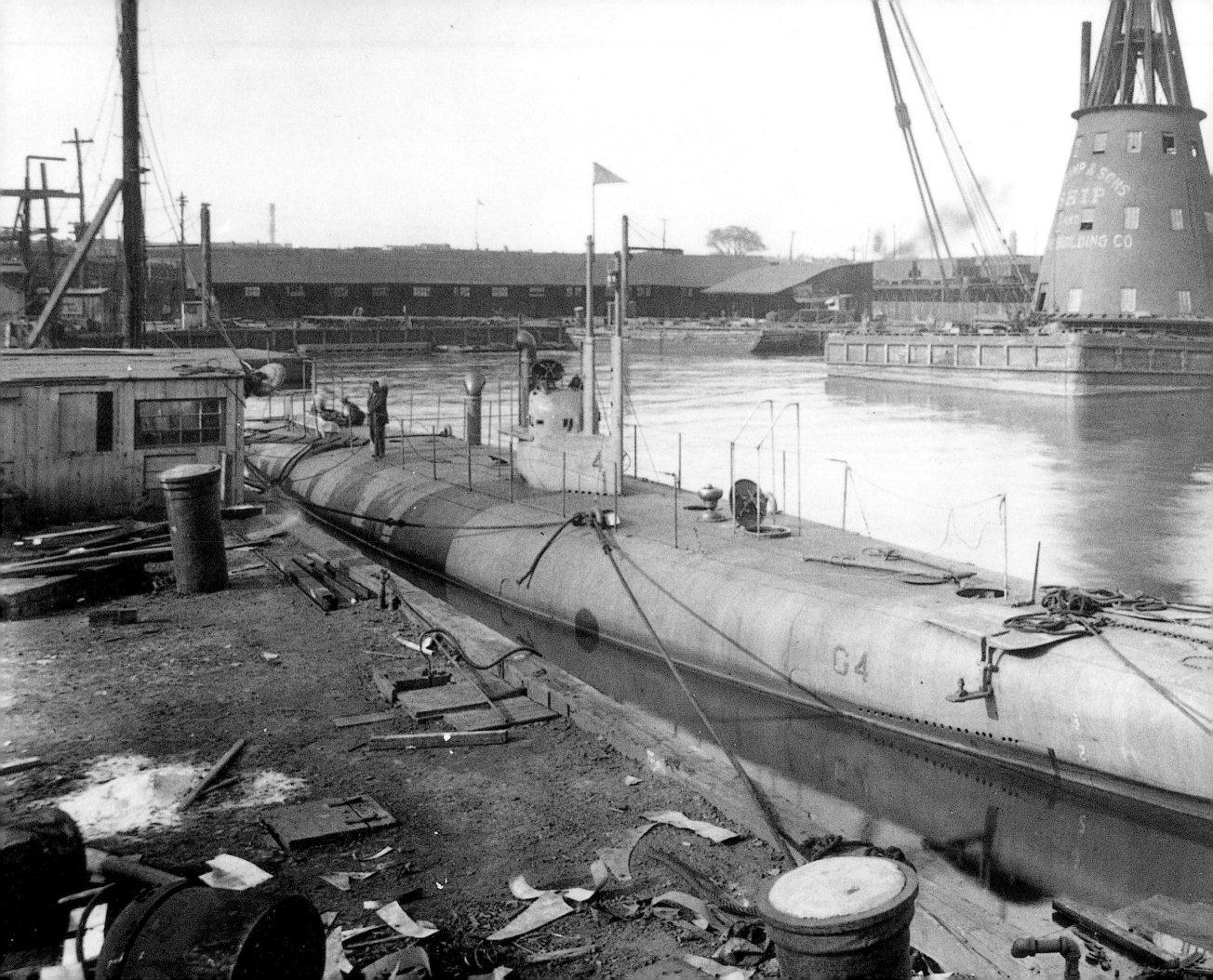

Chapter 1

The Limitations of Technology

HOW TO TRANSPORT SAILORS BELOW THE SURFACE OF THE SEA AND SAFELY bring them back up has perplexed engineers for thousands of years. Ancient Greek and Roman authors recorded many failed attempts to build submersible craft. Muslim, Chinese, and Renaissance inventors reportedly tried similar experiments with wood, oil-soaked animal hide, and hand-powered oars, but they, too, met little success.

The first authenticated machine was created by Cornelius Drebbel, a Dutch inventor working for James I in England. Drebbel built a wood and greased-leather submersible in 1620. Later reports include a forty-man Russian submersible made of wood and cowhide that tried to attack Turkish ships in 1643, and a cone-shaped, copper-plated wooden diving bell that John Lethbridge used to make descents in Marseille harbor in 1730. Because these devices either wallowed just a few feet below the surface or did little more than drift with the tide, they offered little military or practical value.

The end of the eighteenth century saw the first substantial progress toward a modern submarine. Improvements in the iron industry enabled inventors to tinker with submersibles built with iron plates, gears, and other metal parts. Originally, iron ore was forged using charcoal fuel and water-powered leather bellows, and tempered by a blacksmith pounding it with a hammer. Lack of wood for charcoal, contaminants in the little charcoal available, and tired blacksmith arms made iron a rare, brittle, and expensive product.

The replacement of charcoal with coking coal, which had fewer impurities, and the development of steam-powered machine hammers and bellows lowered the cost dramatically, while simultaneously increasing both quality and reliability. By 1784, the Englishman Henry Cort had established a coal-powered and steam-heated rolling mill that produced a stronger, more standardized, and cheaper iron than ever before.

Britain's shift to iron, steam, and coal power provides a good analogy for the development of working submarines. The first improvements in metal and steam engines were made by men who knew little about the science of metallurgy and the discipline of mechanical engineering. Science followed technology in those first ventures, with theory trailing the invention. Engineers were like amateur cooks who learn what

G4, later *Thrasher* (SS-26), lying unfinished at her building yard, William Cramp & Sons, in Philadelphia. The photograph was taken on October 2, 1912, six weeks after launching and over a year before her commissioning on January 22, 1914.

A fanciful drawing of a wooden submersible. The lion pennant and the Dutch ensign on the ship in the background confirm it as the "Rotterdam ship" of 1654. Presumably, it was intended to defend that port against the English.

Nautilus and obtained a grant in 1800 to build it for Napoleon. Cigar-shaped, it had a three-man crew, a sail for movement on the surface, and a single hand-cranked propeller for underwater propulsion. Like Bushnell's *Turtle*, Fulton's *Nautilus* was quite slow and the French government eventually grew impatient and gave up on the project.

Over the next half century, other inventors experimented with similar submarines. William Bauer, a Bavarian artilleryman serving at the port of Kiel in 1849, during the Schleswig-Holstein War, sketched plans for an underwater boat to fight the Danish blockade. The following year Bauer built *Der Brandtaucher* (literally, Diving Incendiary), using iron plates over a wood-and-iron frame. This submarine had hand-powered water pumps, a single rudder, and a treadmill-powered propeller. During trials in Kiel harbor, however, *Der Brandtaucher* descended too far,

Below: Robert Fulton's *Nautilus* is a far more elegant vessel. The large heptagonal construction above the conning tower is a folding sail, provided for surface propulsion. Note the "horn" protruding vertically out of the tower. Like Bushnell's *Turtle*, this device would allow a torpedo to be attached to the bottom of an enemy vessel.

works long before they learn why. As the whys became clearer in both metallurgy and engineering, the inventor built on that knowledge to create new wonders for theorists to explain. Industrialization, and the development of early submarines, came as much from an infinite number of small advances as it did from dramatic new ideas.

Submarine experiments in the late 1700s progressed along with the growth of general industrialization in western Europe and America. Advances in mathematical and engineering principles led to an understanding of fundamental submarine issues such as water pressure, buoyancy, metal gears, and construction tolerances. In 1776, David Bushnell built the *Turtle*, an iron-banded oak submersible, to fight the British blockade of Boston Harbor. The *Turtle* stealthily crept just under the water surface by using a floodable ballast tank and two hand-cranked propellers. However, copper-sheathing on the British warship hulls frustrated three attempts by *Turtle* to attach a gunpowder charge to the blockading ships.

But the submarine concept still seemed sound to the era's inventors. Twenty years later, Robert Fulton designed a three-man metal submarine called

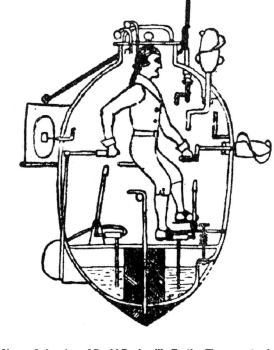

Above: A drawing of David Bushnell's *Turtle.* The operator is holding the rudder with his left hand while turning the horizontal propeller with his right hand. The vertical propeller is just above that, and the screw for attaching a "torpedo," or underwater bomb, to an enemy hull points vertically toward the top of the picture. A very ungainly contraption.

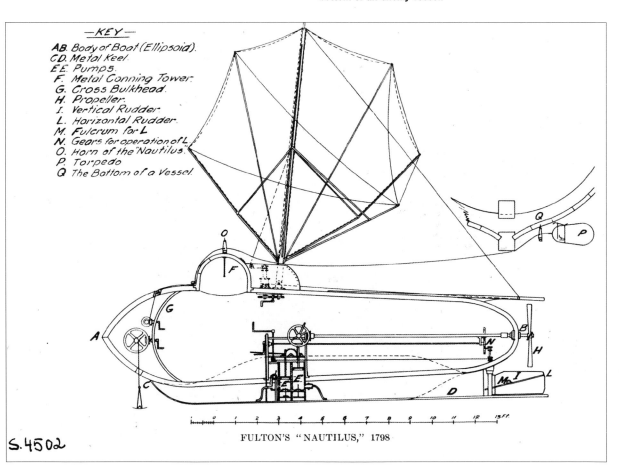

— KEY —
AB. Body of Boat (Ellipsoid).
CD. Metal Keel.
EE. Pumps.
F. Metal Conning Tower.
G. Cross Bulkhead.
H. Propeller.
I. Vertical Rudder.
L. Horizontal Rudder.
M. Fulcrum for L.
N. Gears for operation of L.
O. Horn of the 'Nautilus'.
P. Torpedo.
Q. The Bottom of a Vessel.

S. 4502

FULTON'S "NAUTILUS," 1798

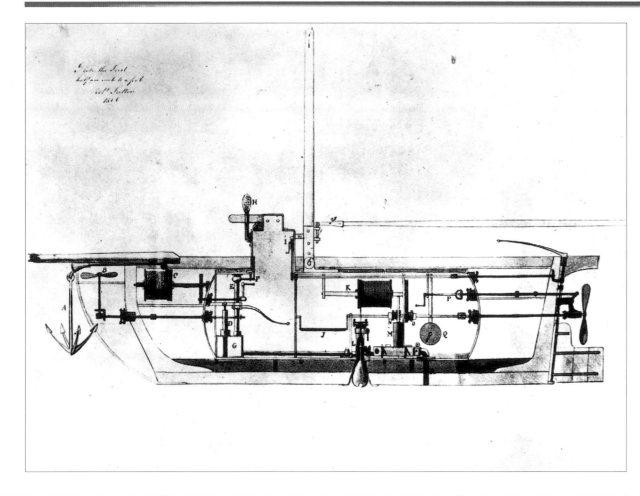

The drawings above, left and right, are plates from Robert Fulton's *Drawings and Descriptions*. On the left is an interior view of one of his submersible ideas, while the plate on the right shows the same vessel, pictured submerged (below) and under full sail. Fulton, despite the primitive state of his technology, had grasped the essential idea that a submersible needed a conning tower for viewing the surface, a rear propeller, and some sort of motive power (a hand crank below water, sails above) to provide movement. Submarine designers would struggle with these issues for almost another century before a practical submarine was realized. Left: This undated woodcut illustrates William Bauer's idea of using an underwater boat to attack the Danish Navy's ships blockading Kiel in 1849. The picture shows a submersible delivering an explosive charge against a Danish ironclad. It was probably pictures like these that helped Bauer sell his ideas to the Russian Navy.

and with leaking valves and blown rivets, took on water and sank to a depth of forty-nine feet (14.7m). Incredibly, after waiting six hours for the pressure to equalize, Bauer and two crewmen were able to open the hatch and float to the surface in a bubble of air.

All these boats, including others that Bauer built for Russia in 1855 and two twenty-foot (6m) craft that Lodner Phillips built and tested in Lake Michigan in 1851, shared several basic limitations. First, human muscles simply could not propel a submarine more than a very short distance without exhausting the crew and, incidentally, quickly using up all the available air. Second, the wood and iron materials made it difficult to produce a waterproof craft, and, even if watertight on the surface, most of these submarines could not stand the water pressure of even ten to twenty feet (3–6m) without leaking alarmingly.

The American Civil War

Soon after the outbreak of the American Civil War, the southern states found themselves facing the far superior Union navy. Unable to fight back with conventional naval forces, the Confederacy turned to the efforts of submarine and ironclad builders to help lift the North's blockades. Ironclads—wooden ships fitted with iron plates along the sides—supposedly ensured invulnerability to most guns of the time.

Submarines, meanwhile, were seen as supplementary craft for safely attacking the wooden ships of the Union blockade force. When the Union reacted to the Confederate construction of ironclads with a much larger program of its own, the submarine became even more attractive to the South, since it promised a way around the heavy side armor of the new Union ironclads. By submerging, the submarine could attack the ironclads where they were most vulnerable—below the water line.

In 1861, two small hand-powered submarines were built in New Orleans and Mobile. Constructed of old boiler iron, and propelled by a single hand-crank, both were lost before they could mount an attack on Union warships. One of the sponsors of those early boats, Horace L. Hunley, financed the construction of a third submarine at Mobile in the spring of 1863. Built under the direction of two Confederate army engineers, Lieutenants W. A. Alexander and G. E. Dixon, the thirty-foot (9m) long and four-foot (1.2m) wide submarine had a single propeller driven by a hand-powered crankshaft. Eight crew members turned the crank while a ninth navigated via glass portholes. In August 1863, the submarine was sent by rail to Charleston, South Carolina, for testing.

During trials the boat sank twice, drowning thirteen men, including Hunley. Raised and reconditioned after the second disaster, engineers adjusted the ballast so that the submarine floated with only portholes showing above the water. The intended target, the Union blockader *New Ironsides*, lay anchored in shallow water; the Confederates equipped the submarine with a spiked-charge on a pole ahead of the bow. The idea was to ram *New Ironsides* with this spar torpedo and explode the gunpowder charge against the enemy hull. For more than three months the submarine tried to close on a block-

Left: The *David* torpedo boat aground in Charleston Harbor. Note the steam-engine stacks rising vertically out of the cigar-shaped hull and the wicked looking spar-torpedo forward. An explosive charge would be attached to the end during operations. Above: This photograph, taken September 4, 1924, shows Frederick Wehner, a Confederate veteran, standing next to *Pioneer*. The submersible had been raised from New Orleans harbor, sent to Camp Nicholls, the Louisiana Home for Confederate Soldiers, and put on display as shown. Wehner is leaning on the propeller shaft.

ader, but failed every time because of tides, strong winds, and the exhaustion of the crew.

Named CSS *H.L. Hunley* in honor of its doomed designer, the boat made another attempt on the night of February 17, 1864. Under moonlight, the Confederate submarine managed to approach the USS *Housatonic*, a steam sloop-of-war anchored in the shallows. The *Housatonic*'s crew failed to see the submersible until it had come too close to be hit with the sloop's big guns. In a vain attempt to avoid damage, the Union sailors slipped the anchor cable and attacked the submarine with small arms, but *H.L. Hunley*'s torpedo struck just abaft the mizzenmast and tore a gaping hole in *Housatonic*'s hull. *H.L. Hunley* was also damaged by the explosion and went down with all hands, but it holds the distinction of being the first submarine to sink a warship in combat.

Meanwhile, other Confederate engineers in Charleston were working on a steam-driven submarine design. Like the modified *H.L. Hunley*, these boats were not even submersibles in the strict sense of the word. Designed to take on water ballast and

operate very low in the water, the fifty-foot (15m) cigar-shaped boats carried a sixty- to seventy-pound (27–31kg) explosive charge on the end of a spar fixed to the bow. One submarine, named *David* in a pointed biblical reference, had a small steam engine for propulsion. On October 5, 1863, *David* attacked the Union blockader *New Ironsides*, damaging but not sinking the ironclad steamer when the torpedo exploded too high on the hull.

David survived the attack, however, and over the next six months made at least two other runs on Union ships. Neither of these attacks succeeded and no other attempts appear in the Confederate records. The Charleston shipyards produced several other craft of this type, but like *David*'s, their ultimate fates remain unknown.

The victorious Union navy was also interested in this technology, and experimented with a hand-cranked submersible called *Intelligent Whale* after the war, but during trials it proved to be neither intelligent nor whale-like, and the experiments came to naught when the navy rejected the craft in 1872.

Though these boats are better viewed as the first moveable mines rather than the first submarines, they did point the way toward nonhuman means of propulsion. However, twenty years of technological advancements would be needed to make machine-propelled submarines practical.

THE PRACTICAL SUBMARINE

Over the next three or four decades, as industrialization continued, European and North American engineers generated an explosion of inventions and manufacturing processes. The marriage of science and technology helped solve many of the old problems of submarine construction.

With the widespread adoption of Henry Bessemer's new refining methods, steelmaking gained great improvements. Rolling mills sped the output of standardized iron and steel, which made stronger hulls and fittings. Industrial lubricants and ball bearings enabled steel machine tools to cut and shape metal to ever-finer tolerances, permitting designers to count on waterproof seams and leakproof valves. And the transformation of shipyards from wood to iron-and-steel construction created a pool of skilled workers who could build a watertight submarine hull.

On the propulsion side, the steam engine underwent several changes in the late nineteenth century. By 1870, compound steam engines and high boiler pressures greatly increased fuel efficiency, and the introduction of triple-expansion steam engines allowed even small surface ships to do away with their sails. These innovations also let engineers tinker with such engines in submarines. Several inventors, including John Holland in America and George Garrett in England, built steam-powered submarines in the late 1870s. Both discovered that, with the high steam pressures now possible, one could extinguish the furnace on the surface and, with a full head of steam in the boiler, dive and propel the submarine underwater for some time. These boats performed well on the surface, but, underwater, heat from the boiler tended to suffocate the crew.

As steam engines remained quite large, a better solution for the confines of a submarine was the internal combustion engine. More compact and energy efficient than steam engines, gas piston engines provided more power as well. Available in a small enough size by the 1890s, these gasoline engines, although extremely dangerous, were nevertheless installed in submarines. Some navies, particularly the German, experimented with the safer kerosene engine, but it took Rudolf Diesel's invention to dramatically improve engine safety and reliability. First built in 1898, the diesel engine had greater fuel economy and burned a cheaper and, most importantly, a far less flammable fuel than a gasoline engine.

Meanwhile, battery technology had become both practical and economical. Lead-acid or nickel-cadmium storage batteries, often called "accumulators," were capable of powering electric engines for many hours.

By the late nineteenth century, these improvements in combustion and battery technologies caused the more advanced navies of the day to look at submarines a little more closely. At first, the development of surface-ship construction and weapons had stalemated: the ironclad warship was invulnerable to gunfire unless attacked by large cannon at very close range. But each innovation in gun construction, such as rifling or ballistically shaped projectiles, was quickly countered by an improvement in steel or compound (steel with an iron backing) armor. This dynamic, and the lack of major advances in gunnery science, meant rounds had to be fired at very short

ranges to be effective. One alternative to gunfire was the underwater mine. The difficulty lay in convincing the enemy to run over them. The solution was to build a mobile mine.

Alfred Whitehead did just that when he introduced the first practical self-propelled mine in 1868. Working with an Austrian firm in Fiume, Whitehead produced a cigar-shaped weapon, called a torpedo, which was propelled by a compressed air reservoir. With a range of a few hundred yards, the torpedo matched the gunnery ranges of the time, instantly making it a severe threat to surface ships. In the days before ship compartmentalization and effective damage control, a hit below the water line was usually fatal. Moreover, the torpedo's range grew quickly: by 1876, it had a range of six hundred yards (540m). Gradual improvements, including heating the compressed gas to provide more thrust and, in 1905, the introduction of gyroscopes, more than tripled the range to over 2,100 yards (1,890m).

To take advantage of the new torpedo weapon, several countries began building steam-powered patrol boats for coastal defense. Small and fast, these torpedo-armed boats were a cheap way to counter blockading enemy warships. By the mid-1880s, larger torpedo boats were designed for open sea operations. In 1886, the British Admiralty actually announced

Above: The shipyard workers prepare the 64-ton (57.6t) *Holland* for launch in 1898. The U.S. Navy purchased it from John Holland in 1900. **Right:** The Holland Submarine Company basin, showing five of the A-class boats at New Suffolk, New York, in 1903. The three front boats are (left to right): *Plunger* (Submarine No. 2), *Porpoise* (Submarine No. 7), and *Adder* (Submarine No. 3); while the two in the rear are *Shark* (Submarine No. 8) and *Moccasin* (Submarine No. 5).

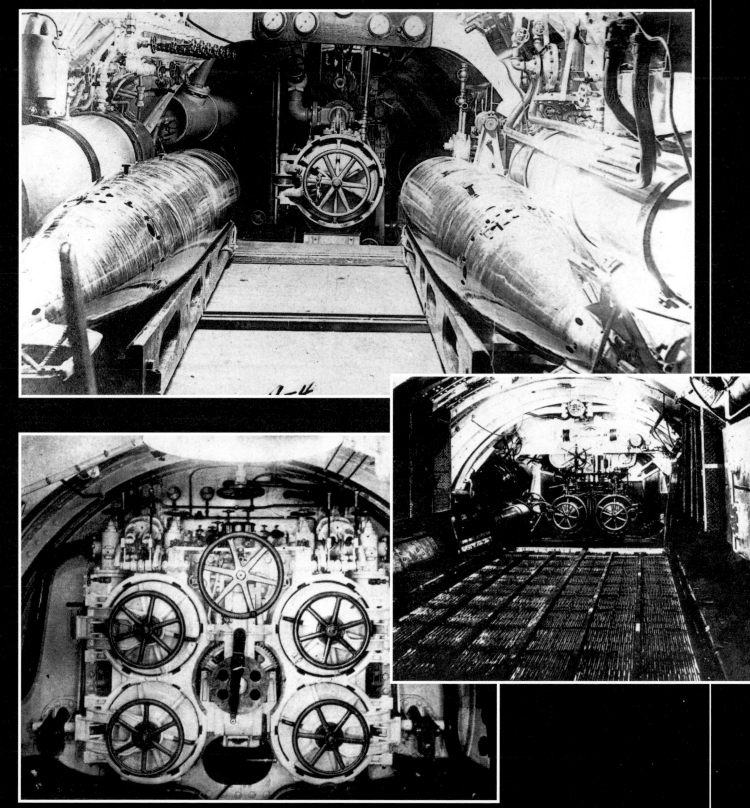

Top: An interior view of *Adder* (Submarine No. 3) at Manila Bay, Protectorate of the Philippines, in 1909. The two torpedoes are reloads for the single 18-inch (45cm) torpedo tube forward. Bottom: Taken prior to World War I, the photo on the right shows the interior of one of the three B-class boats built in 1907 under Electric Boat Company contract at Quincy, Massachusetts. Note the double 18-inch (45cm) torpedo tubes. The bottom left photograph of the forward torpedo room bulkhead, with four 18-inch (45cm) torpedo tubes, could be any of the fifteen D, E, F, G, or H class submarines built between 1909 and 1915.

Top: *Holland* (Submarine No. 1) preparing for launching at Elizabethport, New Jersey, in 1898. Note the steering and diving planes inboard from the propeller, itself protected by a shroud ring.

that it would no longer build large warships, on the theory that little torpedo boats had longer-range weapons that rendered battleship guns ineffective.

The threat of torpedo boats forced designers to counter with rapid-firing, breech-loading guns equipped with hydraulic recoil systems. These arms greatly increased the chance of hitting a torpedo boat at longer range. When turn-of-the-century propulsion and metallurgy improvements led to a new type of warship called a "torpedo boat destroyer," which was bigger, faster, and more heavily armed than the torpedo boat, the balance began to swing back in favor of large surface ships.

Built in sufficient numbers, these destroyers, armed with quick-firing guns, could easily counter the torpedo-boat menace. Other technical developments, such as the replacement of black powder with cordite and metal cartridges, increased the rate of fire still further, improved accuracy, and allowed more and lighter gun mounts on small ships. All of this meant, for those navies interested in cheap coastal and harbor defense, the torpedo boat had to seek safety off the high seas and go underwater. And that meant building submarines.

In France, for example, where interest in building a vessel to prevent a close blockade was almost a national obsession, an all-electric submarine called the *Gymnôte* was constructed in 1888, under the direction of Gustav Zédé. With a crew of two, and displacing a mere thirty tons (27t), the little craft served solely as an experimental platform. It illus-

trated several key principles, including the concept of reserve buoyancy, by which the boat is kept underwater only by the action of horizontal rudders.

Gymnôte proved that batteries, fitted in large enough numbers, could safely propel a submarine under the waves. As they steered their electric submarine through the deep, the French no doubt believed they had an answer to the Royal Navy and "perfidious Albion." It was not yet Leviathan—not even close—but little *Gymnôte* pointed the way to the future.

Another French design, proposed by the engineer Labeuf in 1896, prefigured the standard submarine design of the early twentieth century. Called *Narval*, it had the shape, speed, and buoyancy characteristics of a normal, steam-powered torpedo boat, but it also had an airtight interior pressure hull within its outer hull. In 1900, Labeuf followed up this design with the diesel-powered *Aigrette*. Equipped with Rudolf Diesel's engine, Labeuf's new design proved far superior to gasoline- or kerosene-fueled boats. This combination of double hulls and diesel-electric engines became the standard submarine design of the early twentieth century.

John Holland and the Italian designer Caesare Laurenti, among others, copied these features when they submitted similar designs to the U.S. Navy. The French also built two larger electric vessels, *Sirène* (renamed the *Gustav Zédé* upon the engineer's death in 1891) and *Morse*, but soon settled on experimenting with combustion engine submarines.

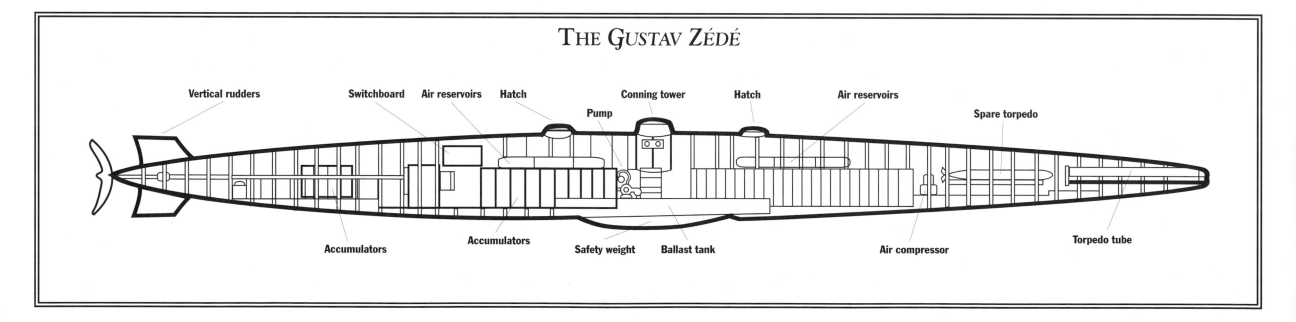

THE GUSTAV ZÉDÉ

Vertical rudders • Switchboard • Air reservoirs • Hatch • Pump • Conning tower • Hatch • Air reservoirs • Spare torpedo

Accumulators • Accumulators • Safety weight • Ballast tank • Air compressor • Torpedo tube

Three early submarines. Top: The *Gustav Zédé,* with the French tricolor flying and passengers (note the berets) crowding the deck, cruises on battery power off Toulon in 1893. Bottom left: A heavily retouched photograph of *Gymnôte* sailing on the surface sometime in the 1890s. This submarine, like the *Gustav Zédé,* served as an experimental platform in the French Navy well into the twentieth century. Bottom right: Unlike the two French submarines on this page, this Swedish-built *Nordenfelt* submarine was equipped with a steam engine, hence the smokestack forward the conning tower. The three passengers seemed to be enjoying the smooth ride in Stockholm harbor.

The Russian battleship *Retvizan* looms behind *Holland* (Submarine No. 1) at the New York Navy Yard in October, 1901. While the diminutive *Holland* would end its career as a target, and ultimately was sold as scrap in 1922, the *Retvizan*'s service life ended far earlier. The pre-dreadnought was sunk at Port Arthur by Japanese artillery fire on December 6, 1904.

French tactical experiments with these boats soon revealed tiny *Gymnôte* to be virtually invisible to surface ships, even when on the surface. The narrow conning tower was also very hard to hit with quick-firing guns, and just four inches (10cm) of water above the hull safely ricocheted incoming shells. These defensive characteristics, remarkable by themselves, were matched by excellent offensive capabilities. During war games in 1901, the *Gustav Zédé* was fitted with a primitive periscope and towed to sea off Ajaccio, Corsica. Once there, it set off to attack the battleships blockading that port. No one spotted the diminutive boat; the first sign of its presence came with the shock of a practice torpedo striking the flagship *Charles Martel*, as the Minister of Marine sat at dinner.

HOW DOES IT WORK?

An object dropped into the sea displaces water. That displacement creates an upthrust as the molecules of water compress against their neighbors. When the object displaces enough water to equal its weight, the squished molecules push back hard enough that the object floats. The density or solidity of the object is also important. Normally, anything denser than water will sink. But if the volume of the object is large enough, no matter how heavy, it will push enough molecules out of the way to float on the surface. This explains why a thin steel disk, like a manhole cover, will sink like a stone, but a high-walled or enclosed steel barge will float. So, with the displacement caused by weight, both an iron-clad monitor and a steel submarine will float, because of each vessel's respective volume.

But submarines, obviously, have to do more than float on the surface. They need to sink beneath the waves and, unlike other ships, rise back to the surface. Moreover, submarines must also hover at different depths while underwater. A submarine's rise and fall is accomplished by altering its weight, and thus its density, through a series of ballast tanks built within, or attached to, the hull.

When these tanks contain air, the submarine, with a density less than seawater, will float on the surface. Conversely, when the tanks are flooded, the boat's weight increases and it sinks, because its density equals or exceeds the density of seawater. By precisely regulating this process, the submarine can approach neutral buoyancy and hover underwater in much the same way a helicopter can hover in air. The submarine rises to the surface when compressed air forces the seawater out of the ballast tanks. Once there, the crew refills the compressed air tanks and the process can begin again.

The submarine also has to maneuver both above and below the surface. A diesel-electric boat developed before 1914 used a diesel engine for surface propulsion and electric power for underwater movement. The diesel engines propelled the submarine at a relatively high speed, since the partially submerged hull and sleek design along the sides and bottom offered less water resistance. The diesels also

Above: Submarines and their tender at the Dewey drydock, Olongapo Naval Station, Protectorate of the Philippines, circa 1912. Sent across the Pacific after 1908, these three A-class boats served with the Asiatic Fleet through World War I. The boats, and their seven-man crews, conducted experimental work until 1914, when the boats patrolled the entrance to Manila Bay and convoyed ships moving out of local waters. The *Mohican,* an old steam sloop of war, served as their supply and maintenance ship until 1915. **Right:** An undated photograph showing a Simon Lake submarine mounted on a railway carriage. Intended for sale to the Russians, it looks ready for shipment. Rail travel would later prove useful for transporting submarines, either whole or in parts, when sea or canal transport was unavailable (part of the way between the Baltic and the Black Seas, for example) or too dangerous (such as German transfers to Austria during World War I).

DIVING AND SURFACING

Ballast tanks
Trim and compensation tanks

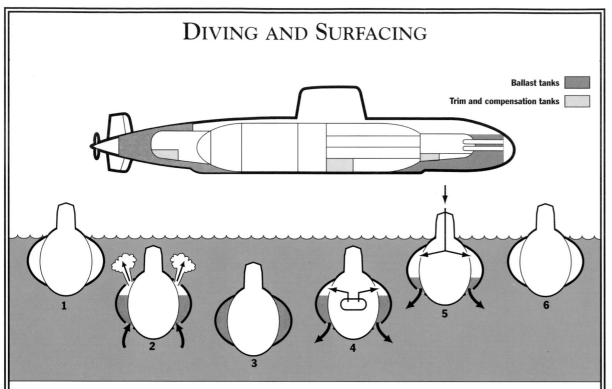

The six stages involved in submerging and surfacing a submarine. 1. The submarine lies on the surface, the reserve buoyancy barely keeping the hull above water. 2. The ballast tanks are opened, and water pressure forces seawater into the ballast tanks, expelling air. 3. The submarine uses compressed air and diving planes to adjust the vertical and horizontal trim—resulting in the ability to "hover" and move up or down underwater. 4. When surfacing, compressed air tanks force out the seawater in the ballast tanks, lightening buoyancy and causing the submarine to rise. 5. Additional air can be brought in via an air pump to the surface, if available, to fully blow out the ballast tanks. 6. The ballast tanks are closed and the submarine again floats on the surface.

The early Austrian submarine *U-2*, photographed while diving in the Adriatic Sea. The water spouts are caused by seawater rushing into the air-filled ballast tanks.

recharged the batteries. When submerged, the submarine switched to electric power, because there was no air for the internal-combustion diesel. The huge banks of batteries in these boats produced far less power than the diesels, and the submarine moved much more slowly underwater. Bulky deck equipment and nonstreamlined hulls further reduced speed and range of these early boats.

Like surface ships, a submarine is equipped with a propeller that provides forward (and backward) movement. A rudder provides lateral movement. In addition, since a submarine moving underwater operates much like an airplane in air, fins or hydroplanes are attached by swivels to the front and/or rear of the hull to provide lift. Under power from the electric motor, a submarine crew can alter buoyancy and, using hydroplanes and a rudder, swim through the water.

STRUGGLING WITH TECHNOLOGY

Just building a workable submarine, however, was not enough. Regardless of whether it is watertight or equipped with acceptable engines, its ultimate test must take place at sea. But the sea is not a docile environment: it requires constant diligence by those who travel on or through it. The sailors who went down in these early boats had to struggle with faulty batteries, leaky valves, and shoddy machinery. All too often sloppy maintenance or simple lack of attention caused a problem like a clogged valve or an unsecured hatch, which in turn led to disaster. Other dangers, such as storms and other ships, could be just as lethal. It is this hard-earned experience at sea that inspires the motto at the U.S. Naval Academy in Annapolis: "The sea does not care if you are sincere."

On March 18, 1904, for example, the British submarine *A-1*, with a crew of fourteen, was accidentally rammed by the liner *Berwick Castle* and sank with all hands. A pair of gasoline explosions killed seven on *A-5* in February 1905 and, later that year, *A-8* flooded and suffered a battery explosion. Nor were the British alone in suffering from fatal accidents. In June 1905, twenty-four lives were lost when a passing steamer swamped the Russian submarine *Delphin* in the Baltic Sea.

The French *Farfadet* was lost with all hands in July 1906 after submerging with an unsecured hatch. And, in January 1911, three men were killed in the German *U-3* when it sank, because of valve failure, in Kiel harbor. Even with the losses, however, these accidents attracted little attention. The number of dead was low, especially when compared to the hazards of industrial accidents as a whole. And, understandably, it was assumed the chance of drowning was an occupational hazard of going underwater.

In addition to these dramatic failures, there were the many heartaches and frustrations of actually getting submarines to work at all. The challenges facing one American boat, the *Thrasher* (G-4), present a litany of common troubles. The keel of the boat, a Laurenti design, was laid down on July 9, 1910, by William Cramp and Sons Ship and Engine Building, in Philadelphia, Pennsylvania. The builders had some problems with construction and, in 1912, they were forced to admit to the U.S. Navy that "the difficulty which we have experienced . . . has been due to the lack of experience on our part in this character of work. . . ."

During engine tests and sea trials, several problems were discovered: the rubber jars containing the batteries leaked, allowing water in and creating deadly chlorine gas; incorrect weight distribution inside the boat led to instability; the engine-room

The British submarine *A-1* cruising on the surface. The first Admiralty-designed submarine, its conning tower (not included on the Holland boats) proved a great advantage in navigation, steering, and visibility. Built by Vickers at Barrow-in-Furness, it carried a single 18-inch (45cm) torpedo tube forward. The submarine met an early end when rammed by SS *Berwick Castle* in 1904. She was later salvaged but sank again during sea trials in August 1911. Overall, the A-class boats were somewhat unlucky: five of the thirteen built either sank or ran aground between 1905 and 1920. Inset: A heavily retouched photograph of *Akula* in the Baltic before the war, probably 1913–14. Unsuccessful on her early war patrols in the Baltic, the submarine was converted to a mine-layer in mid-1915. On her first mission, however, *Akula* disappeared south of Libau. The armored cruiser *Rurik* appears in the background. The *Akula* is shown on the building way at the Baltic Works, St. Petersburg, in 1908. The Chief Engineer stands in the foreground.

Above: A drawing of French divers attempting to communicate with the crew of the sunken submarine *Farfadet*. Despite the chains and air hoses, none of the crew survived. Right: The drawing of submarine cross-sections shown at right illustrates the great variety of hull shapes common to early submarines. Note the almost universal reliance on a circular hull, with the *Narval*-type the first to rely on an interior pressure hull surrounded by a streamlined outer hull containing ballast tanks. That trend, common to all submarines until the 1950s, was reversed with the advent of nuclear-powered submarines. The latter, ironically enough (like the *Ohio*, included for comparison), are shaped somewhat like John Holland's first boats.

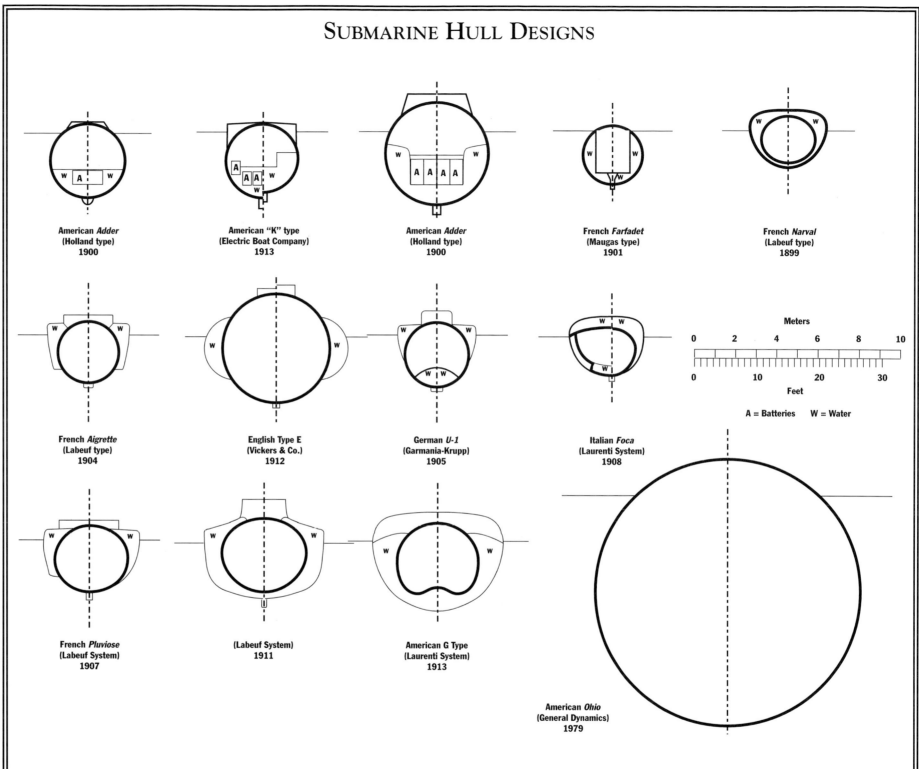

SUBMARINE HULL DESIGNS

American *Adder*
(Holland type)
1900

American "K" type
(Electric Boat Company)
1913

American *Adder*
(Holland type)
1900

French *Farfadet*
(Maugas type)
1901

French *Narval*
(Labeuf type)
1899

French *Aigrette*
(Labeuf type)
1904

English Type E
(Vickers & Co.)
1912

German *U-1*
(Garmania-Krupp)
1905

Italian *Foca*
(Laurenti System)
1908

French *Pluviose*
(Labeuf System)
1907

(Labeuf System)
1911

American G Type
(Laurenti System)
1913

American *Ohio*
(General Dynamics)
1979

Meters

A = Batteries   W = Water

ventilation system failed, sickening the crew with noxious gases; several pistons cracked when the engines ran at full power. When submerged, the engines tended to fill with water through the exhaust lines and saltwater leaked into the oil system. *Thrasher* also rolled excessively when on the surface, so much so that some thought "she is of no military value." It says much for the state of technological expectations of the time that the submarine was fully accepted from the contractor by the Navy on March 7, 1916.

WHY BUILD SUBMARINES?

The author H. G. Wells, in light of the many submarine accidents of the time, wrote "I must confess that my imagination . . . refuses to see any sort of submarine doing anything but suffocate its crew and founder at sea."

Despite the numerous flaws that more or less existed in every boat of the time, submarines were still purchased in large numbers. Why, then, did submarines prove so attractive? Why did navies spend money on an unproven invention when there were plenty of other, less risky projects that demanded attention?

Certainly there was the lure and romance of something new. The submarine symbolized the march of progress and the conquest of yet another natural frontier by science. Popularized by Jules Verne in his 1869 novel, *20,000 Leagues Under the Sea*, submarines caught the eye of the public and naval officers alike. Some navies were simply enthralled by the

idea of any cheap but effective weapon. Others joined in the rush to order submarines out of concern about coastal defense or saving money.

Boarding submarines became something of a fad as well. National leaders of all stripes wanted to see if submerging beneath the sea was as adventurous as Jules Verne had described. On September 23, 1903,

Prince Heinrich of Prussia went down in the kerosene-powered Krupp submarine *Forelle*. Nor was President Theodore Roosevelt immune. On August 23, 1905, he went aboard *Plunger* (A-1) when it was conducting trials off Oyster Bay, New York. He spent three hours onboard, and enjoyed several dives before he disembarked. Later, he wrote that never in his life had he experienced "such a diverting day . . . nor so much enjoyment in so few hours." He did comment, however: "I believe a good deal can be done with these submarines, although there is always the danger of people getting carried away with the idea and thinking they can be of more use than they possibly could be."

A somewhat more personal concern was expressed by the Princess of Wales, who supposedly remarked, after her husband, the future George V, descended into the murk in an early British submarine, "I shall be very disappointed if George doesn't come up again."

It is perhaps this combination of technological progress and (mostly) untempered enthusiasm that led to the wholesale construction of submarines. Soon, watertight valves and reliable electric motors, along with depth meters and a periscope, made submerged navigation reasonably successful. Combustion engines gave the submarine good surface endurance. The Whitehead torpedo gave it a weapon capable of sinking battleships. And the underwater capabilities of the submarine would counter the high speed and quick-firing guns of the destroyer. The submarines could bypass the destroyers by submerging, leaving them behind like dogs chasing a false scent, while the fox slipped quietly into the chickenhouse.

PREWAR SUBMARINE STRATEGY

The submarine began to fill its unique niche in naval strategy shortly before the Great War. Just as countries have different uses for the sea, they subsequently have different uses for their navies. These needs influence what types of ships, and how many, a nation will build or purchase. A navy built to protect a fishing fleet, or to patrol a small amount of coastline, will be very different from one designed to protect transoceanic merchant shipping.

For example, Denmark did not have the financial or economic strength to build a dreadnought battleship in 1900. But, because of the restricted geography of the country's position at the mouth of the Baltic Sea, the Danes did not need such a warship. Instead, the Danish navy built or purchased patrol boats and submarines, which provided a far more cost-effective defense of its small but important coastline. The same dynamic applies to most naval powers and, at the end of the nineteenth century, the fleets of the three largest European naval powers— France, Britain, and Germany—illustrated this principle perfectly.

In France, support for the navy was all the rage. The navy represented progress and was a symbol of the machine age. It was also a key factor in the nineteenth-century competition between France and Great Britain, which, in the words of one historian, was called the "Second Hundred Years War." This period was marked by continuing tensions over colonies, political disagreements over the European balance of power, and lingering resentment from the Napoleonic and earlier wars.

These disagreements, combined with numerous diplomatic incidents, created a more or less constant naval arms race between France and Britain throughout the late nineteenth century. The persistent strategic problem, however, was France's inability to challenge Britain's superior industrial strength.

This insufficiency had plagued France since the seventeenth century. French armies, forced to deal with continental threats, had always absorbed the bulk of the nation's resources. The French navy simply could not compete with the Royal Navy, backed as it was by the superior financial and industrial strength of Britain. But if France could somehow change the rules of the game—alter the pattern of competition—the nation might stand a chance at sea. By making technological innovation the central element of their naval designs, the French hoped to force obsolescence upon the Royal Navy's ships. With this strategy, which tried to eliminate Britain's financial and economic advantages, the French remained on the forefront of incorporating industrial and technological innovations into nineteenth-century navies.

These innovations included shell-firing guns, steam-powered engines, and ironclads. At first, whenever the French introduced such an innovation, the British simply adopted the same technology. Britain's superior maritime industry allowed it to match every French improvement. By the 1870s, somewhat tired of this game, many French naval theorists argued that innovation had to be more radical

Two American submarines moored at Iloilo, Philippines, circa 1912. Note the awnings, intended to provide at least some protection from the tropical sun.

in order to have any lasting effect. They concentrated on developing innovations that had either no defense available or would require a substantially greater expense to defend against. The torpedo and the torpedo boat were steps in this direction. But, by the 1890s, British destroyers had neutralized the French advantage in torpedo boats and yet another advance was needed.

The submarine seemed to be the answer. Nearly invisible, submarines could easily challenge British warships if they blockaded French ports. And, with the help of Russian allies, the French might even drive the Royal Navy from the English Channel and enable an invasion of southern England. By 1900, with this vision before them, the French began building submarines in earnest. And then, ironically, just as submarines became practical, the diplomatic and strategic situation altered dramatically.

The meteoric rise of Germany scared both Britain and France, forcing informal talks that settled many of the competitors' old grievances. The submarines, much less useful against the German navy than they had been against the British, were instead deployed in the Mediterranean. The French planned to use the boats, based at Toulon and Ajaccio, against the growing Italian and Austro-Hungarian navies. By 1914, the French navy had sixty-seven submarines in service.

The British built submarines for entirely different reasons. Initially, the Royal Navy rejected short-range submarines, considering them ineffective for a navy with global commitments, especially when the main threat to the British Empire seemed to be swift French and Russian cruisers. By 1905, though, the British began to build submarines. Unlike the French, who needed to challenge a larger navy through innovative thinking, the Royal Navy built submarines for financial reasons first, strategic requirements second. The roots of this decision lie in the increasing cost of warships.

For most of the nineteenth century, the cost to maintain the superiority of the Royal Navy was not unreasonable. But the adoption of steam engines, new weapons, and armor raised the price of warships considerably. And, after 1885, the fast rate of technological change, combined with increasing rates of foreign construction, forced British naval expenditures up at a rate far greater than the growth in state income. This financial crisis reached a peak in 1904,

after the Boer War.

The British Admiralty appointed Sir John Fisher as First Sea Lord in October, 1904, with the hope he could find savings within the naval budget. Fisher responded by introducing a radically different naval policy. Instead of relying on expensive squadrons of battleships to defend Britain's far-flung maritime interests, Fisher proposed a dual track approach to the problem. First, by relying on British advances in technology, including an over-optimistic understanding of fire-control advances, the Royal Navy would build small numbers of revolutionary capital ships. These battlecruisers, whose speed and long-range firepower would enable them to defeat all known French and Russian commerce raiders, would provide cheaper trade protection than the obsolete gunboats then in place. Second, the battle fleet would be reduced by the establishment of numerous torpedo-boat and submarine squadrons in home waters. The submarines and torpedo boats would deter invasion, therefore freeing all the heavy ships from home defense and allowing them to hunt down enemy raiders.

In 1905, however, as Germany began to surpass Russia and France as Britain's main enemy, these plans changed. But, despite a shift toward dreadnought construction in order to counter German heavy warships, submarines were still built in large numbers. Fisher had not only envisioned them as a defense against invasion, but also imagined them "infesting" the North Sea and the Baltic. And, since recent maneuvers had demonstrated that a close blockade of enemy ports with surface ships was impossible because of mines and submarines, British patrol submarines were intended to help shut the German fleet in port. Cheap and plentiful, there were roughly seventy-three British submarines in service by 1914.

The Imperial German Navy, meanwhile, had its own unique reasons for building submarines. In contrast to the innovative policy of the French, or the financial goals of the British, the Germans were guided by tactical considerations. Led by Admiral Alfred von Tirpitz, the German navy underwent a vast expansion in size and strength during the fifteen years before 1914. This huge peacetime building program, meant to force Britain to accept Germany as a great maritime power, initially neglected submarines. Tirpitz was hesitant to build them, partly because they were untried and partly because they would divert money and manpower from the battle fleet.

But German fears of being "Copenhagened"—a reference to the British preemptive strike against the Danish fleet during the Napoleonic wars—gave the submarine a role in harbor defense. In addition, German naval planners believed, incorrectly as it turned out, that the British would institute a close blockade of the German coast. The submarine, therefore, along with mine-layers and torpedo boats, was enlisted to wear down the Royal Navy through *kleinkrieg*, a naval guerilla war waged with mine and torpedo. Then, when the German fleet was on equal terms with the Royal Navy, a climactic surface battle might defeat the British. By 1914, with this strategy in mind, there were thirty-one German submarines in service.

Left: Britain's *D-1* cruising on the surface at perhaps 16 knots. The crew, attired in their white submarine jerseys, seem to be enjoying the air. An armored cruiser, possibly *Aboukir,* appears in the background. *Aboukir* fell to German submarine torpedoes in 1914, while *D-1* survived to be decommissioned and sunk as a target in 1918. Above: An early photograph of Mare Island Navy Yard, California, prior to World War I. The submarines are in drydock, where major overhaul and maintenance work can be done out of the water. Note the heavy crane on the right. A good view of just part of the industrial infrastructure needed to maintain a steel navy.

X HULK ACHERON

Chapter 2

The Great War

I N THE YEARS PRIOR TO WORLD WAR I, SUBMARINE CREWS PRACTICED open sea navigation, seamanship, and all the other skills needed to make the submarine an effective warship. They also learned the highly complex tasks peculiar to submarine operations. These included diving drills, the loading of torpedo tubes while submerged, and careful use of the periscope. Conditions within submarines made these difficult duties even harder to accomplish. The boats were so dark, wet, and cramped inside that one German officer complained, "between close quarters, foul air, and crazy rolling and pitching, a rowboat was palatial compared to the inside of one of those diving dories."

An American medical officer made similar comments after he found submarines "a serious menace to the health of the members of the crew." According to him, half the crew of any boat was always seasick. Rotten food, as well as bad toilet conditions, created foul air that incapacitated the rest. During cold weather, electric heaters could barely keep the boats warm and nothing could dry the pervading dampness. The highly skilled crews endured the abysmal conditions, however, because submariners had a special, almost elite, reputation. Their desire to prove themselves to their surface compatriots, who viewed the undersea men with scorn, overshadowed the daily trials of life beneath the waves.

HOW TO SHOOT A TORPEDO

The most decisive way for a submariner to prove himself, of course, was to sink enemy warships. But hitting a fast-moving and occasionally zigzagging target with a torpedo was a challenge. Even when the submarine lay on the surface, the kill was not easy. Torpedoes of that day, after all, traveled in a straight line, at a constant speed, and only worked if they physically struck the target. From a submerged ship, the complex calculations needed became even more difficult. Looking through the periscope, the commander had to determine the correct speed and course of the target, then accurately relay this information to the crew in time to obtain a successful torpedo shot.

The submarine commander first had to account for the course and speed of both the submarine and the target. Then he developed a firing solution (the angle setting for the torpedo gyro) by comparing the

Eight German U-boats moored next to the supply hulk *Acheron*. The clearly visible exhaust stacks and naval ensigns give this photograph the air of a prewar photograph, although the anti-torpedo net booms (the diagonal slashes along the hull) on the armored cruiser in the background suggest otherwise. As the *U-12* was rammed and sunk by the British destroyer *Ariel* in March 1915, the picture may be an early wartime photograph.

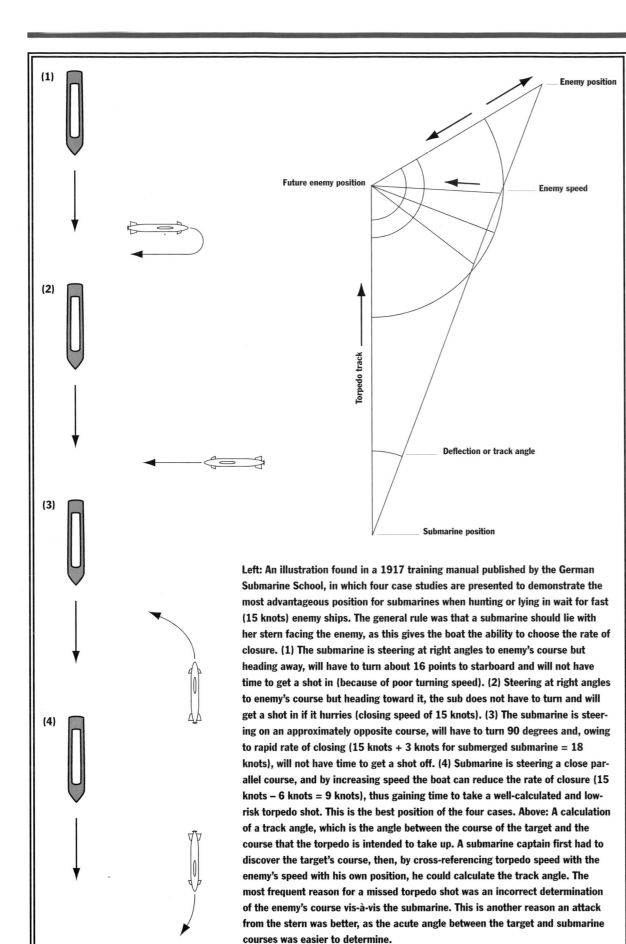

Left: An illustration found in a 1917 training manual published by the German Submarine School, in which four case studies are presented to demonstrate the most advantageous position for submarines when hunting or lying in wait for fast (15 knots) enemy ships. The general rule was that a submarine should lie with her stern facing the enemy, as this gives the boat the ability to choose the rate of closure. (1) The submarine is steering at right angles to enemy's course but heading away, will have to turn about 16 points to starboard and will not have time to get a shot in (because of poor turning speed). (2) Steering at right angles to enemy's course but heading toward it, the sub does not have to turn and will get a shot in if it hurries (closing speed of 15 knots). (3) The submarine is steering on an approximately opposite course, will have to turn 90 degrees and, owing to rapid rate of closing (15 knots + 3 knots for submerged submarine = 18 knots), will not have time to get a shot off. (4) Submarine is steering a close parallel course, and by increasing speed the boat can reduce the rate of closure (15 knots – 6 knots = 9 knots), thus gaining time to take a well-calculated and low-risk torpedo shot. This is the best position of the four cases. **Above:** A calculation of a track angle, which is the angle between the course of the target and the course that the torpedo is intended to take up. A submarine captain first had to discover the target's course, then, by cross-referencing torpedo speed with the enemy's speed with his own position, he could calculate the track angle. The most frequent reason for a missed torpedo shot was an incorrect determination of the enemy's course vis-à-vis the submarine. This is another reason an attack from the stern was better, as the acute angle between the target and submarine courses was easier to determine.

range, speed, and bearing (or compass course) of the target with the position of the submarine, and figuring in the speed of the torpedo. This had to be done quickly, with pencil and paper or in the commander's head. For safety's sake, only a few glances were allowed through the periscope. If the submarine commander performed all these calculations correctly and the crew managed to fire the "fish" on time, the torpedo and the target would reach the same place at the same time.

Submarines had additional reasons to take extra care when shooting a torpedo: torpedoes were expensive and a submarine could only carry a dozen or so, sometimes fewer. Technical limitations forced attacks to take place at roughly 250–300 yards (225–270m); any less and the torpedo might not level in time, any more and the chance of a miss increased dramatically. Firing astern at the target offered the best angle of attack. A position to the rear also helped to avoid getting rammed by the target. In addition, there was less chance that the target would spot the track made by the torpedo's compressed air tanks, making evasion less likely. The best place to hit a ship was off-center and well below the water line, but that required very careful aiming and depth-setting on the torpedo. It also meant a successful hit would unbalance the target ship and lead to rapid sinking.

THE FIRST SUBMARINE WAR

When World War I broke out, it seemed submarines might not get the chance to sink enemy warships. The British deployed most of their boats to defend the Channel troop convoys from German incursions. The French and the Russians also placed their boats in defensive positions, the French covering their North African troop convoys and the Russians protecting St. Petersburg. The Germans stationed their U-boats around the naval base at Helgoland to repel possible British bombardments; the seven Austrian boats did the same at Pola in the Adriatic. Ironically, the expected attacks on each others' bases did not materialize, confounding the prewar plans on all sides.

Over time, the various admiralties released their submarines to explore enemy waters. The first torpedo shot of the war came in the North Sea on August 8, 1914, when the German *U-15* fired a torpedo at a passing British dreadnought, but missed the target. Unfortunately for the U-boat, while patrolling

the area the next day, it was sighted on the surface by the cruiser *Birmingham*. Caught by surprise, the submarine had no time to dive, and the cruiser closed at flank speed to ram the U-boat. The first pass struck only a glancing blow, but after a full circle the *Birmingham*'s second run hit *U-15* directly amidships, cutting it in half. First blood thus went to the Royal Navy.

STALEMATE IN THE NORTH SEA

Despite the complexities of firing a torpedo at a warship, and the dire fate of *U-15*, it did not take long for German submarines to score. On September 5, 1914, the *U-21* fired a single torpedo at the British scout cruiser *Pathfinder*. The torpedo exploded amidships and the resulting explosion detonated the cruiser's powder magazines. It sank quickly, taking 259 crew to the bottom of the sea. *U-21* had made the first submarine kill of the war.

Eight days later, however, the British evened the tally when *E-9* spotted and then sank the old cruiser *Hela* off Helgoland. But these victories, remarkable for the time, paled in comparison to the most spectacular submarine attack of the war, one that dramatically illustrated the power of the little "steel fish."

On the September 22, 1914, the *U-9*, commanded by Lieutenant Otto Weddigen, was patrolling a sector of the North Sea off the coast of Holland. An early boat, *U-9* was propelled on the surface with two kerosene motors, which, as one crewman wryly noted, "smoked like the very deuce." Luckily, Weddigen saw the black smoke of enemy ships on the horizon before they spotted his. *U-9* submerged and lay in wait. Examining them as they sailed closer, Weddigen thought that the three British ships were light cruisers of the *Birmingham* class. His second-in-command, Lieutenant Johann Spiess, whispered, "Revenge for the *U-15*!"

Weddigen watched the cruisers through the periscope, (which crew members affectionately called the "asparagus") and waited as the four-stack cruisers drew closer. At about five hundred yards (450m), Weddigen ordered a long-range but well-calculated shot at the middle cruiser. After the heavy torpedo left its tube, he quickly dove deeper in order to keep the boat from broaching and revealing his presence. His well-aimed torpedo hit, mortally wounding the cruiser.

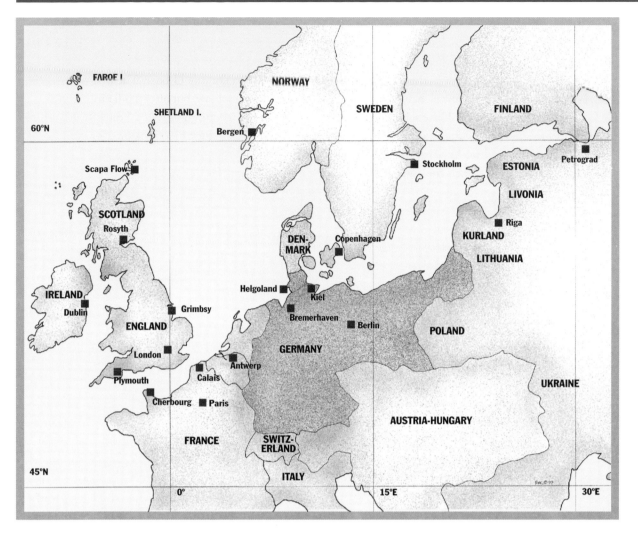

This map of western Europe shows the North Sea, including the British Isles, the northern coast of France, Denmark, and the Baltic Sea, with the main ports marked.

As the crippled cruiser sank stern first, the other two warships, believing the first had struck a mine, closed to rescue survivors. Weddigen could not believe his luck. He ordered the bow torpedo tube reloaded. (Some of his crew had other duties, they were needed as ballast to keep the U-boat level, and they ran from bow to stern inside the boat as required.) Thirty-five minutes after the first attack, he ordered two torpedoes launched against the second cruiser. Both hit the target. Weddigen, aware he was running out of battery power, ordered the submarine's course changed so that the stern tubes could be fired while the crew loaded the last bow torpedo. As the submarine's stern came into position, two more torpedoes left their tubes. One missed, but the other struck the hull of the third cruiser.

The U-9 slowly came around at periscope depth and, once the bow faced the listing British warship, Weddigen ordered the last torpedo fired. After the hit, Speiss recorded that this cruiser rolled over to port as its crew "climbed like ants over her side and then, as she turned turtle completely, they ran about on her broad, flat keel until in a few minutes she disappeared beneath the waves."

The U-9 had actually torpedoed three old *Bacchante*-class armored cruisers. *Cressy*, *Aboukir*, and *Hogue* had been cynically dubbed "the live bait squadron" by their fellows, as they stood little chance against modern warships. Instead, the warship to fear proved to be a submarine. Having caused the loss of

What's in a Name?

Various navies have different ways to identify their warships. Identification depends on tradition, experience, and bureaucratic inertia. Sometimes ships are named, such as the famous *Dreadnought*, and other times simply assigned an alpha-numeric code, like *DD-44* for "Destroyer Number 44." Submarines, perhaps because they are direct descendants of small torpedo boats, usually received a simple alpha-numeric code. The Imperial German Navy and the Austro-Hungarian Navy called them *Unterseeboote*, or U-boat for short. Submarine Number 21, therefore, was identified as *U-21*. Different types, called a class, were usually identified by changing the letter codes. U, UB.I, UB.II, UC.I, UC.II, UC.III, U-cruisers, UE, and UF were all different classes of U-boat.

The British and the Americans also labeled their submarines by class, except that they changed the first letter to identify different models. The seventh E-class boat to be built, for example, would bear the name *E-7*. The British had B-, C-, D-, E-, H-, K-, and W-class submarines in service during World War I; the Americans had A- through L-class boats. The French and the Italians, on the other hand, gave their submarines names just like other warships. The Russians, oddly enough, followed both rules, or none, depending on your point of view. Some Russian submarines received names and others an alpha-numeric code.

An undated view of British submarine *C-44* cruising on the surface. The bold white letters and the safety rails suggest that this is a peacetime photo. At the outbreak of the war, these small submarines were stationed at the Humber (near Grimsby), the Nore (the Thames estuary), and Dover. Along with other light forces, torpedo boats and old destroyers, their main purpose was coastal defense, offshore patrol, and screening the troop convoys to France. In 1916, four of these boats were towed to Archangel, loaded on barges, and sent down the rivers and canals of north Russia to Petrograd. There they conducted patrols against German forces in the Baltic until April 1918, when they were scuttled to avoid capture after the Russian surrender.

Above: A very famous photograph of the German armored cruiser *Blucher* capsized at the end of the Battle of Dogger Bank on January 24, 1915. The crew can be seen scrambling like ants over the hull, much like the description given by Lieutenant Speiss after the *U-9* torpedoed the *Cressy*, *Aboukir*, and *Hogue* on September 22, 1914.

Taken on April 28, 1918, this photo of *U-28,* an Austrian submarine, shows the bent base of the periscope just aft of the conning tower. The periscope had been sheared off when a steamer tried to ram the submarine. The bright circular disk in the foreground is a recognition mark for Austrian aviators, intended to decrease the chances of a friendly fire incident.

three cruisers, sixty-two officers, and 1,397 men in little more than an hour, the submarine suddenly became the main threat to British superiority at sea. As if to prove the point, on October 13 Weddigen located the cruiser *Hawke* off Scotland and sent it to the bottom. The British First Sea Lord, Admiral Sir John Fisher, noted caustically that with those four ships he had "more men lost than by Lord Nelson in all his battles put together." Weddigen, meanwhile, became a national hero and the Kaiser awarded him Germany's highest honor, the Pour le Merite, or "Blue Max." Weddigen was not able to savor his medal for long. He was lost when the British battleship *Dreadrought* rammed and sunk *U-9* in March 1915.

Damage to the Royal Navy did not stop there. On October 31, 1914, *U-27* sank the seaplane carrier *Hermes* off Calais. The U-boats tallied another success by destroying the pre-dreadnought *Formidable* on January 1, 1915. During gunnery exercises in the English Channel, the warship crossed the sights of *U-24* and received a new year's gift of a torpedo, sinking with 557 men. The British submarine squadrons, dis-

advantaged by the small number of German ships at sea, had only a single shot at the dreadnought *Posen* on December 16, 1914. The torpedo ran deep and missed.

By early 1915, attacks like these encouraged both sides to keep their heavy ships out of the North Sea. The British, by now aware the German fleet would not challenge their control of the North Sea, left the region to light minesweeping and patrol forces. The British also abandoned as too difficult plans to attack the German High Seas Fleet in its base at Wilhelmshaven.

The Germans, especially after experiencing several small but bloody surface battles, felt more determined than ever to avoid a costly surface engagement. Despite dramatic successes like Weddigen's, the guerilla war of mine and submarine could not sink enough British warships to make battle a feasible risk. Thus, the North Sea by 1915 had become a watery no-man's-land, empty of capital ships, but criss-crossed by minelayers and minesweepers, and ruled by submarines.

During the first months of the war, U-boats stalked enemy warships but left merchant vessels unmolested. The Kaiser's submariners had not made any plans to sink merchantmen, and they feared damage to shipping could turn the opinion of neutral countries (like the United States) against Germany. In October 1914, however, the commander of the U-boat flotillas, Korvettenkapitan Hermann Bauer, conducted a feasibility study and recommended an attack on Britain's vulnerable shipping routes. The German Admiralstab took no immediate action but later events in the war would push them towards such a course.

1914–1915: COMMERCE WAR BEGINS

The Royal Navy had long used blockades to strangle the coastal and overseas commerce of their enemies. Warships and patrol craft would stop merchant vessels to determine cargo and destination. If the cargo was classified as war contraband (a definition liable to infinite expansion), they would confiscate it by diverting the ship to a friendly port. When the British declared foodstuffs contraband in the early days of World War I, this blockade stopped virtually all merchant traffic to German ports.

Though the Germans continued to obtain some goods through neutrals such as Denmark and Holland, the British blockade cut off overseas food supplies and began the slow process of starvation in central Europe. The Germans called this an illegal "hunger-blockade" and looked for ways to retaliate with their own form of commerce war, or *guerre de course*, against the British.

The prewar German navy, like other naval powers, had not considered the submarine a weapon for the *guerre de course*. Beginning in late 1914, however, in retaliation for the British hunger blockade, the Admiralstab ordered its U-boats to attack enemy merchant ships within the constraints of international law. The first such attack occurred off Norway on October 20, 1914, when the *U-17* stopped the British merchant ship *Glitra*. Once the U-boat's commander identified the *Glitra*'s cargo as contraband, in this case iron plates, coal, and oil, he ordered the merchant crew to abandon ship. Allowing ten minutes to load lifeboats, he then ordered his crew to sink the merchant ship. With the Norwegian coast

beyond sight, *U-17* took the lifeboats in tow towards land, releasing them when close enough for the British to row to shore.

This attack was conducted according to the Prize Regulations, a set of strict conventions outlining how combatants should conduct wartime attacks on merchant ships. It also demonstrated how complying with these regulations would cost the submarine the twin attributes of stealth and surprise that made them so effective. The regulations called for a warship to first stop the merchant vessel, check the vessel's papers and cargo, and if it determined that the merchant ship carried contraband cargo, either put a prize crew on board or sink it without harming the crew.

The small size of submarines prevented them from putting a prize crew on every merchant vessel they stopped. Worse, surfacing to secure the safety of the merchant crew, as *U-17* had done with the *Glitra*, was very dangerous, given the vulnerability of submarines to gunfire and ramming.

By early 1915, it became clear that both the German offensive on the Western Front and the *kleinkrieg*, or guerilla war, against the Royal Navy had failed. Given that frustration, and the initial effects of the British blockade on the civilian population, the German press began to call for a more intensive submarine campaign against the English. On February 4, after his naval advisors suggested an unrestricted commerce war might break the stalemate, the Kaiser declared the waters around the British Isles a war zone: merchant ships sailing in these waters were now subject to attack without warning—a campaign for which submarines were ideally suited. But with only seventeen modern submarines available, the German navy lacked the numbers to cause sufficient damage. The immediate future held no real prospects either. Only thirty-four large submarines, and another thirty coastal and minelaying U-boats, were under construction or ordered, and increased production would reap no benefits for nearly a year.

Those few U-boats in service, however, made up for their limited numbers through ruthless attacks. Over the first three months of the campaign, the U-boats sank 115 ships, at the cost of only five submarines. The construction of three bases along the Belgian coast aided these efforts, bringing the smaller coastal and minelaying U-boats closer to

Top: An unidentified German U-boat lies on the surface near the British steamer *Parkgate*. Complying with the Prize Regulations, the merchant crew is put off in lifeboats and the freighter sunk with scuttling charges or the deck gun. As can be seen by the closeness of the two vessels, a submarine stopped on the surface was very vulnerable to hidden guns, a sudden decision to ram, or the surprise appearance of a warship. Bottom: A British merchant ship sinks beneath the waves. The sharp angle indicates the ship was probably torpedoed; the smoke is most likely from the flooded boilers. Scenes like these were common in the spring of 1915.

British trade routes and permitting longer patrols in operational areas.

This unrestricted campaign had immediate and dramatic diplomatic repercussions. U-boats sank ships of several neutral nations by accident, including Swedish, Norwegian, and Dutch vessels, but the most important incidents involved ships from the United States. Although several American citizens had been killed in earlier attacks, the submarine action with the most profound implications for the course of the war did not take place until May 1915.

In late April 1915, under the command of Walther Swieger, the *U-20* got underway with orders to enforce the blockade against Britain. Swieger was well liked by his crew, which included three dachshunds brought along for good luck. They must have worked, because Swieger's patrol area, off southwest Ireland, proved fruitful—*U-20* sank three ships before turning for home. Then on May 7, while running on the surface in a heavy fog, Swieger spotted what appeared to be two destroyers on the horizon. As the ships closed the range, he realized he had targeted a large four-funneled ocean liner. It was the Cunard ship *Lusitania*, bound from New York with 1,257 passengers, including 197 U.S. citizens. The *U-20* submerged and prepared for an underwater attack.

Swieger fired a single torpedo at the liner when it came into range. It hit forward and detonated. Soon after, he heard a second explosion and the ship began to sink by the bow. Swieger prepared to fire a second torpedo but withheld the shot, noting later, "I could not have sent a second torpedo into the crowd of those passengers who were trying to save themselves." Peering through his periscope, Swieger saw hundreds of people struggling to swim as the *Lusitania* dove bow first to the bottom. "There was a terrible panic on her deck. Overcrowded lifeboats, fairly torn from their positions, dropped into the water. Desperate people ran helplessly up and down the decks. Men and women jumped into the water and tried to swim to empty, overturned lifeboats. It was the most terrible sight I have ever seen. . . . The scene was too horrible to watch, and I gave orders to dive to 20 meters, and away."

The Cunard liner *Lusitania* in an American port, probably New York City. This large passenger liner carried travelers, mail, and some small cargo shipments to and fro across the Atlantic. The sleek lines and powerful funnels are signs of her high speed, but that quickness did not save the liner. On May 7, 1915, Kapitanleutnant Walther Swieger (shown in inset) in *U-20* put a single torpedo into the liner and the great ship sank quickly. The incident set off a major diplomatic crisis between Germany and the United States.

The loss of 1,201 lives set off a major diplomatic incident. The Germans claimed the *Lusitania* had carried munitions, making it a legitimate target of war. The British countered that it was carrying passengers only and Swieger's action amounted to nothing less than piracy. Most Americans believed the British arguments and many, including former president Theodore Roosevelt, demanded the United States declare war against Germany. Efforts at diplomatic damage control mollified President Woodrow Wilson, and the Germans promised not to conduct any more surprise attacks against merchant ships.

Above: This photo presumes to show a U-boat halting an American steamer. The photo was sent to the United States sometime in 1917–18 by an American naval attaché stationed in Paris. The differences in the clarity of the flags, the odd sea surface, and other lines suggest the photo is a fake. Still, it was incidents like these that inflamed American public opinion. Right: The poster admonishes German civilians to "Give to the U-Boat Fund." Such patriotic posters, whether they asked citizens to buy war bonds or airplanes or naval vessels, abounded in the countries fighting, and trying to finance, World War I.

Nevertheless, American opinion began to swing against Germany. Gone for the moment were the numerous business complaints against the Royal Navy for their strict and, some argued, high-handed blockade that limited U.S. trade with the Central Powers. In the minds of many, unrestricted submarine warfare was piracy of the worst sort, and the Germans were the only country guilty.

By mid-September, even with the tighter restrictions on U-boat attacks, the Germans had still sunk another 365 merchant ships for a loss of only ten submarines. Most of the kills did not involve a surprise torpedo attack. Gunfire and scuttling charges did the work just as well and this helped to prevent dramatic incidents, like the *Lusitania* disaster, which might have triggered more bad press and further hindered the U-boats' goals.

But neutral civilians still died, killed by gunfire, drowning, or starving while adrift in lifeboats. Fearing reprisals for the deaths of American citizens and not wishing to offend other neutrals, the Kaiser canceled the unrestricted campaign on September 18, 1915. Many of the U-boats then departed for service in the Mediterranean (fewer American citizens), the Baltic, or the Black Sea.

Above: This picture of *U-53* at Newport, Rhode Island, was taken on October 7, 1916. With the United States still neutral, Kapitanleutnant Hans Rose invited American naval officers on a tour of his submarine, and several accepted. A few hours later, *U-53* departed and, after moving into international waters, proceeded to sink five foreign ships off Nantucket. The sinkings were witnessed by American destroyers, who hurried in to rescue the merchant crews. Rose then asked one destroyer to move out of the way so he could torpedo a Dutch ship. All in all, it was a striking demonstration of the remarkable range of a "modern" diesel submarine.

THE MEDITERRANEAN

In July 1914, the naval balance in the Mediterranean Sea was very unstable. Because France and Britain had agreed to work together, the British had withdrawn most of their fleet to the North Sea. The French Mediterranean fleet, meanwhile, did not equal the combined fleets of Italy and Austria. The diplomatic situation at the outbreak of war had left it uncertain whether Italy and its twenty submarines would join the Central Powers.

When Italy declared neutrality in August 1914, the Mediterranean naval situation eased considerably for the western powers. Only the still neutral Turkish fleet, which had no submarines, and the greatly outnumbered Austria-Hungarian fleet at Pola remained as threats. The French navy instituted cruiser sweeps out of Malta to protect friendly supply lines to Montenegro, and quickly bottled up the Austrians in the Adriatic Sea.

The Austrians, with only five operational submarines in the Adriatic, faced a situation very similar to the German navy's predicament in the North Sea. Unable to break the French blockade of the Adriatic, and worried about nearby Italian forces, the Austrians began waging a *kleinkrieg* of their own against the French. Based out of Pola and Cattaro, submarines raided the nearby French patrol zones. On December 21, 1914, the Austrian *U-2* heavily damaged the French flagship *Jean Bart* off the coast of Montenegro. The attack convinced the French to retreat past the Straits of Otranto, a decision painfully reinforced on the night of April 26–27, 1915 when *U-5*, commanded by Lieutenant Georg Ritter von Trapp, sank the armored cruiser *Leon Gambetta* with 684 sailors. The French, meanwhile, lost one of their own submarines, the *Curie*, during a daring attempt to penetrate the Austrian defenses at Pola.

Contrary to Allied expectations, Italy's entry into the war on their side in May 1915 did not break the Adriatic stalemate. The Austrian *U-4* heavily damaged the British cruiser *Dublin* on June 9 and, four weeks later, the little *UB-14*, with a crew of Germans, sank the Italian armored cruiser *Amalfi*. Lieutenant von Trapp added to his kill score by torpedoing the Italian submarine *Nereide* off Pelagosa.

The Austrians did not escape unscathed. The *U-12* struck a mine off Venice on August 12, and the

Above, left: A closeup of the Austrian *U-5*. The boat had struck a mine on May 16, 1917 but was salvaged and repaired, surviving until 1920. During her career, she had torpedoed two transports, the French *Leon Gambetta* in April 1915 and the Italian *Principe Umberto*. Above, right: The Austrian *U-1* in March 1917. Note the details on the conning tower such as the hatch and periscope mountings. The *U-1*, the first Austrian submarine, was built by Germania Werft in Germany and commissioned in 1909. Small and unseaworthy, the boat spent the entire war defending the naval base at Pola and never left the northern Adriatic. Right: The French transport *Santay*, a 7,247-ton (6,522t) steamer, was sunk sometime in 1916-17.

Above: The Austrian *U-25* (ex-German *UC-13*) lying at Pola in 1915. Although flying an Austrian flag, this submarine was crewed by Germans. Austrian officers and crew served on board as trainees. Transferred to Constantinople in October 1915, *U-25* conducted several patrols to the eastern end of the Black Sea. On November 29, the boat ran aground and was wrecked off the mouth of the Sakaria river along the Anatolian coast.

U-3 was sunk a day later by a French destroyer. Meanwhile, a squadron of British submarines at Venice helped keep the Austrian fleet in port. By the end of the summer, the steel fish had closed down the Adriatic to all comers. As in the North Sea, the threat of the mine, the torpedo boat, and especially the submarine, kept the seas free of warships. Deadlock, it seemed, was not the sole purview of the trenches.

THE DARDANELLES

In the spring of 1915, British, Australian, and French troops launched a bold campaign to seize the Dardanelles, take Constantinople, and drive Turkey out of the war. The attack stalled in the face of stiff Turkish resistance, however, and the ground troops on the Gallipoli peninsula could not expand their beachhead.

The supporting Allied naval forces off the Dardanelles proved as vulnerable to submarine attack as their peers in the North Sea and the Adriatic. More, to some extent, because they were tied down supporting the ground troops. The Austrians did not have long-range submarines, so the Germans dispatched the veteran *U-21*, under the command of Otto Hersing, to the Mediterranean. No German submarine had ever made such a long voyage, but Hersing, by careful rationing, arrived in Cattaro on May 13, with only 1.8 tons (1.6t) of fuel remaining from his original 56.5 tons (50.9t)—the submarine equivalent of running on fumes! German engineers took apart two other boats, of the small UB class, and sent them to Pola by rail for reassembly.

The British, meanwhile, had intercepted wireless messages sent to *U-21* at Cattaro. They warned the warships located off the Dardanelles to expect a U-boat in their area at any time. The battleships, anchored close off the beaches in order to bombard the Turks, hung antitorpedo nets for protection. Small craft were put on alert and began to watch for any sign of the German U-boat.

On May 25, as the *U-21* crept submerged near the Gallipoli peninsula, Hersing sighted three Allied battleships bombarding the Turkish positions. "Rare game for a U-boat," he noted. He moved in closer and, barely three hundred yards (270m) away, took aim at the *Triumph*. He fired a torpedo, set for a surface run, and ordered full submerged speed. The single torpedo bounced over the torpedo nets and fatally

Above: A drawing of *Triumph*, an old British battleship, which is shelling, and being shelled by, Turkish coastal batteries during the Dardanelles campaign. The armored crow's-nest atop the forward mast allowed the fire-control officers to spot the fall of shot for the guns. Below: This photograph reveals the large hole caused by a torpedo striking a ship underwater. The canvas and rope hanging in front of the ship is similiar to antitorpedo netting, although by the end of the war such nets were made of steel wire.

Fishing for Torpedoes

Antitorpedo nets, which look like very heavy fishing nets, were carefully hung off buoys and wooden spars to completely surround an anchored warship. When set up correctly, these nets could prevent a torpedo from striking the warship.

Unfortunately, if the nets were not very carefully maintained they offered little protection. Rotting nets, slack in the ropes, or wave action could compromise the defense by knocking the nets out of alignment.

struck the battleship's hull. As destroyers swarmed near his position, Hersing daringly sailed under the crippled battleship and escaped. Soldiers from both sides of the trenches were able to watch the *Triumph* as it slowly capsized and sank. One of them remembered, "That sinking battleship was a terrible sight. The water was filled with struggling men, and boats trying desperately to pick them up. In the midst of them was the overturned battleship, still floating bottom up. It looked for all the world like a giant whale."

Two days later, Hersing returned to the same area and encountered the *Majestic* surrounded by patrol boats. The rough sea helped camouflage the "asparagus" as he plotted the attack, and again, Hersing was not spotted. The *U-21* fired another single torpedo, lowered the periscope, and made its escape. This time the torpedo tore its way through the torpedo nets to detonate against the battleship's hull. The *Majestic* capsized within four minutes.

After this second disaster, the British and French diverted even more small craft to the area, laid stronger net and boom defenses, and used shallow-draft monitors instead of battleships for shore bombardment. While these extensive defenses made German U-boats much less effective, they also illustrated how costly antisubmarine measures could be: a single U-boat had sunk two battleships that cost twenty times as much. Stopping the menace required a wholesale effort involving dozens of warships and extensive static defenses.

The British and French navies, meanwhile, waged their own submarine war against the Turks with similarly effective results. On December 13, 1914, the British *B-11* sank the ancient Turkish pre-dreadnought *Messudiyeh* near Cape Hellas. Beginning in April 1915, submarines also traveled up the Dardanelles for operations off Constantinople. Though the French and the British lost four submarines each to net defenses, mines, and enemy submarines, several British boats operated very successfully in the Sea of Marmara. A submarine sank the Turkish battleship *Barbarossa* on August 8 and, by the end of the campaign in January 1916, one destroyer, five gunboats, eleven transports, and twenty-five steamers had suffered a similar fate at the hands of British submariners. In addition, *E-11* and *E-14* had both shelled the coastal road in an attempt to cut the Turkish supply line to Gallipoli.

THE BLACK SEA

Although the Russians treated this region as a backwater, they still had a stronger Black Sea fleet than the Turks. In 1914, the fleet included four old and short-range submarines initially assigned to the defense of Sevastapol and the Russian coast. When several new submarines entered service in 1915, however, matters changed. These boats, along with destroyers and seaplane carriers, spread havoc along the Turkish Anatolian coast. *Krab*, an early mine-laying submarine, successfully planted numerous minefields off the Bosphoru and the Bulgarian coast. These attacks paralyzed Turkish shipping until the two revolutions of 1917 disrupted Russian naval operations.

The Turks, who could not build their own submarines, tried to counterattack using a few small German submarines sent through the Mediterranean in the summer of 1915. They patrolled the Russian coast, and although they forced the Russians to divert many destroyers to defensive convoy duty, the boats lacked endurance and sank only a few Russian ships. Larger boats, such as the *U-33*, which arrived in the spring of 1916, had similarly bad luck. Clear water, a lack of targets, and excellent Russian lookouts plagued the U-boats. To make matters worse, four submarines were lost to mines in late 1916. Unlike the restricted waters elsewhere in Europe, German submarines accomplished very little in the Black Sea.

THE BALTIC SEA

The restricted geography of the Baltic, to a much greater extent than the Black Sea, was more suited to mines and submarines. This became apparent very early in the war. The Germans blunted offensive sweeps by the Russian fleet when *U-26* torpedoed the armored cruiser *Palladia* on October 10, 1914. It sank with no survivors. German patrol sweeps were restricted, in turn, when they learned that British submarines had entered the Baltic. In 1915, both sides tried to lay submarine traps, in which enemy forces were lured in front of lurking submarines, but the tricks were largely unsuccessful. Extensive minelaying also made offensive operations difficult. The best targets, in a reversal of other theaters in World War I, proved to be German merchant ships.

In the summer of 1915, all of Germany's seaborne commerce, including the important iron ore trade with Sweden, took place in the Baltic. Such shipping activity did not go unnoticed by the British. By the end of the year, three British submarines had disrupted the trade by sinking fourteen steamers. E-8 also torpedoed the German armored cruiser *Prinz Adalbert* on October 23. The hit detonated the warship's magazines and left only three survivors. More British submarines followed in 1916, but harassment by swarms of German patrol boats and aircraft made them ineffective. Russia, meanwhile, had only a few submarines with the range to operate off the Swedish coast. They lost three submarines, *Bars*, *Lvica*, and *AG-14*, in attempts to disrupt the Swedish ore trade. As in the Black Sea, they had more success with surface forces.

A CRUEL WAR

Ever since November 1914, when Otto Hersing in *U-21* left the survivors of a British merchant ship to die at sea with the remark, "war is war," the World War I submarine campaign has been labeled a cruel and inhuman affair. Although somewhat ironic, given the slaughter of millions on the battlefields of Europe, that label has stuck. This reputation comes partly from the horrible image of innocent women and children drowning at sea. But that image was reinforced, one could even say enforced, by effective Allied propaganda. The British blockade, it was argued, only interfered with property, which could eventually be returned. But a life taken by submarine torpedoes fired from "unsporting ambush" was gone for good. Sympathy and international public opinion sided with Britain and France.

Several particular events also colored public perceptions, producing heroes and scoundrels on both sides of the submarine war. One U-boat commander, who became internationally famous for his chivalry, was Lothar von Arnauld de la Perière. He and his *U-35*, on a single patrol in the Mediterranean, sank fifty-four vessels. Von Arnauld and his crew, with their mascot, a monkey named Fipps, ended the war with the highest score of any submariner. A total of 195 ships fell to von Arnauld's gunfire and torpedoes, approaching nearly 500,000 tons (450,000t). He was known for always strictly obeying the Prize Regulations and going far beyond reasonable efforts to provide assistance to survivors, such as radioing the location of lifeboats to Allied authorities. His honorable tally was marred only on February 26,

1916, when he torpedoed the French liner *Provence* off Greece. The ship listed immediately, rendering many lifeboats unusable, and more than one thousand French troops drowned

Most submarines, especially when far out to sea, knew they could not help survivors, but grimly proceeded to sink ships anyway. The *U-202*, commanded by Adolf K.G.E. von Spiegel, torpedoed an animal transport in April 1916. Looking through the periscope he saw:

> . . . All her decks lay visible to me. From the hatchways a storming, despairing mass of men were fighting their way on deck, grimy stokers, officers, soldiers, grooms, cooks. They all rushed, ran, screamed for boats, tore and thrust one another from the ladders leading down to them, fought for the lifebelts and jostled one another on the sloping deck. All amongst them, rearing, slipping horses are wedged. . . . Then —a second explosion . . . the white steam drove the horses mad. I saw a beautiful long-tailed dapple-grey horse take a mighty leap over the berthing rails and land into a fully laden boat. At that point I could not bear the sight any longer, and I lowered the periscope and dived deep.

The survivors, like countless others, faced a miserable struggle for life in open boats, exposed to the waves and bitter cold, and most probably a slow death from starvation and thirst.

But the tales told by ragged survivors who had lived despite the loss of their ship and the merciless sea were not the only reports of atrocities. On August 19, 1915, the *U-27* surfaced to search the merchant ship *Nicosian*. A British armed steamer, the *Baralong*, approached under American colors and, when hidden behind the merchantman, hoisted the white ensign. It then moved into view and opened fire. The submarine received repeated hits and began to sink. A dozen U-boat sailors managed to swim to the mer-

The Russian submarine *Akula*, built in 1908, shown on the building ways at the Baltic shipyards, St. Petersburg. The officer in the foreground is the designer, Bubnov.

Above: The American-flagged naval transport *Covington* sinking off Brest on July 2, 1918. The ship had been built in 1908 at a shipyard in Danzig, seized by U.S. customs officials at Boston in April 1917, and handed over to the U.S. Navy. Between October 1917 and July 1918, the troopship had safely transported over 21,000 soldiers from Hoboken, New Jersey, to France. Ironically, the German-built ship was sunk by a German torpedo fired from *U-86* on July 1, 1918.

chant ship. The *Baralong* opened fire on them and, after six managed to clamber aboard *Nicosian*, sent a boarding party of Marines who hunted down and killed the unarmed Germans. This affair, like the "piracy" of the U-boats, hardened animosities on all sides.

1916: THE TWILIGHT PHASE

For most of 1916, the German government grappled with the problem of how to hurt the British without harming neutrals. They ordered more submarines, including some very long-range boats, and by March 1916 had fifty-two boats in service. Although under orders not to sink unarmed or neutral vessels, the U-boats still claimed 352 merchant ships by the end of April. But even this campaign ebbed. After the sinking of the *Sussex* off Dieppe in March 1916, which killed twenty-five American passengers, President Wilson told the Kaiser that the United States would sever relations with Germany if the campaign continued. The Kaiser, unwilling to push the issue, backed down after a month of pressure. Tighter restrictions on U-boat operations lowered the tally to 126 ships in May and June.

The German government, still worried about diplomatic incidents, refused to countenance a return to the unrestricted measures desired by the U-boat captains. The Kaiser's military strategists, however, particularly General Erich von Falkenhayn, did not believe they could win the war without help from the U-boats at sea. They continually pressed the Kaiser to reinstate the unrestricted submarine war, believing that by cutting off supplies to Britain and France they would ease the pressure the German armies faced on the western front.

In June 1916, the British and German battle fleets fought the inconclusive naval battle of Jutland in the North Sea. Stung by the failure to break the Royal Navy's blockade, the German admiralty now argued that if the U-boats were liberated from all restrictions they could bring Britain to her knees. Britain, they noted, had only eleven million tons (9.9 million t) of shipping to supply Britain and its continental army. By sinking 600,000 tons (540,000t) a month and terrorizing neutral carriers, the U-boats might reduce traffic by roughly forty percent. U-boats, after all, were already sinking large numbers of ships, even when they followed the

restrictive Prize Regulations. The Admiralstab hoped that "real" unrestricted warfare would reduce British commerce to intolerable levels.

In September 1916, new submarines, such as the UB-II long-range boats, joined the Flanders flotilla and ranged throughout the western approaches to Britain. More submarines were sent to the Mediterranean and a few others operated off the Atlantic coast. By January 1917, these increased patrols had sunk an incredible 929 merchant ships in six months, all for the cost of only ten U-boats. But the British merchant marine, because of new construction and additional leased ships from neutral powers, was still 94 percent of its size at the start of the war. Holtzendorff, chief of the German admiralty, decided that only a completely unrestricted campaign could sink enough merchant shipping to force the Allies to the peace table. The final campaign, conducted with a force of 105 U-boats, was launched on February 1, 1917.

1917: UNRESTRICTED SUBMARINE WARFARE

With this decision, the Germans gambled they could win the war before American troops could contribute to the Allied effort. General Ludendorff's sentiments were: "What can she do? She cannot come over here! . . . I do not give a damn about America." The U-boats, which had reached 125 in service by the year's end, departed with their new orders and began to wreak havoc on merchant shipping. Freed from the restrictions of the Prize Regulations in early 1917, the U-boats attacked any ship (aside from some neutrals off Spain and Greece) in the seas around the British Isles, the Mediterranean, and the Russian Far North. They enjoyed huge success. In February, 254 vessels fell to U-boat attacks; in March another 310 ships went under. April saw the greatest U-boat score, when 413 ships went to the bottom. In that three-month period, the U-boats sank a staggering 977 merchant ships, at the cost of only nine of their own submarines.

The Austro-Hungarian navy joined in this effort by increasing its efforts in the Mediterranean. Assisted by German U-boats, the two dozen or so Austrian U-boats attacked the Gibraltar-Suez trade routes with a vengeance. Over the course of the war, 108 enemy merchant ships fell victim to these submarines.

In April 1917, the submarines seemed favored in the campaign. The sinking rate was more than adequate, and the terrorized neutral shipping would not sail. Although ruthless diplomatic and shipping-control efforts by Britain forced most neutral nations to continue trading, ships were sinking so fast that the total available tonnage kept shrinking. The inability of British shipyards to construct and repair enough merchant ships made matters doubly worse. Steel and labor shortages in private shipyards, both caused by the demands of the Royal Navy, left about one million tons (900,000t) of shipping in port at any one time. When asked about the German campaign, the first sea lord, Admiral Sir John Jellicoe, remarked, "They will win, unless we can stop these losses, and stop them soon."

ANTISUBMARINE OPERATIONS

Earlier in the war, the British had outfitted heavily armed vessels and disguised them as harmless merchant ships. Known as "Q-ships," these vessels lured U-boats to the surface by having part of the crew pretend to abandon ship, and then attacked the submarine with hidden guns. The *Baralong*, which sank *U-27* and *U-36* in 1915, was a Q-ship. This tactic was defensive, for the Q-ship had to passively wait to be attacked, and dangerous, for the Germans showed no mercy once they saw through the disguise. In fact, U-boats sank sixteen Q-ships in 1917 alone. Another variation involved having a trawler tow a friendly submerged submarine on a cable. When a U-boat stopped the trawler the hidden submarine would torpedo the unsuspecting German. The British *C-24*, towed by the trawler *Taranak*, sank the *U-40* on June 27, 1915 with just such a tactic.

But Q-ships and friendly submarines alone could not stop the hemorrhage. U-boats continued to sink Allied merchant ships at a frightening rate. Offensive patrols by destroyers and patrol sloops proved disappointing. President Wilson said it was "like finding a needle in a haystack," and festooning ships with primitive hydrophones, hoping to hear the submarines, proved even less useful.

In another effort, the Allies laid minefields, also called barrages, from the French "barrier," across suspected U-boat transit routes, including one enormous project that called for laying seventy thousand mines

across the North Sea. Other minefields were laid along the north German coast, east of Dover and Flanders, and off Otranto, Italy, to seal these areas. These huge efforts required tens of thousands of mines and countless numbers of small patrol craft.

Improved antisubmarine weapons offered still another answer. In 1916, the British began to use depth charges, first developed from an idea by Admiral Sir Charles Madden. The depth charge was simply a three hundred pound (135kg) explosive bomb that used a pressure sensitive detonator to explode at a preset depth. This revolutionized antisubmarine efforts because escorts no longer had to lure a U-boat to the surface to ram and shoot it with gunfire. The U-boat crews, who took a serious pounding when subjected to a depth-charge attack, nicknamed them "sugar plums."

Another especially useful innovation was the antisubmarine aircraft patrol. Aircraft could search wide areas of ocean and, on occasion, be deadly. On September 15, 1916, for example, Austrian aircraft bombed and sank the French submarine *Foucault* off Cattaro. This sinking was unusual, however. The aircraft's most important function, accomplished simply by flying overhead, was to force submarines below the surface. By slowing the submarine to a submerged crawl, thereby effectively blinding it, aircraft protected merchant shipping in the area. Patrols proved so useful that by November 1, 1918, there were 285 seaplanes, 272 landplanes, and one hundred airships assigned to antisubmarine duty.

Although helpful, these antisubmarine efforts did not offer truly effective means of stopping the shipping bloodbath. The solution, which the British Admiralty stumbled on during the summer of 1916, was to convoy merchant ships in groups from port to port. This was an old idea but one that had been difficult to implement during the war. First, neutral shipping had to cooperate. Waiting around until a convoy formed tended to frustrate shipowners. It took time to gather enough convoy escorts, and lost time meant lost money. If too weakly defended, moreover, a pack of slow merchant ships simply presented a nice opportunity for a U-boat to sink them all at once. Other problems included organizing the rendezvous points, the slow speed of some ships, the difficulties of formation sailing, and congestion in ports. If the Royal Navy could solve those problems, however, convoying might slow the losses.

Top: A remarkable photograph of a British steamer about to take its final plunge to the bottom of the sea. Torpedoed by a U-boat, the crew has had time to man the lifeboats. Note the seaman hanging from a rope toward the top of the picture. Bottom: French marines investigate the mangled remains of an unidentified U-boat on the beach near Calais. The damage was caused by scuttling charges set by the German crew as they abandoned ship. Although unclear, it is possible this is one of the fourteen U-boats destroyed by the Dover Barrage, a vast system of patrol boats, searchlights, drift nets, and minefields set up across the English Channel to prevent U-boats from reaching the Atlantic.

The British Admiralty's opinion about convoys shifted once the United States entered the war. Orders for more escorts went out to American shipyards, and a half-dozen American destroyers, with thirty-six more on the way, joined the escort forces in May 1917. Emboldened by American entry into the war, and impressed with that country's industrial production, the British Admiralty finally authorized two "experimental" convoys, one traveling to Britain from Gibraltar and another from the United States. Both sailed in May and, save for one straggler that dropped out of formation, neither lost a ship.

That summer merchant ships sailed in convoys with continued success. The U-boats found convoys difficult to attack and the dramatic sinking rate of the spring declined. Losses were still very heavy, averaging roughly 460,000 tons (414,000t) a month through the end of the year, but in the face of improved convoy defenses, such as patrol aircraft and wireless communications, losses declined. Meanwhile, increased Allied construction, the reduction of port congestion, and the concentration on

importing only essential materials greatly increased the efficiency of global shipping. By the middle of 1918, it was clear that the unrestricted submarine warfare campaign had failed.

TRANSATLANTIC OPERATIONS

In an effort to stem the flow of men and material to Britain and France, Germany modified a number of large "mercantile" submarines, which had been used to run the British blockade, into U-cruisers. These were submarines capable of traversing the Atlantic and attacking shipping off North America. The first to make the attempt was the *U-151*, under the command of Lieutenant Commander Heinrich von Nostitz und Janckendorff, in April 1918. Foreshadowing the disaster that would occur during World War II, *U-151* laid mines off Baltimore and Delaware harbors before attacking shipping. While off the coast of New York, Janckendorff joked with his men about going ashore, "taking a night off along

Above: This 1920 painting shows the armored cruiser *San Diego* going down off Long Island, New York, on July 19, 1918. Although often ascribed to a torpedo, *San Diego* was actually sunk by a mine laid by *U-156*. Like most of the major warships in the U.S. Navy, the cruiser had spent her last year escorting convoys from New York to Halifax and beyond. Left: Three grimy and tired crewmembers of *E-2* returning to Norfolk after a long war patrol during the summer of 1918. In an effort to find German U-boats operating in American waters, *E-2* conducted four such patrols off Cape Hatteras between May 21 and August 27.

Above: The flag indicates the *UB-88* is one of the four ex-German submarines taken over by the U.S. Navy in early 1919. The American crew sailed her from Britain to New York, and then took the submarine on a long "war bond" cruise down the East coast, up the Mississippi, and eventually through the Panama Canal to California, Oregon, and Washington. On March 1, 1921, the ex-U-boat was taken out to sea and sunk by *Wickes* (DD-75) during a gunnery exercise. Over her almost two-year career in the Imperial German Navy, the coastal submarine sank thirteen merchant ships while serving in the Flanders Flotilla at Zeebrugge, Belgium. Right: A German U-boat lies stranded on the coast of England. This is almost certainly one of the seven U-boats that foundered while being towed to Harwich following the surrender of Germany in November, 1918.

the Great White Way. Fire Island Beach was also a temptation." Instead, he and his crew began destroying enemy ships.

U-151 took twenty-six prisoners off three fishing schooners before sending the American vessels to the bottom, cut two underwater telegraph cables, and sank six ships off New Jersey. On June 2, 1918, it attacked the passenger liner *Carolina* . By the end of his rampage, Janckendorff had sunk twenty-three ships and his mines took four more to the bottom. Prophetically, he noted, ". . . for the day will come when submarines will think no more of a voyage across the Atlantic than they do now of a raid across the North Sea. America's isolation is now a thing of the past."

THE END OF THE GREAT WAR

Despite the success of *U-151*'s raid on America and the ensuing disruption of coastal trade, stepped-up American patrols reduced future efforts by the U-cruisers to lackluster results. Other events, meanwhile, hastened the collapse of the German U-boat campaign. Crews aboard warships of the German navy mutinied in October 1918, paralyzing the surface fleet. In response, the Admiralstab ordered loyal U-boats to sink any German warship that was flying the red flag, the adopted symbol of revolt. Only the armistice, which was signed on November 11, 1918,

prevented this fratricide. The peace negotiations then scuttled, scrapped, or divided up the warships of the Imperial German Navy among the victorious Allied powers.

The U-boat war had been costly in both men and material. The U-boats sank ten capital ships, eighteen cruisers, and 5,078 merchant ships. More than fifteen thousand merchant seaman and civilians perished. Thousands of Allied sailors and soldiers died in submarine attacks. In turn, 178 U-boats with more than 5,300 sailors were lost.

Moral outrage at the depredations of the U-boats brought the nations of the world together to outlaw unrestricted submarine warfare. As with poison gas, the world hoped to never again witness such carnage. Navies, however, studied the military results of the U-boat campaign with great care. Unlike poison gas, which had ultimately proven a weapon of greater horror than effect, the submarine had delivered measurable military results. Against all prewar expectations, the submarine had almost shut down the seas. It was a lesson no one thought could be forgotten.

Chapter 3

Interlude 1919–1939

UNDER THE TERMS OF THE 1918 ARMISTICE, THE IMPERIAL GERMAN NAVY surrendered 184 of its U-boats to the victorious Allies. Another 149 submarines still under construction were scrapped in the shipyards. Most of these U-boats were sunk as targets or salvaged over the next few years, but each Allied country kept a few submarines as war prizes. Allied naval engineers scrutinized captured U-boats for technical details and many of the German design and engineering features were integrated into postwar submarines. The United States, for example, took six U-boats and studied the German diesel and electric engines to improve their own power-plant designs.

As a result of these investigations, the dangerous gasoline engines common in American submarines were replaced by the safer and more reliable diesel engines. A number of countries, including France and Japan, incorporated the captured U-boats directly into their own operational submarine fleets.

Naval analysts also pondered the more strategic impact of the submarine on sea power: the boat had proved itself a potentially war-winning weapon. In combination with minefields, the submarine had not only shut down shipping in European coastal waters, but had virtually eliminated warship operations near enemy coasts. In addition, a ruthless *guerre de course* campaign had caused heavy merchant ship losses, disrupted global shipping patterns, and forced the Allies to implement costly defensive measures. World War I illustrated that a navy could successfully wage a war on commerce with submarines. That the Allies defeated the German effort because of greater wealth and resources did not invalidate this conclusion. It only meant that a huge effort would be needed should another war occur.

The implications of another war were particularly unsettling for Great Britain. British strategists suspected that a great maritime coalition, like the one that defeated the Kaiser's U-boats, might not be assembled again. That was a problem because the submarine, unlike the battleship, was important not because it was unsinkable, but because it was replaceable. The German navy during World War I had steadily increased their submarine numbers, despite sometimes alarming losses, and they had manned this force, as one historian put it, "by fewer men in the U-boats than in a single army division. . . ."

These four ex-German U-boats, obviously spoils of war, are shown moored at the Brooklyn Navy Yard in April, 1919. The American flags indicate the boats are in U.S. Navy commission, a practice of the time to allow American crews to sail the submarines home from Germany. The crowd gathered on the wharf includes civilians, who paid to tour the infamous U-boats and helped pay off war-bonds in the process. The twin lattice-masts in the far background are the fire-control towers on an American battleship.

The thought of having to endure such an attack again, when it could be mounted so cheaply and so effectively, led Britain to press for the abolition of submarines as a weapon of war. The Versailles Treaty, which effectively ended World War I, eased British anxiety by forbidding Germany to possess submarines.

In 1921, when the nations of the world convened to negotiate a worldwide reduction in naval armaments, the British continued the campaign for the complete abolition of submarines. From the British perspective, the potential danger submarines posed to commerce far outweighed any advantage the Royal Navy might gain from the submersible craft.

The French and the Americans, less threatened by the idea of a submarine war against merchant shipping (maybe because most of the world's shipping was British) resisted these demands. U.S. Senator Elihu Root suggested that restrictions on the conduct of a submarine war might be incorporated into the arms reduction treaty, but the U.S. Navy objected, saying such restrictions "introduced ambiguities in the rules governing their [submarine] use." American submariners were already thinking how useful submarines could be, against the commerce of both Japan and Britain, should it be necessary. The final treaty, signed in 1922, limited the number of warships in the various navies, particularly battleships and cruisers, and limited the size and armament of major warships. The question of submarines was left unresolved.

Over the course of three more naval disarmament conferences, held in 1925, 1930, and 1935, the British persisted in trying to eliminate submarines altogether. Once again, however, the smaller naval powers voted against the idea. The conferees did have more success in limiting the total number of submarines each country could build, as well as limiting the size and armament of each type. The United States, Britain, and Japan agreed to limit the number and size of the boats in their submarine fleets. Neither France nor Italy signed the London Naval Treaty, but each agreed to limit new submarine construction.

Of more particular interest to submariners, however, was article twenty-two of the treaty, which reinstated the regulations governing commerce warfare. The Prize Restrictions again became the law of the sea. Although few submarines were actually built in the 1920s and early 1930s, because of the arms limitation conferences and the global economic depres-

sion, the world's industrial navies still struggled with such questions as how many submarines to build, how to incorporate new technology, and who the enemy would be.

THE ROYAL NAVY

Though they had scrapped most of their wartime fleet in order to save money, the Royal Navy maintained a small submarine force during the 1920s. Like other navies, the British incorporated some German U-boat technology into postwar designs, but also experimented with new ideas about weapons, sensors, and communications.

The primary focus of the submarine force remained on antisubmarine (ASW) operations. British engineers concentrated on building boats with small silhouettes, high underwater speed, and quiet machinery—all designed to give Royal Navy submarines an advantage against enemy boats. In addition, Britain built eighteen long-range submarines for operations in the Indian and Pacific Oceans. Improving communications equipment and rescue gear remained a concern, especially after the entire crew of the *M-1* perished when it was run over by a steamship off Devonshire in 1925.

After failing to put an end to the building of submarines through the disarmament conferences, the British continued to refine their ASW measures during the 1930s. In addition to using their submarines to hunt enemy submarines (a familiar tactic from World War I), they also fielded ASDIC devices on a large scale. A ship equipped with the acoustic sensor could send out a sound pulse and, by analyzing the echoes produced by a submarine's hull, determine the rough bearing and range of the target. The Royal Navy placed great faith in the device, even to the point of stating that an ASDIC-fitted destroyer "could do the work of a whole flotilla." Although not quite the panacea the British thought it was, ASDIC finally provided the means for locating submerged submarines and seemed the answer to the upstart weapon.

WEIMAR AND NAZI GERMANY

The Germans continued to view the submarine as both a commerce destroyer and an equalizer uniquely suited to help small naval powers. Although restricted by the Treaty of Versailles from owning submarines, German officials felt this restriction was

Left: Another captured submarine, the minelayer *UC-5*, lying in the Thames River, London, with a few British sailors enjoying the sun.

intolerable, given the hostility of Poland and France toward Germany. The German navy feared that coastal islands and fishing rights would be lost to enemies in much the same way that a defense vacuum had encouraged Polish encroachments in Silesia during 1919.

The German navy was forced to maintain its submarine technology, and its experienced engineers, by subterfuge. A dummy corporation, staffed partially by German engineers, was set up under Dutch auspices to develop submarine technology in 1922. The company built submarines for the Finnish, Turkish, and Spanish navies, and gained valuable experience in design and construction not possible within Germany. Advisors, designers, and workers were also sent to companies in Japan and Argentina.

All these projects supplied test data to a clandestine U-boat department. It studied new technology and construction procedures, and developed plans to re-create the German U-boat fleet should the international situation permit. These updates included work on powerful new diesel engines, safer batteries, and improved underwater controls. Plans were begun in 1932 to construct a few U-boats in secret, but naval discussions with Britain on arms control slowed progress. There were also voices of dissent against the submarine in the German naval command: some officers questioned the value of U-boats—given the British deployment of ASDIC—and felt the submarine should not be the sole weapon in a war of commerce destruction. It was not until 1936, when the Versailles restrictions were repudiated, that German shipyards began to construct U-boats.

Several new designs had been proposed over the years and in 1935 two coastal craft, the Type IIA and IIB, were ordered. These were small 126-foot (38m) boats, with a crew of twenty-five, and could make only thirteen knots on the surface. With only six torpedoes, and a range of less than two thousand nautical miles (3,706km), these boats were designed solely for defensive operations off the coast. A larger Type IX, roughly 230 feet (69m) long, was built for long-range operations in the Atlantic. With a range of 8,100 nautical miles (15,011km), and a surface speed of eighteen knots, it had the endurance to be a successful commerce raider.

But slow diving speed and poor underwater handling convinced U-boat designers to build the Type VII. Smaller, with a range of 6,500 nautical miles

(12,046km), it turned out to be a very maneuverable patrol submarine. The Type VII was the most numerous of all German U-boats built during World War II; it became central to determining the limits and possibilities of German submarine strategy. A few larger minelayers, seaplane carriers, and very long range U-cruisers were also built.

THE AMERICANS

The success of the U-boats during World War I did not go unnoticed by the U.S. Navy. Nor did the failures—mechanical breakdowns, low endurance, and poor seakeeping—of their own wartime operations in the Atlantic and off the Philippines. Indeed, those failures reinvigorated navy planners to develop a more reliable ocean-going submarine. Since the most likely enemy of the United States was Japan, the two main submarine types developed during the early 1920s were designed with Pacific Ocean operations in mind. The first was a small coastal submarine intended to patrol important coastal areas, such as the Panama Canal, and to protect other U.S. possessions, such as Hawaii, Guam, and the Philippines. The second kind of submarine was the larger fleet-type, to accompany the battle fleet, gather intelligence about enemy movements, and strike at enemy warships before a major engagement at sea.

Above: One of the first periscope pictures ever taken, this photo was shot by Lt. W.M. Young, USN, from an R-boat at Pearl Harbor in 1919. Below: In an attempt to enhance the submarine's scouting mission, many navies experimented with submersible aircraft hangars. The Martin MS-1 floatplane, shown on the deck of the U.S. Navy's *S-1* (SS-105) in 1923, was a single-seat reconnaissance plane capable of quick assembly on the deck of the submarine. When launched, the plane could extend the submarine's search radius by many hundreds of miles. After returning to the submarine, the plane could be rapidly disassembled and stored in the waterproof hangar fitted aft of the conning tower.

New ideas for U.S. submarine development came from the Submarine Officers Conference (SOC). The SOC, established after World War I, consisted of submarine officers chosen by the chief of naval operations (CNO). The group's first designs used American-built diesel engines but because of engineering problems, none of the submarines built in the 1920s were very successful: the boats could not reach high enough speeds to cooperate with the battle fleet.

In addition, the American submarines were slow to dive, prone to oil leaks, and plagued by diesel engine breakdowns. The Navy then obtained a license to build German-style diesel engines, which, the Navy believed, were better than anything domestic manufacturers could produce. Once installed, however, these engines proved just as troublesome. The inability of the fleet submarine to function with the fleet forced the Navy's submarine experts to completely rethink the role of American submarines.

Submarine proponents, such as Captains Thomas Hart and Charles A. Lockwood, proposed placing submarines ahead of the battle line to gather intelligence for the fleet. As a long-range scout, the submarine required a large fuel storage space, many torpedoes, and roomy living conditions for the crew, who might be at sea for up to sixty days at a time. Surface speed, on the other hand, would not be as important.

So began the concept of the long-range patrol submarine operating deep within enemy waters and independent of the battle fleet. Capitalizing on the development of high-powered diesel engines for the railroad industry, the Navy moved ahead with a new medium-sized submarine design. Starting with *Dolphin* in 1929, this type of long-range patrol submarine was built with the large interior spaces for the engines, crew, and armament common to World War II American submarines.

During the 1930s, when the U.S. Navy received more funds to increase fleet size, twenty-six new submarines were built, all of the *Porpoise*, *Sargo*, or *Salmon* classes. They were roughly 310 feet (93m) in length, carried a crew of about fifty-five, and were armed with four twenty-one-inch (52.5cm) forward torpedo tubes. The *Porpoise* class also had two stern tubes, the *Sargo* and *Salmon* classes had four. Each also mounted a three-inch (7.5cm) deck gun and a few fifty-caliber machine guns (later upgraded to a five-inch [12.5cm] deck gun and 40- and 20-millimeter machine cannons) for antiaircraft defense. Perhaps more importantly, given the hot weather in the Pacific, the submarines were equipped with air-conditioning. By late 1941, eighty-seven more submarines, designed along the same lines, were built or on order.

American submarines also received the newly designed torpedo data computer (TDC). The analog computer calculated a torpedo's gyro angle based on the target's range, bearing, speed, and course. As with the more primitive fire control of World War I, that information was still gathered from short glances through the periscope. But once plugged into the computer, the firing solution was automatically generated and electronically transmitted to the torpedo gyro. Later models of the TDC were even equipped with a small radar to help determine the target's position. Since all this data could be changed up to the moment of firing, the new equipment produced a very accurate firing solution.

By the end of the 1930s, American submarines had become quite sophisticated in construction. The pressure hull was all welded, eliminating the need for rivets, and made from high-grade steel alloys. The interior piping and electrical systems, as well as the crew quarters, were very advanced for the time. In addition, an escape breathing apparatus was supplied to all submariners. Two accidents had illustrated the

Top: This photo of *O-2* (SS-63), shown here on November 26, 1943 during dive training exercises off New London, Connecticut, clearly reveals the spray kicked up by expelled air venting out the back of the ballast tanks as seawater rushed in the front. The speed at which the ballast tanks flooded helped determine how fast a submarine could dive. Below, left: When all else fails . . . rig sail! Early submarine engines were notoriously fickle, as the crew of *R-14* (SS-91) discovered in early May 1921. While cruising far southeast of Hawaii, the power plant failed and repairs at sea could not coax the engines back to life. The crew responded by fitting a swath of battery-covers to the periscope and sailed home, arriving at Hilo on May 15, after five days under sail.

Above: The bow of *S-48* (SS-159) points vertically out of the waters of Long Island Sound on December 9,1921. The submarine had suffered battery flooding during acceptance trials the night before and had come to rest on the bottom of the shallow waters off Bridgeport, Connecticut. The mixed navy and civilian crew lightened the bow until it protruded from the water, crawled out a torpedo tube, and attracted the attention of Standard Oil Company's Tug No. 28, which rescued them.

To All Submarines at Sea

A technological advance with crucial implications for submarine operations was the establishment of reliable long-range radio communication. Electronic and quartz crystal technology enabled radios to be small enough for installation in submarines. Instead of subs going out on patrol and remaining essentially blind to new developments, radio allowed shore-based commanders to issue new orders after the boats had left port. Entire submarine flotillas could now be directed by one commander and the boats could also communicate with each other while at sea. But radio communication became a double-edged sword: not only could it help submarine commanders find and destroy many more targets, it could also be intercepted by enemy forces.

Above: A submariner clambers into an air lock, a small cylinder with hatches at both ends, which permits underwater escapes without flooding the rest of the submarine. The sailor is wearing an under-water breathing device to supply him with oxygen once he leaves the submarine for the surface. Left: The growing reach of American submarine cruises is revealed in this photo of *V-2* (SS-164) passing through the Panama Canal during the 1930s. The canvas tarps indicate this submarine was used to operating in the hot climate of the Caribbean and the Pacific, while at the same time revealing the lack of air conditioning inside the hull.

need for such a device. On September 25, 1925, the S-51 had been rammed by the merchant steamer *City of Rome* off Block Island, New York. Thirty-three crew members died, partly, it was thought, because of a lack of rescue gear. Then, on December 17, 1927, the S-4 was accidentally rammed by the Coast Guard ship *Paulding*. Rescue and salvage operations were begun immediately and six survivors were discovered by divers in the forward torpedo room. Severe weather thwarted the rescue efforts, however, and the six men eventually suffocated. In all, forty crew members were killed in the disaster. In the aftermath of the tragedy, the Navy realized some sailors might have lived if some type of breathing apparatus had been available to them. Soon afterward, a new rescue device called a Momsen Lung was developed, which enabled submariners to escape from stricken submarines up to two hundred feet (60m) below the surface.

THE RISING SUN

Between the naval alliance with Britain in 1902 and the victory over Tsarist Russia in 1905, Japan became the predominant power in the Far East. Its initial submarine force was a dozen submarines purchased from various European countries, but in the 1920s, the Imperial Japanese Navy began building its own submarines.

In 1919, the Japanese received seven German U-boats as war prizes. With the help of German specialists, many of them former U-boat officers who were lured to Japan by high salaries, a submarine construction yard was established at Kobe, Japan, in the 1920s. Initial production was slow, as these submarines were mostly experimental, but by the 1930s the yard was well established. Over the next decade, the Japanese navy built close to fifty submarines at Kobe.

Submariners wearing German oxygen "lungs," similar to the American Momsen Lung. This apparatus allows the men to breathe bottled air in case of flooded batteries, which release chlorine gas, or to rise to the surface if their submarine is disabled on the bottom.

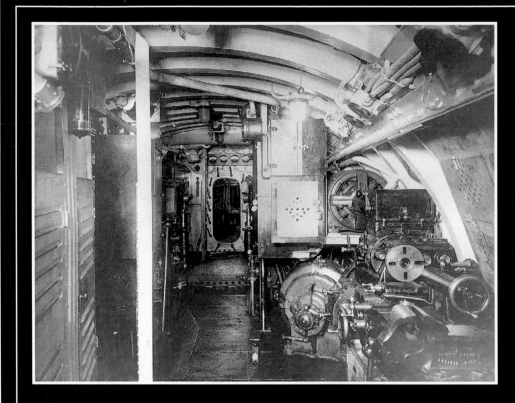

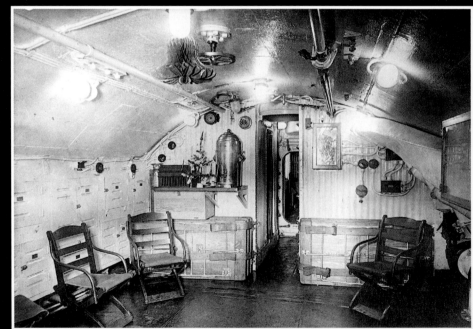

Top, left: This is the view from the aft end of the electric motor room of *S-4* (SS-109). The batteries, which supplied the generator on the right, lie under the steel hatches in the middle of the deck. Note the many levers around the hatch in the rear of the compartment; these were strong enough to seal the closed hatchway in case of flooding further aft. Bottom, left: This shot of *S-4*'s wardroom is misleading regarding the amount of space available to the crew because it has been cleared in preparation for a Christmas party. Note the little tree near the brass coffee pot and the tables stowed underneath. Right: The battered *S-4* lies in dry dock at the Boston Navy Yard in March 1928. The workers are releasing the huge pontoons used to raise the submarine from the bottom off the coast of Massachusetts. Note the severe damage just forward of the gun mount where USCG *Paulding* struck *S-4* on December 17, 1927.

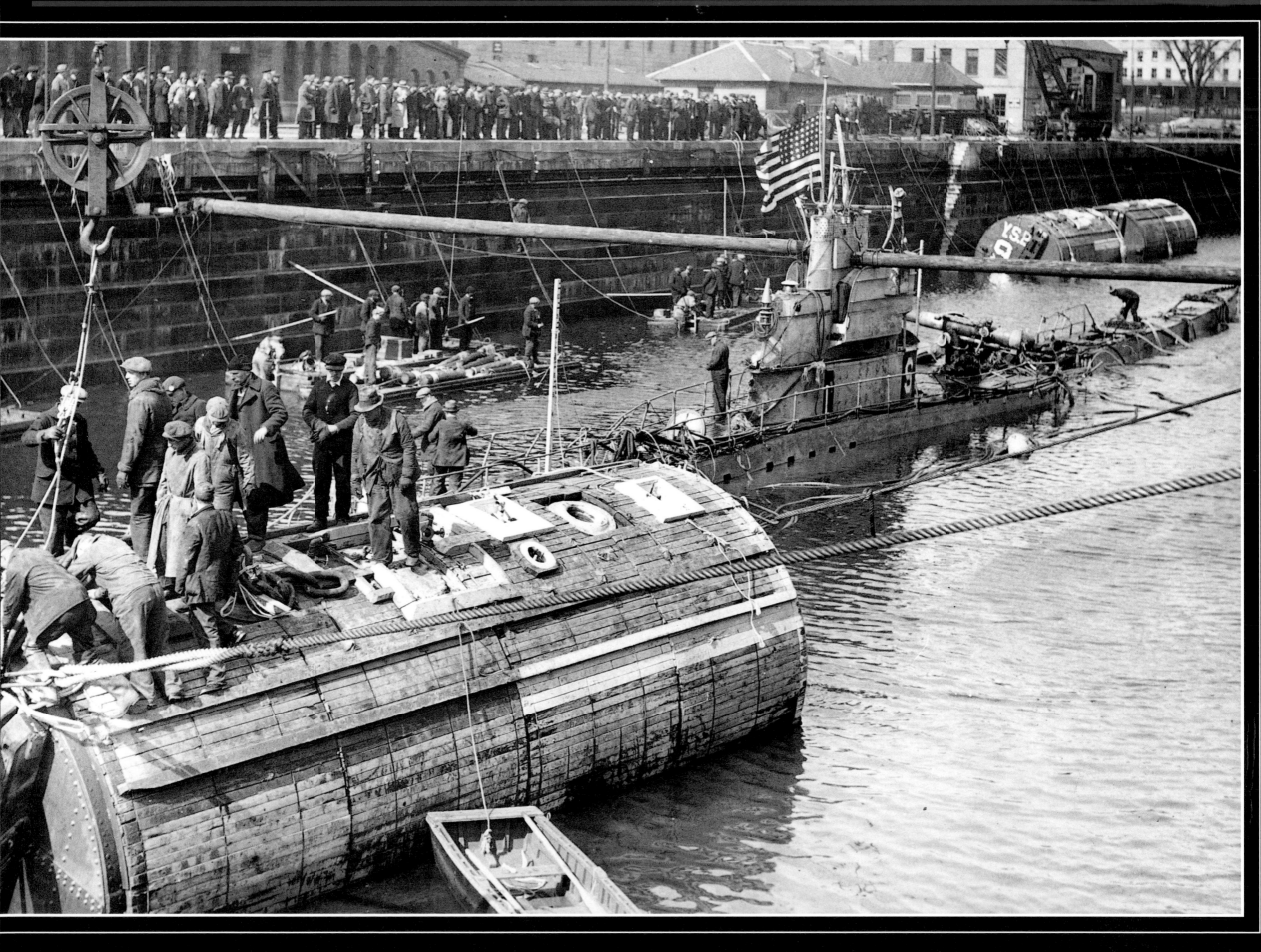

The *Seal (SS-183)* lies in the Anacostia River at the Washington Navy Yard on July 26, 1938. This *Sargo*-class boat was on its shakedown cruise when this photo was taken. A patrol boat, *SC-185*, is moored astern. The very same quay has now been turned into a museum park and, since 1981, is home to the display ship ex-USS *Barry* (DD-93).

The boats were principally of two classes: a large fleet-type, known as the "I" or First Class; and the smaller "RO" or Second Class. Similar to submarine designs in the United States and Britain, the large boat was designed for extended cruises across the Pacific; the smaller type was more suitable for coastal and shallow-water operations. Both types had the usual diesel-electric engines, deck guns, and multiple torpedo tubes. Like the Americans, they also had computer fire-control systems. But the newest Japanese torpedo, the famous Long Lance, was far superior to western designs. With a pure-oxygen fueled engine providing it with a six and a half–mile (9,000m) range, the Long Lance proved a devastating weapon during the Pacific war.

Once the United States was identified as the main hindrance to expansion in Asia, Japanese submarine operations began to mirror the U.S. Navy's operational plans. Japan, too, developed long-range submarines to gather intelligence, and believed the boats would be used chiefly against enemy capital ships. But, unlike the Americans, who had gradually adapted their submarine strategy to long individual patrols, Japanese submariners stubbornly clung to the

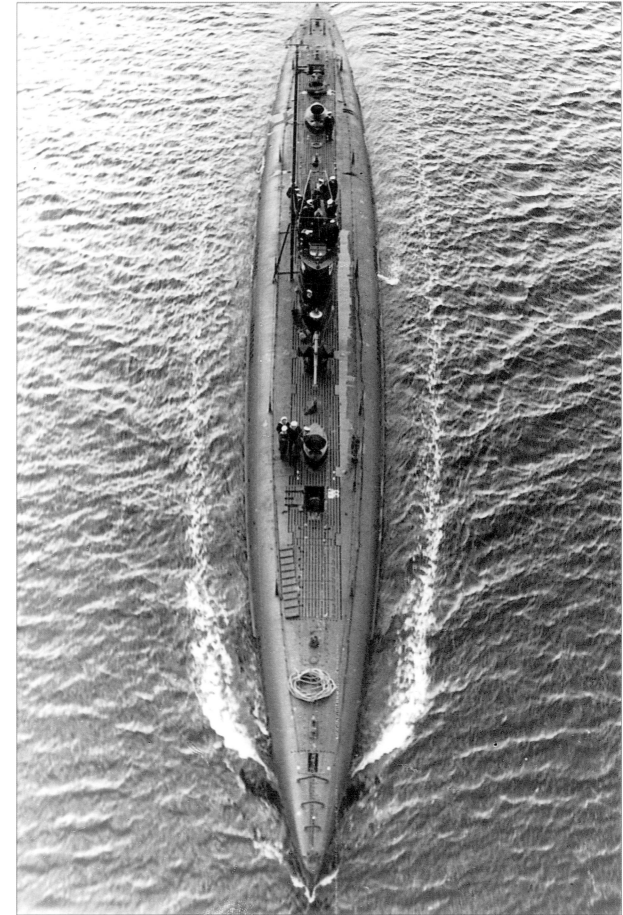

Top: Two sailors demonstrating the use of the 3-inch (7.5cm) deck gun on the *Montgolfier* at Cherbourg soon after World War I. Note the simple gun mount and rudimentary sights common to submarines of this time. Above: A French *Diane*-class submarine, one of the larger boats, being launched sometime during the mid-1930s. These types had a radius of action of 3,000 miles (5,556km) at 10 knots on the surface. Right: An undated photo of a Swedish submarine, probably a *Draken*-class boat, underway in the Baltic. Note the large radio antenna and the grooves, for traction, cut into the deck.

notion of attacking the U.S. battle fleet in one massive, decisive encounter.

There was good reason for such thinking: outnumbered by the larger American navy and overpowered by American battleship superiority, Japan had to wear down U.S. capital ship strength. The long-range submarines, in a manner similar to the German *kleinkrieg* strategy of 1914–1915, were to track enemy warships, repeatedly ambush them, and try to whittle down the superior American battle fleet through attrition.

THE SECOND TIER POWERS

The weaker naval powers continued to build and maintain submarines during the 1920 and 1930s. This activity, as they argued successfully at the various disarmament conferences, was to compensate for a lack of battleships and cruisers.

Italy, hoping to implement a sea denial strategy, built eleven medium-sized, *Marcello*-class submarines for central Mediterranean operations. The 239-foot (73m) submarines had eight torpedo tubes, four forward and four in the stern, and two one hundred-millimeter deck guns. A few large cruiser-type submarines, the 283-foot (84.9m) *Balilla* class, had a range of thirteen thousand nautical miles (24,092km) and were designed for operations off Italy's African colonies in the Red Sea and Indian Ocean.

The French, meanwhile, remained steadfast to their old idea of the submarine as a commerce raider. During the 1930s, they built a large number of medium and small submarines for antishipping operations. The *Diane* class was engineered for short-range operations in the Mediterranean and was considerably smaller than most fleet submarines, measuring only 211 feet (63.3m) in length. The most numerous of France's submarines was the larger *Redoutable* class, 302-foot (92m) ocean-going boats designed to conduct long-range patrols in the Atlantic; thirty-one were built during the 1920s and 1930s. The French navy also experimented with a submarine commerce raider called the *Surcouf*. A huge submarine, it was

The *Nautilus* (SS-168), moored fast to the wharf, probably at Pearl Harbor, in April 1931. The *Narwhal*-class submarine, as the large radio antenna indicates, was one of the newer boats built for long-range reconnaissance missions. For self-defense and anti-merchant ship operations the submarine also carried two 6-inch (15cm) deck guns.

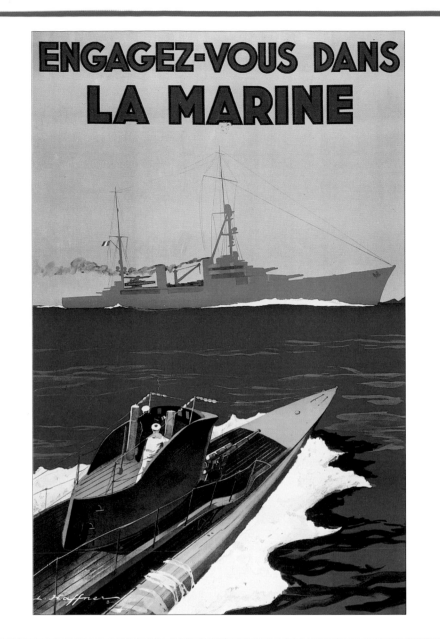

394 feet (119m) long, and was armed with eight tor-pedo tubes and two eight-inch (20cm) deck guns. It also carried a seaplane, a small boat, and a holding cell for prisoners.

Other small naval powers followed either a strategy of numbers or of cost-effectiveness, with the Soviet Union and Holland providing the best examples. The Netherlands, as befitted a small country with a colonial empire in the East Indies, built only a dozen or so long-range submarines. These boats, rela-tively cheap and not too demanding in terms of man-power, supplies, or equipment, were ideally suited for operations amid the vast Indonesian archipelago.

The Soviets, on the other hand, were not con-cerned with long-range operations. Worried about the security of their Baltic, Black Sea, and Far Eastern coasts, the Soviets built some 150 small coastal submarines for inshore operations. These boats, as one historian put it, were designed "as a sort of projection of the army frontier guard into the sea."

Top, left: Obviously influenced by the avant-garde, this French navy recruiting poster was meant to convey an impression of speed, modernity, and dashing adventure. **Top, right:** A group of French officers stand on an unidentified submarine, probably a *Redoutable*-class boat, at Brest or Cherbourg in the mid-1930s. Note the rotating torpedo tubes just under the officers and the port in the superstructure amidships for another set of revolving tubes. **Bottom:** The cruiser-type French submarine *Surcouf* underway at sea. The massive submarine, with a radius of action of 10,000 miles (18,520km) at 10 knots, was the only one of this type built by the French navy.

By the 1930s, despite at least a half-dozen accidental sinkings during the interwar years, submarines had become well established in every major navy. More efficient welding, improved valves and engines, and simple experience made submarines much more reliable. Other changes improved the chances of to escaping stricken submarines. During the First World War, only a handful of crewmen had escaped from the German *UB-57* and *U-51*. Both U-boats had sunk in shallow water, but chlorine gas, caused by water flooding the batteries, suffocated much of the crew. Improvements in escape-hatch fittings and plentiful supplies of escape gear made that dreadful experience less common during World War II.

On the eve of World War II, all the modern navies had capable and well-equipped submarine forces at their disposal. The boats were similar in size and shape; the diesel-electric combination led to a standard design. The boats were safer and more reliable than their World War I counterparts. Most of these submarines shared the same function—scouting and attacking enemy warships. And with interwar improvements in weapons, communications, fire-control systems, and range, the submarine had developed into a devastating weapon.

Above, left: The Italian submarine *Tricheco* being prepared for launch at the navy yard near Rome in the early 1930s. The name translates to "Walrus." Note the folding hydroplanes. Above, right: Three submarines of the *Balilla* class moored at Boston during their March-to-October 1933 transatlantic deployment. Note the 4.7-inch (11.7cm) gun housed partially inside the sail. Its position served the dual purpose of protecting the crew from splinters and the gun from the elements. Bottom: A photo of the *Antonio Sciesa*, another *Balilla*-class boat, just after launching at Spezia, Italy. The bulge along the side is the top portion of the port ballast tank.

Chapter 4

The Second World War: Submarines Triumphant

T HE HISTORY OF SUBMARINES DURING WORLD WAR II IS DOMINATED BY
the fleets of two warring nations: Germany and the United States. Other navies had large numbers
of submarines; the British, for example, operated extensively in the North Sea and the
Mediterranean. But none came to dominate the public's imagination—and the naval planners'
nightmares—more than the "Grey Wolves" of the German U-boat fleet and the American "Steel Sharks"
in the Pacific.

Although the two nations had many submarines at sea at the same time, they rarely encountered
each other. Instead, German and American submarines tore into the mercantile and naval fleets of their
respective enemies, killing thousands of seamen and sending hundreds of ships to the ocean floor. The
cold North Atlantic became the Grey Wolves' primary hunting ground, while the Steel Sharks fed in the
vast open waters of the Pacific.

OPENING MOVES

When the first shots of World War II echoed over the border between Germany and Poland, the
Kriegsmarine had but fifty-seven U-boats ready to fight the Allies. The primary tools for waging a commerce war against Great Britain (France was spared, for diplomatic reasons) were the newest Type VII
and Type IX U-boats built in the late 1930s. Both these designs, with long cruising ranges and carrying
more than a dozen torpedoes, were capable commerce destroyers.

Most remarkable was their ability to dive to well below five hundred feet (150m), which took them
deeper than the deepest settings of early British depth charges. Despite their seaworthiness, the small submarines were still cramped. One U-boatman complained about "the heat, the stench of oil. Lead in my
skull from the engine fumes . . . I feel like Jonah inside some huge shellfish whose vulnerable parts are
sheathed in armor." Karl Doenitz, the admiral commanding the U-boat arm, said of the Type VIIs: "The
comparatively small and maneuverable Type VIIC proved itself excellent for night attacks. The great

Left: This painting, titled *Victory Returning U-boat*, shows a Type VII submarine carried home by a following sea. The forbidding cliffs, framed between the U-boat and the escorting patrol boat, suggests the Atlantic coast of France or Norway,
both home to German submarine bases after June 1940.

Top: A Type IX U-boat lies in the bombproof submarine pen at St. Nazaire, France, in May 1945. The submarine had just returned from a 110-day cruise to Japanese waters. Note the twin AA-gun mounts, made indispensable by Allied air superiority over the Bay of Biscay and the rest of the Atlantic. Below: A German U-boat enters a patch of debris. The wreckage is from an unknown American steamer, sunk in July 1942 when convoy *PQ-17* scattered in the Barents Sea. Note the survivors clinging to wreckage in the middle distance.

U-boat aces of the war, such as Kapitanleutnants Prien, Kretschmer, and Schepke were all 'VIIC' drivers." To facilitate long-range missions, some Type IXs were modified as submarine supply vessels, known as "milch cows," from which patrolling U-boats could replenish their fuel, torpedoes, food, and spare parts, as needed.

Of the fifty-seven U-boats in commission in 1939, there were only twenty-five large submarines (eighteen Type VIIs and seven Type IXs). The other thirty-two were small coastal boats unsuited for a blockade of Britain. And maintenance, training, even the time required to cruise to and from patrol stations, meant only a third of the boats could actually be on patrol. So, maybe eight submarines, supported by perhaps a dozen coastal boats (mainly used as minelayers), could actually attack British ships on any given day. This was quite a small number of submarines to begin a naval war against one of the strongest maritime powers on earth. Yet though the number of submarines was insignificant, the German planners knew that even limited attack on commerce would disrupt the flow of trade and force Britain to institute a convoy system.

The Versailles Treaty restrictions, meant to inhibit the development of a submarine force, had ironically allowed Doenitz to hand-pick the very best officers to command his U-boats. Correctly assuming that the British would immediately institute convoys upon the declaration of war, Doenitz helped design submarine tactics to both locate convoys and overwhelm their defenses. U-boats would patrol the seas and, once a convoy was located, concentrate forces against the merchant ships through the use of radio communications. Then, when enough U-boats had located the convoy, the commanders would attack on the surface at night, when the U-boats' low silhouette and high surface speed made them most dangerous.

This night surface strategy had the added benefit of negating British ASDIC. Doenitz used the term "wolf pack" to define these new tactics, and encouraged his young commanders by declaring: "U-boats are the wolves of the sea: Attack, Tear, Sink!" German naval officers realized these tactics, relying heavily on radio, would make the U-boat locations vulnerable to radio intercepts, but presumed the large numbers of U-boats would simply overwhelm any convoy defense. Because of the small U-boat fleet,

however, these wolf pack tactics were not immediately implemented.

In September 1939, the international law governing submarines stipulated they could attack enemy shipping in convoy without warning. Ships sailing independently were to be stopped according to the Prize Regulations as detailed in the treaties signed prior to the war.

Those regulations almost came to naught on the first day of the war, when the *U-30* torpedoed and sank the liner *Athenia*. The *U-30*'s commanding officer, Kapitanleutnant Fritz-Julius Lemp, had mistakenly assumed the *Athenia* was a lone troop transport. Hitler, hoping Great Britain and France would not fulfill their treaty obligations to Poland, had ordered that no passenger liners be attacked.

The Allies, however, did honor their Polish obligations and remained at war with Germany even after the fall of Warsaw. In the face of this perceived Allied intransigence, Germany gradually withdrew restrictions on submarine attacks. By November 1939, torpedo attacks on merchant ships were permitted. The waters around Great Britain were declared a war zone; Hitler remarked, "Every ship without respect of flag in the war zone around England and France exposes itself from now on to the full dangers of war." Restrictions regarding the sinking of passenger ships were lifted by August 1940.

The British, assuming the *Athenia* sinking heralded an unrestricted submarine campaign, had immediately instituted convoys, shipping and port controls, and all the aircraft and warship patrols they had found necessary in 1917–1918. It took some time to translate abstract plans into concrete reality, however, and gaps remained in the establishment and coverage of convoy routes. Many merchant ships, either because they were too slow or too fast for convoys, or their owners wanted to take the risk, sailed independently. These merchant ships relied on the more general protection of patrol boats, squadrons of flying boats, and land-based bombers flown by Coastal Command.

The lack of radar in patrol planes, and the less-than-expected efficacy of ASDIC, allowed the U-boats to pounce on the cargo ships like wolves among straggling sheep. Hunting was so good that this phase of the submarine campaign was called "the Happy Time" by U-boat sailors. By March 1940, when the U-boats were withdrawn for the campaign

TYPE VIIC U-BOAT

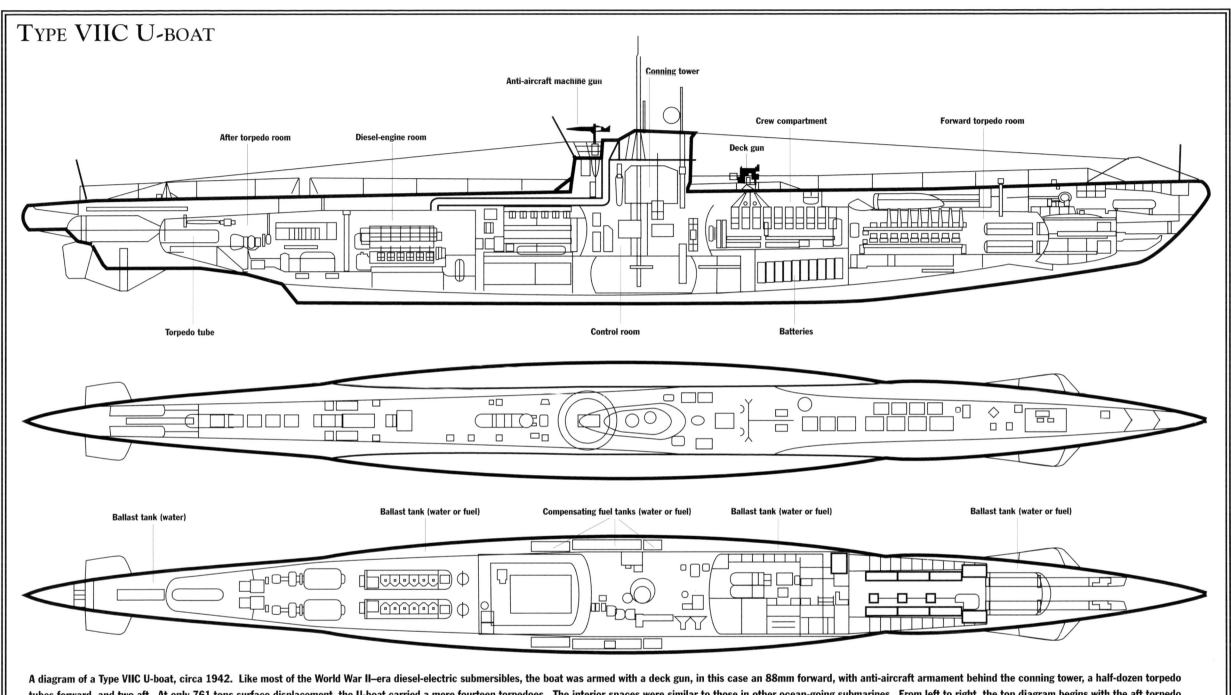

A diagram of a Type VIIC U-boat, circa 1942. Like most of the World War II—era diesel-electric submersibles, the boat was armed with a deck gun, in this case an 88mm forward, with anti-aircraft armament behind the conning tower, a half-dozen torpedo tubes forward, and two aft. At only 761 tons surface displacement, the U-boat carried a mere fourteen torpedoes. The interior spaces were similar to those in other ocean-going submarines. From left to right, the top diagram begins with the aft torpedo tube, followed by the electric motor room, steering gear, diesel engines, galley, the bridge with its deep periscope wells, crew compartment, torpedo stowage, and the forward torpedo room. Underneath, in a long series of compartments, lie the diesel oil tanks and ranks of batteries that fuel the engines either above or below the surface. The middle diagram shows a top view, including the distinctive rail around the AA-guns. The bottom diagram, a top-down view of the interior, nicely delineates the torpedo tubes, the size of the 1,200 hp diesel-engines, and the electric motors aft.

against Norway, 184 merchant and fishing ships were sunk by submarines and another 136 were sent to the bottom by mines. The toll would have been higher, but, in an ironic parallel to the American experience, many German torpedoes failed to explode. The cause was a faulty magnetic exploder inside the torpedo warhead. As a U-boat moved into northern waters, off Norway or above the Artic Circle, the earth's

magnetic field changed, throwing off the settings and causing the torpedo to pass harmlessly beneath the target. The problem was not fully solved until 1943.

THE BRITISH SUBMARINE EFFORT

Meanwhile, the British submarine fleet was ordered to blockade German ports, conduct reconnaissance

off the coast, and operate against enemy shipping. Though merchant ships could be attacked only in accordance with the strict Prize Regulations, warships were fair game. One submarine, HMS *Salmon*, managed to torpedo and sink the *U-36* and damage the German light cruisers *Leipzig* and *Nurnberg*, all during the same patrol. This is a perfect illustration of both the power of the submarine as an ASW weapon, and

the cost-effectiveness of such a cheap warship.

Operations against enemy submarines remained high on the Royal Navy's priority list and, over the course of the war, eleven U-boats were sunk by Allied submarines in European waters. The most spectacular exploit carried out by the Royal Navy's submarine force ever was the midget submarine attack on the German battleship *Tirpitz*. The warship

Midget Submarines

Cheap, easy to build, and needing a crew of only two or three, midget submarines were seen by most nations, particularly Germany and Japan, as expendable weapons. The Italians used midgets to heavily damage the British battleships *Valiant* and *Queen Elizabeth* at Alexandria in December 1941. The Germans, meanwhile, built hundreds of "small attack units" during 1944–1945 in an attempt to prevent the Allies from invading Europe. They had little success, sinking only a handful of cargo ships, a few escorts, and the Polish cruiser *Dragon*, at very high cost to themselves.

In the Pacific, five Japanese midget submarines participated in the Pearl Harbor attack and, though all were lost, the navy continued to develop these diminutive weapons throughout the war. I-boats were modified to carry these midgets to targets, mostly enemy ships in port, and several attacks were carried out in the spring of 1942. The British battleship *Ramillies* was severely damaged by midget submarines while it lay at anchor in Diego Suarez. Other attempts were made to attack Australian ports. Later in the war, when the Japanese desperately turned to suicide weapons in 1944–1945, small manned torpedoes, named *Kaiten*, were put into operation.

Carried into the combat area by a larger submarine, Japanese manned torpedoes were launched and directed at the enemy target by the torpedo's human pilot. Although only a few were successful, sinking the destroyer escort *Underhill* and the tanker *Mississinewa*, there were several hundred submarine suicide weapons deployed in defense of the Japanese home islands at the end of the war.

The midget submarines pictured above lie in a drydock at the Kure Naval Base, Japan, on October 19, 1945. They were but a small portion of the attack units gathered over the summer to repel the expected American invasion. A close look reveals there are four different designs represented among the eighty-four boats visible in the photograph.

The Socony-Vacuum Oil Company tanker *Dixie Arrow*, loaded with 86,136 barrels of crude, burns in the water after being torpedoed by *U-71* off Cape Hatteras on March 26, 1942. Eleven crewmen died in the sinking, twenty-two were rescued. Heavy losses of tankers and cargo ships off North America's east coast, averaging more than one ship a day at times, forced the introduction of numerous convoy links from the Caribbean to Halifax. Implemented on May 15, when enough forces became available, the short, inefficient convoy links were gradually lengthened as more aircraft and convoy escorts were added to the system. The improvement of the convoy system eventually led to the efficient handling of vessels from the Gulf of Mexico, the Panama Canal, or Trinidad all the way to New York, Halifax, and then on to Britain. The increasing number of forces, both patrol ships and aircraft, also led to a dramatic drop in losses.

threatened the northern commerce routes to the Soviet Union from its base at Alten Fjord in occupied Norway. Six small two-man submarines, known as "X-craft," set out in September 1943 and badly damaged the German battleship while it lay at anchor.

The Royal Navy, in reaction to the German antishipping campaign, lifted its restrictions on commerce warfare in early 1940: British submarines now began to attack enemy commerce without warning. Over the next five years, British boats sank forty-seven German merchant ships, severely damaging Germany's coastal trade.

The primary hunting ground for British submarines, however, was the Mediterranean. Over the course of the war, the British sent one hundred submarines, assisted by twenty-four Allied boats, to prey on Axis warships and commerce. By the end of 1944, these had sunk 217 Axis merchant ships, including the troop transport *Conte Rosse*—in which more than a thousand Italian troops drowned. Numerous warships were also sunk, including the cruiser *Armando*

Diaz and the battleship *Vittorio Veneto*, and at least six Italian cruisers were seriously damaged. Though costly, with forty-five boats lost to Italian surface ships and mines, the Allied submarines played a pivotal role in neutralizing the Italian fleet and immobilizing Axis forces in North Africa. The British campaign against commerce also helped knock Italy out of the war in 1943.

COMMERCE WAR BEGINS IN THE ATLANTIC

It was the *Kriegsmarine*, however, that initiated submarine commerce warfare on a global scale. As in World War I, the Germans knew they could not face the far superior British fleet at sea. Instead, they were forced to develop and implement a strategy suitable for a weaker naval power. German planners also realized the Allies, particularly Britain and later the United States, had based their strategic plans on a long war of industrial attrition. The western powers, suported by their experiences in World War I, had set

The heavily modified *U-66*, note the AA armament aft the conning tower, departing on a war patrol sometime after 1942. The crew seems happy for the camera, despite the growing awareness of Allied ASW superiority. This photograph was seized when *U-66* was sunk on May 6, 1944, by aircraft of VC-55 from *Block Island* (CVE-21) and *Buckley* (DE-51). *Block Island* was herself sunk on May 29, while *Buckley* survived the war.

more U-boats could stay at sea, and even the small coastal U-boats began operations against British commerce.

As the bases in France became operational, and more U-boats came into service, Doenitz reintroduced the wolf packs into the Atlantic. An important change from the previous year was centralized control by radio, allowing Doenitz to micromanage each battle from headquarters in Paris and later St. Lorient. He was aided by the German decryption service, which had broken the British low-level convoy and naval codes—Doenitz could locate Allied convoys and direct U-boats to intercept them.

In October 1940, *U-48* located the eastbound convoy SC-7 (the Allies identified convoys by alphanumeric codes; SC-7 stood for Slow Convoy Number 7) and notified Doenitz. The submarine torpedoed and sank two merchant ships before being driven off by aircraft. In the meantime, Doenitz sent five more U-boats to attack SC-7. The boats overwhelmed the escorts and sank twenty-one of the thirty merchant ships in the convoy. Otto Kretchmer, the leading submarine ace of the war, accounted for five of the sinkings. The pack tactics worked beyond all expectations and, by the end of 1940, their seven-month total was an astonishing 343 merchant ships. Doenitz, having lost only eight U-boats, looked forward to a time when he could have one hundred medium U-boats on patrol, rather than the mere dozen at sea at the start of 1941.

BRITISH COUNTERMEASURES

The British responded to these losses by increasing the pace of escort and merchant ship production. In 1941, new escort production was joined by fifty U.S. destroyers obtained by "lend-lease" and the services of ten Coast Guard cutters. This force extended the transatlantic convoy system to the Canadian coast. By the summer, the Royal Navy had more than three hundred ocean escort vessels allocated to protecting convoys. Escort crew training intensified and new radar units were fitted to their warships. More aircraft were released from anti-invasion reconnaissance over the English Channel, and Coastal Command was directed to patrol the convoy lanes. More aircraft were assigned to anti-submarine patrol, and new airfields were built in Canada, Iceland, Ireland, Gibraltar, and West Africa.

their economies on the path to total war. By capitalizing on advantages in research, innovation, and modern production methods, the Allies sought to bury the Axis nations under piles of equipment.

But, reasoned German naval strategists, the Allied policy relied heavily on the free flow of commerce. For Allied strategy to be successful, raw materials and finished equipment produced from the vast resources of the Western Hemisphere and the British Commonwealth had to be shipped all across the globe. And, just as in 1917–1918, these great shipping routes were vulnerable to attack.

The *Kriegsmarine*, given the overwhelming strength of the Royal Navy, could only intercept this commerce with quick surface raids and submarine patrols. The surface ships would tie up the British navy by raiding convoy routes; submarines, submerging when need be, would bypass British patrols and strike directly at Allied commerce. The ultimate German goal was to sink enough merchant ships to force Britain to the peace table. Failing that, the unrestricted German submarine campaign would at least disrupt Allied commerce, forcing the Allies to adopt time-consuming global shipping and cargo controls, and direct vast amounts of military resources into an antisubmarine campaign.

The first wolf pack operation against Britain struck on October 17, 1939. *U-46* located a convoy

sailing from Gibraltar, directed two other U-boats to the location by radio, and in the ensuing attack each U-boat sank a vessel before aircraft drove them off. Other early operations failed, however, because too few U-boats were available at sea.

In June 1940, the Allies suffered a disaster of epic proportions when France was conquered by the *Wermacht*. Important naval bases, such as Brest, Lorient, La Pallice, St. Nazaire, and Bordeaux, all fell into German hands. U-boat operations were shifted from Germany to France, and, with bases directly on the Atlantic coast, submarines were much closer to their patrol areas off Britain and the North Atlantic convoy lanes. With less distance to cover,

In the summer of 1941, more than five hundred aircraft were flying antisubmarine patrols, though there was a shortage of very long-range bombers to cover the mid-Atlantic gap. Aircraft, while not effective at this time in sinking submarines (mostly because the aircraft and weapons were not up to the task), did force U-boats to submerge and therefore lose much of their ability to locate convoys. And it was this inability to locate merchant ships, the vast majority of which arrived safely in Britain, that turned out to be the biggest failure of the U-boat campaign in 1941.

The problem was radio communications: ironically, the device that allowed wolf pack tactics to function properly also proved the U-boats' undoing. The British, improving on earlier intelligence work by the Poles and the French, launched an intelligence effort, code-named "Ultra," to break the German radio ciphers. The German codes were enciphered by a complex machine called "Enigma." But, through mainly mathematical analysis, the British broke the German naval code on a more-or-less regular basis.

British efforts became easier after May 1941, when they captured the *Munchen*, a weather observation trawler, and *U-110*, from which they retrieved ciphers, tables, and naval codebooks. Once German radio messages were decoded and U-boat movements plotted, the British could successfully route their convoys around U-boat concentrations. Extensive use of radio by the Germans, necessary for wolf pack tactics to succeed, simply gave the code breakers more data. Realizing the Germans could break codes, too, the British promptly changed their own ciphers, which set back the German cause even further.

Another vulnerability was radio direction finding. The Germans knew the Allies had shore-based radio direction finders, but felt the long ranges involved would make any locations obtained too vague. The British, however, refined a ship-mounted high-frequency radio direction receiver (HF/DF), nicknamed "Huff-duff," which enabled a warship to obtain a bearing on a U-boat's radio transmissions from as far away as twenty miles (32km).

With radio interception and direction finding stations all over the world, the British located wolf packs as they formed and warned any Allied ships in those areas. Convoys were then routed around the danger area and, when sufficient numbers of escorts were available, some could be detached and sent

down a radio bearing to attack the U-boat, forcing it to break contact with the convoy.

In conjunction with ship-mounted huff-duff, the growing availability of radar on escorts provided another countermeasure to U-boat packs. Radar, which detected ships by bouncing high-frequency waves off their metal hulls, could detect surfaced U-boats well before the Germans could sight the Allied convoys. Again, as with huff-duff, the convoy commander could alter the convoy's course or send an escort to attack the U-boat. A critical advantage radar gave escort ships was the ability to spot surfaced U-boats at night.

So, even if a wolf pack located a convoy, the well-armed escorts could fire on the U-boats as they surfaced to attack. U-boats could not fight it out on the surface, so the submarines would be forced to submerge. Too slow underwater to pursue the convoy, the U-boats were put out of the fight. The escorts could then pin down the U-boat with ASDIC and destroy it with depth charges. Though the supply of detection gear was scarce early in the war, more and more escorts were equipped with radar as production increased. In 1941, smaller radar devices were produced and mounted on antisubmarine aircraft. This sounded the death knell for wolf pack tactics as long-range aircraft spotted and attacked surfaced U-boats

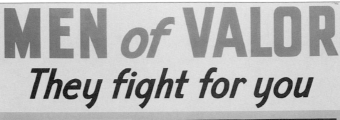

Two-man boarding party from the Canadian corvette 'Oakville' subdues crew of German sub in Caribbean

This stylized propaganda poster was meant as a morale booster during the darker days of the antisubmarine campaign. On August 27, 1942, the *U-94* closed on a convoy in the western Atlantic. Spotted by a Catalina flying boat from VP-92, the submarine was damaged by depth bombs. *Oakville*, a Canadian corvette attached to the convoy, fired on and then rammed *U-94*. The two warships exchanged gunfire and, after *Oakville* rammed the U-boat twice more, the submarine sank beneath the waves.

anywhere within air-patrol range.

New tactics and aggressive escort commanders also made a difference for the Allies. As crews became more experienced and knowledgeable about their enemies, the British escorts began to score against U-boats. In March 1941, aggressive British escorts sank Prien in *U-47* and fellow aces Otto Kretschmer in *U-99* and Joachim Schepke in the *U-100*. One famous escort commander, Captain F. J. Walker of the Royal Navy, countered U-boats by tracking and following any U-boat contact, no matter how elusive. The tactic was simple: he dogged submerged U-boats until they ran out of air or electric power, whichever came first.

Walker knew that a submerged U-boat was very slow, with a speed of four to five knots at most, and could stay down for about thirty hours before its batteries ran down or the crew ran out of oxygen. His tactics, even if there were not enough escorts to harry the U-boat to destruction, would at least drive the submarine off the convoy. Before Walker's untimely death from a stroke in 1944, he was credited with sinking twenty-one U-boats.

These countermeasures began to take a toll on U-boats. Then, in June 1941, the Germans invaded the Soviet Union and Hitler sent U-boats to the Arctic, off the coast of Norway, and the Baltic. Other

submarines were diverted to the Mediterranean to support operations in North Africa, further draining the numbers of U-boats available for patrols in the North Atlantic. In addition, Ultra decrypts, dramatically improved after the cryptanalysis success of early 1941, enabled the Allies to route almost every convoy around the U-boat patrol lines.

By the end of the year, although 429 merchant ships had been sunk by submarine torpedoes and guns, the *Kriegsmarine* was still far from its goal of strangling Allied commerce. They had lost only twenty-seven U-boats in the Atlantic and, more importantly, the number of boats available had grown to seventy-two. But, not knowing the success of the Allied code-breaking efforts and unable to attack commerce in the western Atlantic because of American neutrality, there was little Doenitz could do to increase the sinking rate, except fret. He noted, "The war will ultimately be decided by attacks on Britain's imports, which are the main objective."

THE NORTH AMERICAN "HAPPY TIME"

Following the December 7, 1941, Japanese attack on Pearl Harbor, the German Admiralty pondered the addition of the entire U.S. merchant fleet to the forces against the Axis. The combined Allied shipping fleet now totaled some 5,300 ships of 43.5 million tons (39 million t). And, even more depressing, American shipyards would now increase this figure at a high rate. The *Kriegsmarine* planners calculated German forces would have to sink about 800,000 tons (722,000t) of shipping (roughly two hundred ships) per month to defeat the Allies. Such a tonnage amount had not been met before, the highest being the 155 ships sunk by U-boats, mines, raiders, and aircraft in April 1941.

The U-boats alone needed to sink about 150 ships a month to meet their share of this goal. Doenitz, apprised of this new plan, sent U-boats into American waters before a convoy system or more escort vessels made the venture too risky. Because a number of U-boats were needed to patrol off Gibraltar, only five of the long-range Type IX boats sailed for the American coast. The operation was code-named *Paukenschlag*, or "beat of the drums," and all U-boats sent were manned by veterans and led by aggressive commanders.

U-123, commanded by Kapitanleutnant Reinhard Hardegan, known as a braggart by his fellow officers, was the first to arrive off the U.S. coast. There, in January 1942, he located the British freighter *Cyclops* and sank it with two torpedoes. He saw no convoys, no air patrols, and pitifully few escort vessels.

Hardegan's next victim was a Norwegian tanker, which he torpedoed and sank off the coast of Rhode Island. The U.S. Navy began a desperate search to find aircraft and escort vessels, but, lacking sufficient numbers, could not establish a convoy system for the East coast. Hardegan, who helped sink the twenty-six merchant ships lost in the New York–Cape Hatteras area in January 1942, jokingly told his crew, "We're here like a wolf in the middle of a flock of sheep."

Johann Mohr, commanding the *U-124*, was so successful off the American coast that his crew nicknamed him *Fingerspitzengefuhl*, or "the sure touch." He attacked and sank a British freighter on his voyage to U.S. waters in March 1942, and then wreaked havoc with coastal shipping. His favorite targets were oil tankers and on this patrol he sank eight. In delight, he radioed Doenitz:

> *The new-moon is black as ink*
> *off Hatteras the tankers sink*
> *While sadly Roosevelt counts the score*
> *some fifty thousand tons—by Mohr.*

Throughout the spring of 1942, the U-boats sank merchant ships off North America. In March, the first of the big supply U-boats, or milch cows, carried spare torpedoes, fuel, food, and parts to the western Atlantic. There they could resupply the smaller Type VII U-boats, which could now carry the war into the Caribbean and the Gulf of Mexico, sinking tankers

Top: A Type VIIC U-boat returns to the submarine base at Trondheim, Norway. The flaked white paint suggests the boat has been on a long Arctic patrol, perhaps to the Murmansk convoy route. The navy band welcoming the crew was standard operating procedure. Right: The port side diesel of this Type XXI engine room section awaits installation at the Deschimag Shipyard, Bremen, Germany. The picture nicely illustrates the sectional building technique used on these late war submarines, a method copied from the American shipbuilder Henry Kaiser. The circular plates in the middle of the section form the pressure hull, while the overhead pipes connect to the diesel exhaust pipes, allowing gases to be vented underwater via the snorkel.

and freighters off the coasts with impunity. Since merchant ships sailed singly, and along predictable coastal routes, there was not much U-boat radio traffic and, when the Germans changed their codes in February, Ultra proved of little help.

With burning tankers glowing on the night horizon, the U.S. Navy began to take the offensive. Sailings of merchant ships were limited to certain sea lanes, short port-to-port convoys were instituted in danger zones, and any land-based aircraft that could be found was put on offshore patrol. Finally, in August 1942, a fully interlocking convoy system was established between Key West and Boston. Pickings for the U-boats grew slim and they soon left the waters off North America. In six months, they had sunk 250 merchant ships. In June, the Germans sank in all waters 823,000 tons (742,000t) of shipping, a monthly rate more than sufficient to ensure victory.

WARSHIP KILLERS

In the narrow seas off the coasts of Europe, especially the North Sea and the Mediterranean, submarines proved adept at torpedoing enemy warships. While the British had only limited success, because the German warship fleet was so small, they did manage to torpedo some heavy units, sinking *Karlsruhe* and damaging *Gneisenau*. The British also scored heavily against Italian destroyers and light craft in the Mediterranean, sinking eleven.

U-boats fared much better, if only because there were more targets. Of the 105 Royal Navy warships sunk by torpedoes, one was the battleship *Barham*, blown to pieces by *U-331* on November 25, 1941; five others were aircraft carriers. Another submarine, *U-549*, managed to sink the American escort carrier *Block Island* on May 29, 1944.

THE PRODUCTIVE EFFORT

In late 1942, however, the *Kriegsmarine* began losing their race against time. Earlier in the year, American shipyards had been disrupted by massive wartime construction orders. The shipyards had to cope with a lack of skilled labor, the difficulties of processing and transporting raw materials, and the failures of subcontractors to produce enough critical components, such as ship turbines, electronic equipment, and steam valves. Deadlines were not met—U.S. escort vessel production fell six months behind schedule at one point—but by year's end, the vast output of ships began to turn the tide in the Atlantic.

The Allies' growing power base lay partly in the disparate size of the war economies. In 1942, before the Germans expanded their construction program, fifty thousand workers managed to produce seventeen U-boats a month. Because of the complexity of a submarine and the tight working quarters, it took roughly 500,000 man-hours to build a U-boat. In the United States, the average time to produce a *Liberty*-class merchant ship was 500,000 man-hours and about 750,000 for a tanker. Destroyers ran about 1,500,000 man-hours. The United States, however, had roughly 300,000 workers employed in shipyards in the spring of 1942. That number would double in the following year. This manpower advantage, coupled with a huge resource base, enabled the Allies to overwhelm the Axis. By early 1943, American shipyards were launching four ships per day, a rate the U-boats hadn't a chance of matching.

The number of available U-boats continued to rise as rates of submarine loss did not match that of new boats coming into service. By December 1942, Doenitz had more than two hundred U-boats in service, adding an additional nineteen every month. True, his force lost eighty-five boats during 1942, but the production lines made good the losses. In trade for those eighty-five, his U-boats sank more than six million tons of shipping that year, shipping that would still take the U.S. shipyards time to replace. The decisive battle in the Atlantic—the last opportunity for the U-boats to win the war—would come during the winter and spring of 1943.

THE ATLANTIC

Following the withdrawal from the North American coast, Doenitz prepared to conduct a new offensive in the North Atlantic. In late 1942, the U-boats concentrated in the air gap in the mid-Atlantic, where land-based anti-submarine aircraft could not reach, and tried to disrupt the convoy routes to Britain. There were now roughly fifty U-boats at sea at any one time. British cipher analysts had still not broken the new German codes, so the convoys lacked foreknowledge of U-boat locations. But Allied air cover increased as well: a few squadrons of Liberator bombers were assiged to patrol the Atlantic gap, and

the British had about 305 escorts, many equipped with radar and HF/DF, in the battle area.

Throughout the fall, wolf pack attacks increased as code breakers on both sides struggled to locate each other's forces. So many U-boats were at sea that, even after the German code was rebroken in December 1942, convoys could not be routed around pack locations. The campaign culminated during the winter and spring of 1943, with battles so ferocious it became known as "Bloody Winter."

During February 1943, the U-boats sank 110 ships of more than 633,000 tons (571,000t), and by March 9 they had sunk forty-one more ships of nearly 230,000 tons (207,000t). By that date, after reading the telegrams of the New York harbor captain, German Intelligence deciphered the sailing orders for three Britain-bound convoys. In mid-March, Doenitz concentrated forty-four U-boats into three wolf packs along the convoys' routes out of New York and Halifax. In all, a total of 141 merchant ships began the voyage. One convoy made the crossing after losing just a single vessel, but the other two, convoys SC-122 and HX-229, were located by waiting

U-boats. They signaled Doenitz and stayed on station, trailing the convoys and radioing courses and speeds as other U-boats closed in for the kill.

A merciless gale hit convoy HX-229 and scattered its ships. At least eight U-boats attacked, torpedoing thirteen ships in two days of fighting. Meanwhile, the remaining ships of HX-229 caught up with the slower SC-122. The escorts were reinforced by warships sent from Iceland and some long-range B-24 aircraft. The U-boats nevertheless pressed home their attacks. In a running melee across the North Atlantic, the U-boats sank twenty-two ships, for a combined total of more than 146,000 tons (131,400t). The losses may have been higher had it not been for the Liberator bombers that flew over the convoy—after a nine hundred-mile (1,440km) flight from Northern Ireland. The planes forced the U-boats to submerge and eventually lose the convoys.

Only one U-boat, *U-384*, failed to return to base. Doenitz regarded this incredibly damaging battle as the greatest of the war. Following an attack on a fourth convoy, the wolf packs sunk a total of forty-four ships in a mere ten days. Combined with other losses,

Submarines Sinking Submarines

Submariners hate enemy submarines. The next worse thing to an aircraft diving out of the sky is an enemy boat prowling across a submarine's course.

Usually the first warning of an enemy ambush was the sound of a speeding torpedo or, even worse, the crash of an ear-splitting explosion blowing the doomed craft to bits. Submariners learned that the safest course, if and when an enemy was spotted, was to submerge. Since neither side had sonars or hydrophones good enough to track an enemy underwater, the two submarines usually just crept away from each other.

It took a bit of luck to sink an enemy submarine, although radar and good intelligence—both found only in the American and British fleets—helped immensely. During World War II, one Japanese, sixteen Italian, and twenty-four German submarines were sunk by British submarines, at a cost of five of their own. American submarines sank twenty-one Japanese boats, but lost only one to a Japanese submarine. The Dutch also lost one boat to the Japanese. The French, meanwhile, had the misfortune to accidentally lose one submarine to a British submarine torpedo and two others to German U-boats.

Far left: This dramatic painting shows a U-boat delivering the coup de grâce to an Allied merchant ship, which, judging from the explosion, was presumably carrying munitions. Unlike regular merchant ships, where seamen slept in life vests and waterproof clothes, crewmen on oil tankers and ammunition ships were said to sleep comfortably, knowing they had no hope of escape if the ship was torpedoed. Left: A close-up view of the conning tower of *U-664,* showing the "Happy Sawfish" U-boat flotilla emblem, as the crew prepares to abandon ship off the Azores. The submarine had been crippled by depth charges delivered by carrier aircraft flying off *Card* (CVE-11) on August 9, 1943. Over the course of the war, 79 enemy U-boats were sunk by Allied naval aircraft.

Sinking of the U-175

On April 17, 1943, the *U-175,* while on patrol in the North Atlantic, closed on convoy HX-233. Discovered by the convoy's escorts, the boat was depth-charged for three hours before being forced to the surface.

These remarkable photos, taken by Chief Photographer's Mate Jack January, show (1) the *U-175* on the surface after suffering depth charge attacks by Coast Guard cutter *Spencer.* The damaged U-boat has been taken under fire by the *Spencer,* cutter *Duane,* and many of the merchant ships in the convoy. In the ensuing gunfire, the U-boat was fatally damaged, with many of the crew killed, while nine Coast Guardsmen were wounded, one fatally. Photo (2) shows Midshipmen Walter Weppelmann and Ensign Paul Moller in the water, while (3) shows Seaman 1st-class Dieter Wolf and Peter Wannamacher clambering up a cargo net to safety aboard *Spencer.* Photo (4) shows the damaged U-boat on the surface. Two Coast Guard crewmen boarded *U-175* and attempted to salvage the boat but damage from depth charges, gunfire, and German scuttling charges were too much to overcome and the boat sank quickly. The convoy is on the far right horizon. The Chief Engineering Officer of the *U-175,* Leopold Norworth, is shown in (5) receiving medical attention from Pharmacist Mate 1st-class William Crumbaugh. The other photos show (6) a Coast Guard souvenir photo, (7) stunned survivors eating a meal in *Spencer*'s galley, and (8) some of the forty-one surviving German crewmembers marching into captivity in Greenock, Scotland.

sixty-seven of the 120 ships sunk in March had been sailing in protected convoys, a fact not lost on the British Admiralty. If such losses continued, the entire shipping structure of the Allied coalition would be imperiled. Fortunately for the Allies, this success was to prove the last great howl of the wolf packs.

THE ALLIED COUNTERATTACK

The breakthrough that defeated the U-boats in the spring of 1943 proved to be the Allied cryptographic solution of March 20. Now, instead of routing all convoys around pack locations, the Allies concentrated extra escort groups and long-range aircraft around threatened convoys. There were now enough escorts to create five support groups that would cover threatened convoys all the way to Britain. These surface and air forces led the convoys through the submarine traps and, using Walker's aggressive tactics, hunted U-boats to the death.

The battles over convoys ONS-5 and SC-128 in May illustrate how the campaign had shifted to the Allies' favor. ONS-5 consisted of forty-two merchant ships escorted by six escorts. Arrayed against them

were three wolf packs with more than forty U-boats. Doenitz radioed the crews: "I am certain you will fight with everything you have got."

The escorts tracked the approaching U-boats by radar and the corvettes were released to attack. Air cover was called in from Nova Scotia and Iceland. Eventually, a few U-boats broke through and torpedoed five ships, but not before four U-boats had been forced to withdraw because of depth charge attacks. A severe storm and the air coverage prevented further losses to the convoy. Soon afterward, however, SC-128 was located and nearly forty U-boats massed to close in for the attack. A timely fog bank hid the merchant ships, and only six ships were torpedoed. The escorts, equipped with radar, attacked the surfaced U-boats in the mist and sank five in one night. Two other U-boats collided and sank, bringing the total German losses to seven.

Another convoy, SC-130, was attacked later in the month, but aggressive Allied escorts pinned down and sank six U-boats, while the convoy escaped without loss. Doenitz's son was among those lost in that particular sea battle.

The Allies also began using a new acoustic torpedo during May. Dropped from patrolling aircraft,

the torpedoes homed-in on the sound of a submarine's propellers. Small escort carriers also joined in the defense of convoys, providing continuous air coverage for the entire voyage across the Atlantic. On May 24, Doenitz recognized that he had lost the battle. Thirty-one U-boats did not return after these battles—and the survivors were withdrawn from the North Atlantic.

The success of the Allied countermeasures was paid in more than diverted men, ships, and planes. Sometimes, even with special "no-go" zones, it was very difficult to tell if a submarine was friendly or not. The British submarine *Triton*, thinking its target was a U-boat, accidently torpedoed its *Oberon*-class comrade *Oxley* on September 10, 1939. The vast increase in the numbers of ASW forces, both surface ships and aircraft, led to many other friendly fire incidents. By the end of the war, four British and a Polish submarine were sunk by Allied forces. The French continued to have poor luck, with at least a dozen Vichy French submarines lost to American and British ships during the operations off North Africa and Dakar, while at least one Free French submarine was lost to an Allied patrol bomber. To top it all off, the huge submarine-cruiser *Surcouf* was accidentally

rammed and sunk by a friendly merchant ship in the Gulf of Mexico during 1942.

SACRIFICE IS NECESSARY

For the remainder of 1943, Doenitz sent U-boats out on patrol to feint against the North Atlantic supply line. The only solution against the Allied escorts, it seemed, would be more advanced submarines that could turn the technological battle back in Germany's favor. But, until that time came to pass, Doenitz ordered U-boats to patrol the central and south Atlantic as well as the Indian Ocean.

The crews obligingly went, knowing the odds were against them, and had some success when Allied ASW forces were weak or the region did not possess fully developed convoy systems. Operations in the Caribbean, off Brazil, and in the Gulf of Guinea proved rewarding until American escort carriers made those regions lethal, sinking fourteen of forty-three U-boats sent to the areas. Another group, sent to Indonesia for operations in the Indian Ocean, was also successful until a British convoy system shut down the attacks in August. Between June and August, U-boats sank only eighty-one ships worldwide. This meager score was partially the result of an Ultra-based offensive against the U-boat replenishment points west of the Azores, which sank most of the U-tanker milch-cows, and a Coastal Command offensive against U-boats in their transit areas in the Bay of Biscay.

By this point in the war, the Allies had enough escorts to stay with a located and pinned down U-boat until it was destroyed or forced to the surface. On average, an escort stayed with the contact for thirty hours before the U-boat was forced to surface because of lack of oxygen or electric power. One attack actually took thirty-eight hours, the longest of the war. The Allies had also developed a sonar buoy, which, when dropped from aircraft, permitted tracking submerged submarines by propeller noises. A magnetic anomaly detector, MAD for short, also made its appearance and permitted aircraft to detect a submerged submarine's magnetic hull.

German scientists attempted to counter these Allied measures through radar detection devices that warned U-boat crews when aircraft or ship radar waves came near them—like a radar detector in a car. The radar receivers worked for a time, but, once the

The above picture was taken from the *New York* (BB-34) while cruising in the transport zone off Fedhalla, Morocco, in the evening of November 12, 1942. The two transports attacked in the picture, having unloaded troops for Operation Torch earlier in the day, were struck by torpedoes fired from *U-130*. All told, the U-boat torpedoed three ships that night, *Tasker H. Bliss* (AP-42), *Hugh L. Scott* (AP-43), and *Edward Rutledge* (AP-52), with a loss of 153 lives.

The above photo captures the brutal force of the 660 pounds (297kg) of explosive found in a German torpedo warhead. On May 3, 1944, the *U-371* fired an acoustic torpedo that homed in on and exploded against the stern of the *Menges* (DE-320). The stern was almost entirely blown off, with 31 men killed, but the escort remained afloat. Towed to port and rebuilt by welding the stern of the damaged *Holder* (DE-401) to the remaining two-thirds of *Menges,* the "new" escort served until it was decommissioned in early 1947.

Allies learned to shift the frequencies of their search radars, the U-boat crews lost confidence in the receivers. The Germans were never able to develop adequate radar detection sets for their submarines and the U-boats continued to fall prey to Allied escorts and aircraft.

Trying desperately to attain a technological edge, the Germans also fielded an acoustic torpedo, called *zaunkonig*, which, like the American version, homed-in on the sounds of an escort vessel's machinery or propellers. New antiaircraft armament was also placed on U-boats in the hope they could challenge Allied air cover. In late August 1943, hoping to revive the submarine campaign, Doenitz sent out several U-boat packs as soon as they were equipped with the radar receivers, heavier antiaircraft guns, and the acoustic torpedoes.

The first successful *zaunkonig* attack struck the frigate *Lagan* on September 20, 1943. In the resulting confusion, a number of U-boats penetrated the escort screen and sank two Liberty ships. The American escorts imploded the *U-338* with acoustic torpedoes, but the U-boats struck back, torpedoing the escorts

St. Croix and *Polyanthus* with *zaunkonig* torpedoes. The battle raged on as another escort rammed the *U-229*, sinking it with all hands, while the frigate *Itchen* succumbed to another *zaunkonig*. In all, the U-boats sank six merchant ships and three escort vessels, but lost three of their own.

The Allies quickly countered this challenge by rerouting convoys, increasing air patrols, and deploying a towed decoy, called "Foxer," that neutralized acoustic torpedoes. The escorts, supported by Ultra, aircraft, and escort carriers, then went on a counteroffensive against the U-boats. In the last four months of 1943, sixty-two U-boats were sunk.

THE TWILIGHT OF DEFEAT

The logical response to the Allied hunting of U-boats on the surface with radar, HF/DF, and Ultra was to submerge the threatened U-boat. But submerging left the sub with limited battery power. One way to avoid using batteries was the snorkel, or "snort," a device invented by the Dutch in the late 1930s—basically a long, tubular pole that protruded from the water's surface while the submarine remained just underwater. The tube pumped air for the diesel engines, and vented the engines' exhaust, enabling the U-boat to stay submerged without running down the submarine's batteries.

Though it suffered from initial problems, especially when waves washed over the snorkel head, the first operational snorkel cruise occurred in February of 1944. The submarine, *U-264*, was sunk on this cruise, which did little to encourage other crews, but snorkels were soon installed on a wide scale. The apparatus offered the only hope of continued U-boat operations, because its small radar signature would make Allied search radar essentially useless. When ready, Doenitz sent these U-boats into British waters, where the noisy sea conditions negated most of the Allied sonar advantages.

Germany's last real hope, however, lay in the true submarine, that is, one that would not have to surface, could maintain a high underwater speed, and could carry a heavy armament. The Walter company, led by Professor Helmuth Walter, had been developing a streamlined submarine powered by closed-cycle hydrogen peroxide turbines sine the 1930s. In theory, these engines would propel the submarine under-

A spread of hedgehog projectiles fired from a throw-ahead projector arc over the port bow of an American destroyer escort. The large circular pattern of quick-sinking missiles held several advantages over conventional depth-charges. Because the contact projectiles exploded only on impact with a U-boat, they did not unnecessarily disturb sonar operators tracking the submarine. The forward-throwing projector also allowed the escort to "pin" the U-boat in the sound cone of its hull-mounted sonar, use a fire-control computer to develop an angle for the projector, and deliver an attack at the same time. This practice was impossible with depth charges because the escort had to pass over the submarine to deliver those weapons. The only disadvantage, according to one escort commander, was that "the probability of convincing evidence (i.e., prisoners) after a successful hedgehog attack is not as good as would be the case after a successful depth charge attack, but this matters little."

water at an incredible thirty-knot speed. But the engineering problems proved insurmountable. As an alternative, another company, Broking and Schurer, proposed adding more battery power to a conventional power plant, equipping it with a snorkel, and fitting these into a streamlined Walter hull. Though not absolutely true submarines, these U-boat designs offered the chance to make the entire Allied ASW force obsolete at one stroke.

The final results of research and construction were the Type XXIII coastal submarine and the larger Type XXI. As designed, the larger boats made 17.2 knots submerged, a ten-knot advantage over the older Type VIIs, and were capable of running submerged without utilizing the snorkel for sixty hours. With six tubes forward and twenty-three torpedoes, they could throw a powerful punch. The small coastal boats, although carrying only two torpedoes, managed 12.5 knots submerged.

Both boats were also capable of diving close to nine hundred feet (300m), well below any depth charges then used by the Allies. Constructed in prefabricated sections at dispersed factories and then transported in sections to the shipyards, these advanced U-boats were slow in coming. Problems with steel allocation, lack of skilled workers, and Allied bombing all hindered construction.

After the invasion of Normandy, the *Kriegsmarine* lost their French bases and most of the U-boats were sent to Norway. The nonsnorkel boats suffered heavily during this evacuation and it was deemed suicide to put to sea in such submarines. The old faithfuls, the snorkel-equipped Type VIIs, soldiered on, giving the Allies fits, because air patrols could not spot the snorkel-heads. The U-boats' near-invisibility led to tens of thousands of useless Allied flying hours, and the lack of radio communications with the submerged boats gave the British cipher analysts nothing to decode.

The snorkel-equipped U-boats returned in force to British waters in November 1944, sinking eleven cargo ships and two escorts by the end of the year. By itself, this was not significant, but it foreshadowed what might happen if the new U-boats became operational. The Type XXIs, however, were delayed by air raids and the encroaching Allied and Soviet armies. None of the Type XXIs fired a shot in anger. On the other hand, seven of the simpler Type XXIIIs went into action in January 1945. They carried out several

missions off the east coast of England, sinking five cargo ships, and outran all attempts by escorts to find them.

In 1945, the Allies threw all their escorts, some 426 of them, into the battle in British waters. These ships, combined with crushingly heavy bombardments of U-boat bases and fighter sweeps of the Baltic training areas, sank or destroyed 151 U-boats in the last five months of the war. The agony finally ended on May 4, 1945, when Doenitz ordered his U-boats to cease hostilities. The message read, in part: "My U-boatmen. Six years of war lie behind you. You have fought like lions. . . . Unbeaten and unblemished you lay down your arms after a heroic fight without parallel."

Only two Type XXIs, the *U-2511* and *U-3008*, were at sea when Doenitz's order came over the airwaves. The experience of *U-2511* illustrated what might have been. After hearing of the surrender, the commanding officer, Kapitan Adalbert Schnee, located a British cruiser through his periscope and closed in, submerged. His U-boat remained undetected as it sailed through a ring of escorts at a speed of sixteen knots. He completed a firing solution, but did not fire his torpedoes and returned to base undetected. The U-boat war in the Atlantic was over.

THE PACIFIC WAR

Soon after Japan's Pearl Harbor Strike Force left Hawaiian waters with most of the U.S. battle fleet destroyed, American submarine commanders were surprised to receive a concise order from Washington. It said: "Execute unrestricted air and submarine warfare against Japan," leaving no room for doubt about the wartime mission of the "silent service." With that order, the United States repudiated at one stroke all the international agreements it signed in the 1930s limiting the use of submarines against merchant ships. Like the German attacks in the Atlantic, the American campaign in the Pacific became brutally destructive.

It took some time, however, for the U.S. submarine fleet to warm to this new role: the force was unprepared to wage an unrestricted campaign against Japan's merchant fleet. Like the Japanese, the Americans had prepared to attack enemy warships and scout for the main battle fleets. Prewar tactics called for cautious attacks, because the U.S. Navy,

Top: Seen through the periscope of *Drum* (SS-228), this undated photo shows a Japanese merchant ship lying with decks awash after two torpedo hits. Above: Water and debris shoot skyward as *Scorpion* (SS-278) torpedoes a 600-ton (540t) armed trawler well off the coast of Honshu on April 30, 1943. During the hour and three-quarters fight with the patrol ship, gunfire had been exchanged on both sides and one officer on *Scorpion* was killed. This was the fourth and final ship, in addition to four sampans, sunk by the submarine on her first war patrol. The vertical tube in the foreground is the 3-inch (7.5cm) cannon mounted on the submarine's deck.

The large cruiser submarine *Nautilus* (SS-168) lies off Alaska in November 1943. Converted to carry scouts and raiders, the submarine is pictured above in preparation for landing 7th Army special forces teams during the upcoming invasion of Attu in the Aleutians. The two 6-inch (15cm) deck guns were left on board to supply shore bombardment during these types of raids. Unlike an earlier mission to Makin in the Gilbert Islands, where *Nautilus* was twice attacked by planes and the marine raiders lost 30 of their number in fierce fighting ashore, the May 11 landing on Attu was uneventful.

like their British counterparts, overestimated the ability of sonar to guide antisubmarine craft against submerged submarines. Even frequent use of the periscope was frowned upon. The submarine force concentrated instead on submerged attacks, using passive hydrophones to confirm target data gathered through brief periscope glances.

Japanese attacks during the Pacific war's first hundred days destroyed the American naval base at Cavite, sinking or driving away the valuable submarine tenders, and pushed the twenty-nine submarines out of the Philippines and the Dutch East Indies. The psychological shock of this swift attack, combined with the chaotic disruption of Allied supply and communications, led to a poor performance by American and Allied submarines in the early months of the war in the Pacific.

American submarines could not prevent the invasion of the Philippines or Wake Island nor did they, along with seven Dutch and two British sub-

marines, prevent the fall of the Dutch East Indies. Of small consolation was the sinking of the Japanese destroyer *Natsushio* in the Celebes by *S-37* on February 8, 1942.

The loss of naval bases and lack of supplies contributed to the Allied failure, but part of the problem was the American Mark-14 torpedo. Like the Germans, the United States had developed a magnetic detonator for the warhead. As designed, the torpedo was supposed to explode as it entered the magnetic field of the target, most probably breaking the ship's keel as it passed beneath the hull. But the detonator did not function correctly, sometimes exploding as soon as the torpedo came within a few hundred yards of the target, or not at all.

Detonation difficulties were caused by varying magnetic fields, depending on latitude, which the designers did not account for, and partly by faulty valves, which forced the torpedoes to run deep—sometimes fifteen feet (4.5m) deeper than set.

Eventually, the Bureau of Ordnance sorted out the problem, placing the blame on limited interwar budgets, but it was not until April 1943 that U.S. submarines received a reliable torpedo. Until then, the torpedoes failed at a high rate, causing one Japanese merchant captain to joke that his ship, with a number of dud torpedoes protruding from his hull, resembled a porcupine.

A more serious problem was training and leadership. With the failure of the U.S. submarine fleet to prevent, or even inhibit, the Japanese invasion of the Philippines and Wake Island, timid commanding officers were replaced wholesale. Men too deeply tied to the cautious tactics of the interwar years were summarily removed from command and replaced by younger, more aggressive officers. In addition, officers more experienced with the tactical data computer (TDC) replaced those who had never trained with it or who lacked skill in its workings.

During the first half of 1942, about forty com-

manding officers lost their jobs to younger men—nearly thirty percent of the entire force. This practice continued throughout the war, with fourteen percent of commanding officers removed from command in 1943 and 1944. Signs of improvement were seen in the sinking of the seaplane carrier *Mizuho* by the *Drum* on May 2 and the minelaying cruiser *Okinoshima* by *S-42* on May 11.

The Japanese, meanwhile, remained steadfast to the idea of sinking the American battle fleet, not destruction of Allied shipping. Allied commerce in the Pacific was small compared to the Atlantic, with destinations quite distant from Japan. The Japanese also thought the war would be short. Trained in reconnaissance and attrition tactics against warships, Japanese submarines were primarily deployed against the Allied fleets. Before Pearl Harbor, twenty-seven submarines sailed to Hawaiian waters to seek out warships and cut supply lines to San Diego and Panama. Five were sent to Malaya and the Indian

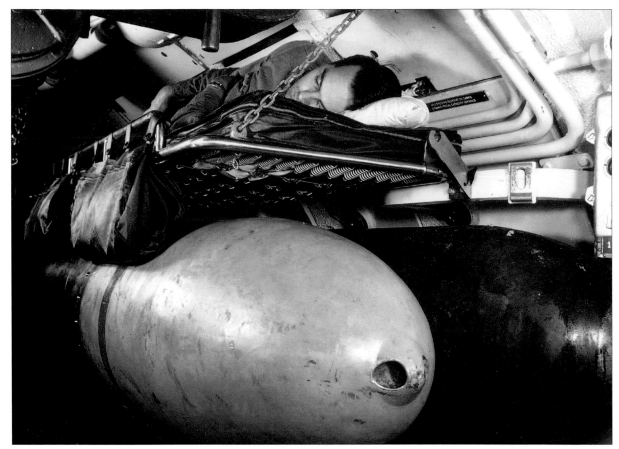

Above: A photo of *Grampus* (SS-207) undergoing post-overhaul sea trials off Portsmouth, New Hampshire, on November 6, 1941. The picture clearly shows the safety railings mounted along the deck. These were removed during war patrols as the cables had a tendency to vibrate, or "sing," when submerged. The submarine was lost in February 1943. Above, right: This picture of a crewman asleep in the torpedo room shows both the sheer size of the warhead and the importance of maximizing space on a submarine. The spare torpedo on the left has a yellow exercise warhead. The notched tip is to attach a winch and cable, required when loading the 1,200-pound (540kg) torpedoes. Right: Manhandling the torpedoes through the forward hatch was a time-consuming process, generally done at port—but it could be accomplished at sea during an emergency. The round disks are access panels, so the torpedo men could maintain the "fish," and the gyro connection port, where the final gyro angle was transmitted before the torpedo was fired.

Ocean to hunt British warships, and others conducted reconnaissance and patrol missions, using submarine-launched seaplanes, off Australia and the west coast of the United States.

Early Japanese successes were promising. The *I-6* located the aircraft carrier *Saratoga* about five hundred miles (800km) southwest of Hawaii on January 11, 1942. One torpedo struck home, flooding three fire rooms, and the carrier was forced to sail to Bremerton, Washington, for complete repairs. It was out of action for five months, depleting the already meager carrier forces of the U.S. Pacific Fleet and missing the critical battles of Coral Sea and Midway. Other I-boats severely damaged the British battleship *Ramillies* with midget submarines as it lay at anchor in Diego Suarez.

Japanese submarines suffered, however, when Americans code analysts broke their radio transmission codes. Nicknamed "Magic," these intercepts, combined with other intelligence, such as traffic analysis and direction finding, gave the Americans an edge similar to the British use of Ultra in the Atlantic. For example, during the critical battle of Midway, in early June 1942, American intelligence warned of a Japanese submarine patrol line forming east of Hawaii. Through early sailings and evasive routing, the American carriers not only avoided these patrols, but, because the Japanese had not been warned, dramatically surprised four enemy aircraft carriers. Other patrol lines were avoided around Hawaii.

But, just like Allied convoys routed around U-boats in the Atlantic, ships still fell prey to submarines through bad luck and enemy perseverance. Submarines also proved useful in knocking off crippled warships. One of the Japanese carriers at Midway was the *Soryu*. Burning after three bomb hits from American dive-bombers, the carrier might have escaped had not the *Nautilus* penetrated the surrounding destroyer screen. It finished off the crippled carrier with two torpedos fired at point blank range.

A stern view of *Gato* (SS-212) at the Mare Island Navy Yard, California, on August 8, 1943. The submarine has just left drydock and is receiving final repairs and alterations before sailing on her sixth war patrol on September 6. She survived the war, having sunk a dozen Japanese ships during thirteen war patrols. Later, she served as a naval reserve training ship at New York and Baltimore in the 1950s, and was finally sold for scrap July 25,1960.

The same fate befell the Americans when the crippled aircraft carrier *Yorktown* was found by the *I-168* under the command of Lieutenant Commander Yahachi Tanabe. He located the damaged *Yorktown* on June 6, after a long, high-speed pursuit. Although it was initially fended off by the destroyer screen, *I-168* finally got within range when the destroyers apparently stopped their sonar searches about noon. Tanabe joked with his crew, "It appears that the Americans have interrupted their war for lunch. Now is our chance to strike them good and hard, while they are eating!" Two of *I-168*'s torpedoes detonated against the *Yorktown*'s hull and a third struck the *Hammann*, a destroyer alongside the carrier, cutting it

in half and sending it to the bottom with eighty-one crewmen. *Yorktown*, flooded from the damage, sank the next morning.

COMMERCE WAR BEGINS IN THE PACIFIC

As the Japanese advance drove American, Dutch, British, and Australian forces out of the Philippines, Malaysia, and the Dutch East Indies, the Allied submarine forces in this region fell back to more secure bases. The two British submarines went to Ceylon; the Americans, under Captain John Wilkes, and a few Dutch submarines, fell back to Java, and then Fremantle, Australia.

Here the submarines were organized into Submarines Southwest Pacific. The Pacific Fleet Submarine Force based at Pearl Harbor was composed of sixteen fleet boats and six S-class submarines under Rear Admiral Charles A. Lockwood. The American submarine offensive took the shape of a dual-pronged attack, with submarines patrolling out of Australia and Pearl Harbor.

During the remainder of 1942, the submarine force learned its new commerce-destroying mission, shaking off prewar misconceptions, and developing effective patrol methods during on-the-job training. Unlike the Japanese submarines, which could not reach the main U.S. shipping lanes, the American *Gato-* and *Tambor*-class boats could easily reach the Japanese commerce lanes in the East Indies and Malaya. Maneuverable, quick to dive, and well-armed, the American submarines also took the war directly into Japanese waters. The U.S. boats were assisted by half a dozen Dutch submarines operating out of Fremantle.

An average of sixty-seven submarines were available to American forces by mid-1942. But diversions to the Aleutians, military operations in the Solomons, and reconnaissance missions in the southwest Pacific meant that only a few boats could patrol against Japanese commerce. The *Gudgeon, Plunger,* and *Pollack* were the first Pacific Fleet submarines to conduct offensive war patrols, but their results were disappointing. Although *Gudgeon* torpedoed the Japanese submarine *I-173* on January 27, only three cargo ships were sunk during a two-month patrol.

Throughout the year, torpedo failings, cautious commanders, and unfamiliarity with commerce-war tactics restricted U.S. sinkings to only about 725,000 tons (654,000t) less than two months' worth of U-boat victims. Japanese imports were only slightly affected, continuing to feed a war machine that conquered most of southeast Asia.

Meanwhile, Japanese anticommerce measures took shape. Though Vice Admiral Teruhisa Komatsu ordered all available Japanese submarines to attack enemy merchant ships in April 1942, in practice, submarines rarely attacked merchant ships. They did force the Americans to adopt convoy measures along the Hawaii-Samoa-Australia supply lines, but did not have the ability to be more than a nuisance.

Only in the Indian Ocean, where targets of opportunity steamed in greater numbers, did groups

Above: The diving officer and two crewmen, handling the stern and bow planes, prepare *Batfish* (SS-310) for a practice dive during May 1945. A war-built *Balao*-class submarine, *Batfish* completed six war patrols before war's end. Right: *Gudgeon* (SS-211) in San Francisco Bay on August 7, 1943. In addition to torpedoing *I-173*, the submarine completed eleven war patrols, sinking 71,047 tons (63,942t) of shipping in the process. Sometime after April 1944, while on her twelfth patrol, the boat was lost, reasons unknown.

Top: A view of the forward torpedo room, and three of the caretaker crew, inside the Japanese submarine *I-58*. This submarine sank the cruiser *Indianapolis* on July 30, 1945, with a loss of 883 lives. Above: An exterior view of *I-58*, showing the effects of weather and lack of maintenance. The pictures were taken on January 28, 1946, by a U.S. Marine when the submarine was moored at the old naval base at Sasebo, Japan.

of submarines foray out of Penang, Malaysia. From there, Japanese I-boats destroyed some fifty merchant ships, but these losses, although high, did not force the British to establish convoys. Instead, American pressure in the Solomons, and later in the central Pacific, forced the Japanese to recall their submarines. They accomplished little else in the Indian Ocean.

JAPANESE SUBMARINES ON THE ATTACK

In the battles for Guadalcanal in late 1942, Japanese submarines conducted missions according to prewar strategy: boats operated as an advance screen for the fleet, radioed coordinates of American ships, and tried to sink any enemy warships spotted, especially carriers. This strategy paid dividends on August 31, when the *Saratoga* again fell victim to a single Japanese torpedo while off Espiritu Santo. The carrier, while undergoing subsequent repairs, would miss the critical battles of October and November off Guadalcanal.

Two weeks later, the *I-19*, under Commander Takaichi Kinashi, located the *Wasp* in the same area. The task group steamed right in front of the submerged submarine and Kinashi fired six torpedoes from about five hundred yards (450m). Three hit the carrier, setting off gasoline explosions that sank the carrier five hours later. The other three torpedoes, Type 95s, with a thirteen thousand yard (11,700m) range, continued on their way, seemingly errant misses.

Five miles (8km) away, unseen by Kinashi, lay the aircraft carrier *Hornet* and its task force. Remarkably, one of the long-running torpedoes hit the battleship *North Carolina* forward, while another heavily damaged the destroyer *O'Brien*. The battleship was put out of action until repaired at Pearl Harbor; *O'Brien* later sank under tow. Kinashi's attack has been called the most successful torpedo salvo in the history of submarine warfare.

On October 26, *I-21* sank the destroyer *Porter* during the Battle of the Santa Cruz Islands. The last Japanese success in the Solomons occurred when *I-26* scored against the cruiser *Juneau* on November 13, detonating the magazines and sinking it in twenty seconds. More than six hundred men were lost.

During the later stages of the Solomons campaign, and in other island groups later in the war,

Japanese submarines were increasingly used as transports to supply isolated garrisons. These operations were very dangerous, given American superiority in radar and sonar, and ten submarines were lost before March 1943, alone. Those submarines not diverted to supply missions were used as a "fire brigade," sailing to whatever islands were threatened by American invasion. Unable to compete with American ASW forces, twenty-three Japanese submarines were lost trying to defend the Gilbert and the Solomon Islands. Only two other major American warships were lost to submarines during the rest of the war: the escort carrier *Liscome Bay*, during the Gilbert operations, and the heavy cruiser *Indianapolis*, in August 1945.

1943: THE PRESSURE BUILDS

In 1943, as U.S. naval intelligence grew better at reading Japanese merchant and naval codes, American submarines could be positioned to intercept merchant ship convoys, and even Japanese warships. Intelligence, combined with geography (the narrow straits found on key shipping routes in the western Pacific), reduced the time submarines spent searching for targets.

U.S. submarines also ran reconnaissance missions before invasions and patrolled off enemy bases, hoping for a shot at heavy fleet units. The Japanese light cruiser *Agano* was sunk off Truk on February 16, 1944 by *Skate* on just such a mission. The main effort of the American submarines, however, was directed at Japanese commerce.

One of the new American submarine officers, who received his command because his old CO was relieved for lack of aggressiveness, was Dudley Walker Morton. "Mush," as he was nicknamed for his yarnspinning, was anything but timid, as the Japanese would soon learn. Before he took his submarine into harm's way in early 1943, he spoke to his assembled crew. He said: "*Wahoo* is expendable. . . . We will take every reasonable precaution, but our mission is to sink shipping. . . ." He then told the crew he only wanted volunteers because "Every smoke trace on the horizon, every contact on watch will be investigated. If it turns out to be the enemy, we are going to hunt him down and kill him." None of his crew took the offered transfer.

Top: *Cuttlefish* (SS-171) cruising on the surface sometime during 1942. Specializing in reconnaissance, this small *Cachalot*-class submarine conducted three war patrols before moving to New London, Connecticut, where she served as a training ship for the remainder of the war. Above: The large submarine *Argonaut* (SF-7) lying at Pearl Harbor. The light-grey paint scheme dates the photo to the late 1930s. After an initial anti-invasion patrol off Midway in December 1941, the submarine was converted to a troop transport and participated in the August 16, 1942 raid on Makin in the Gilbert Islands. On January 10, 1943, after attacking an enemy convoy between New Britain and Bougainvillea, the submarine was sunk by Japanese destroyers.

The above photos are interior shots of *Ling* (SS-297), an American *Balao*-class submarine built by Cramp Shipbuilding Co., at Philadelphia, Pennsylvania. Delivered to the Navy in 1945, the submarine arrived too late to take part in the war. The submarine served as a training ship from 1960 until it was donated as a museum ship in January 1973. Above, left: The maneuvering room, showing throttles and shifting gear for the propellers. Above, right: The control room, showing the dive safety panel, which was called the "Christmas tree" for its green and red warning lights. Below: (from left to right) The cutaway diagram of a *Balao*-class submarine reveals the forward torpedo room (with the folding dive above), the officers' berths and the forward batteries, followed by the bridge, the control and pump rooms, radio, mess, and crew quarters, and finally the familiar diesel engines, maneuvering room, electric motors, and aft torpedo tubes. Designed for operations in the Pacific, the submarine carried 24 torpedoes, in addition to rounds for the 4-or 5-inch (9-11.5cm) deck gun and the four machine guns, and had an endurance of 75 days. Total delivery of this class was 120 submarines.

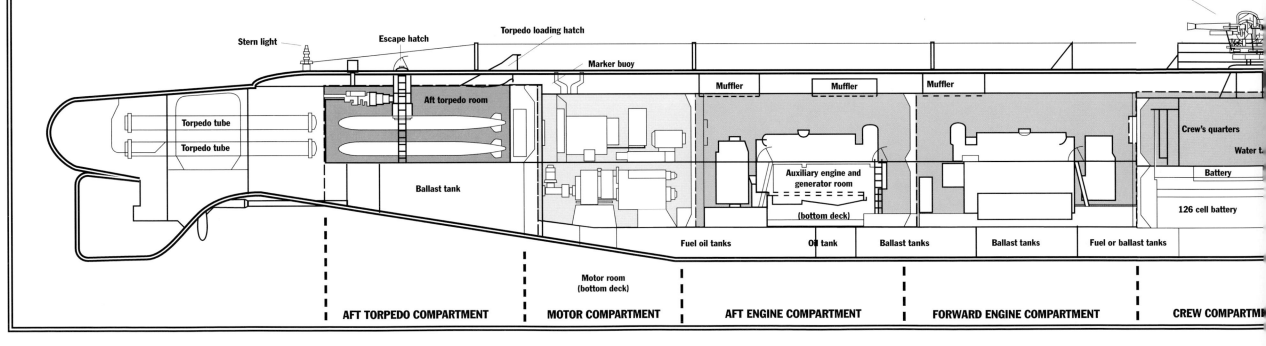

BALAO-CLASS SUBMARINE

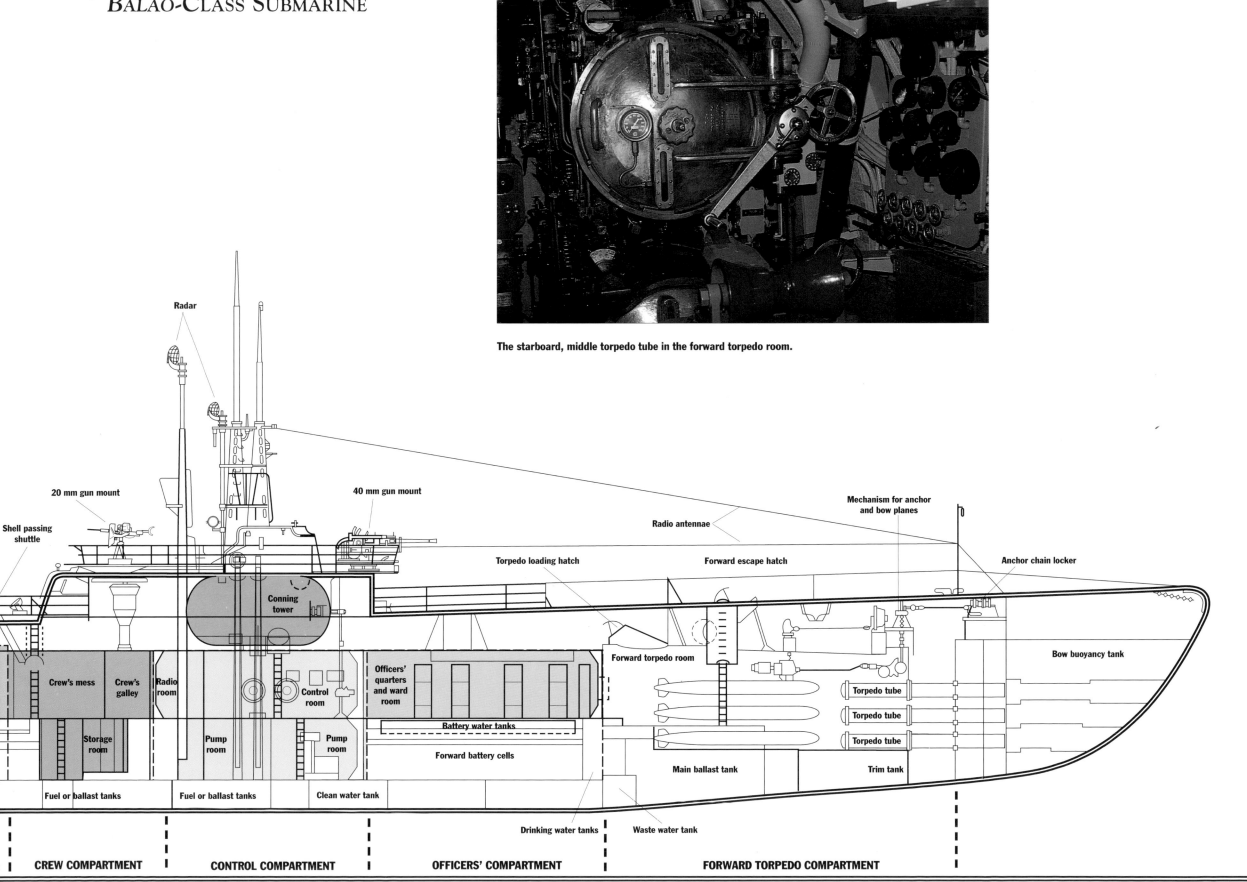

The starboard, middle torpedo tube in the forward torpedo room.

Radar

20 mm gun mount

40 mm gun mount

Shell passing shuttle

Mechanism for anchor and bow planes

Radio antennae

Torpedo loading hatch

Forward escape hatch

Anchor chain locker

Conning tower

Forward torpedo room

Bow buoyancy tank

Crew's mess

Crew's galley

Radio room

Control room

Officers' quarters and ward room

Torpedo tube

Torpedo tube

Torpedo tube

Storage room

Pump room

Pump room

Battery water tanks

Forward battery cells

Main ballast tank

Trim tank

Fuel or ballast tanks

Fuel or ballast tanks

Clean water tank

Drinking water tanks

Waste water tank

CREW COMPARTMENT

CONTROL COMPARTMENT

OFFICERS' COMPARTMENT

FORWARD TORPEDO COMPARTMENT

On his first patrol, Mush took the *Wahoo* off northern New Guinea and conducted a reconnaissance of Wewak by sailing into the harbor to see what he could sink. On January 24, 1943, he spotted a destroyer just underway, but missed with his first four torpedo shots. The destroyer, whose lookouts spotted the torpedo wakes, headed directly toward the Americans. Mush held his ground and attempted to shoot "down the throat," hoping a torpedo would hit the destroyer's bow. The range between the two warships closed—it was down to eight hundred yards (720m) when Mush fired the fifth and last torpedo in the forward tubes. The crew soon heard a terrific explosion as the "fish" broke the back of the destroyer. This strategy of fighting it out with Japanese escorts would bring great dividends: during 1943, American submarines sank seventeen Japanese patrol boats and escorts.

The next day the *Wahoo* located a four-ship convoy consisting of two freighters, an oiler, and the large troopship *Buyo Maru*. Mush attacked and hit the two freighters with his first salvo. One began to sink. A three-torpedo spread then stopped the troop transport, while another shot was needed to keep from being rammed by the wounded second freighter. Meanwhile, the troop ship, with help from two more torpedoes, blew up amidships, spilling the occupants into the sea. As the tanker and the wounded freighter fled, Mush surfaced the *Wahoo* to recharge batteries.

The Japanese troops, meanwhile, struggled into twenty lifeboats and some troops shot at the *Wahoo* with rifles. What happened next became one of the most controversial actions ever carried out by an American submarine: Mush ordered his gunners to shoot the lifeboats and machine-gun the survivors, an order his crew unquestioningly carried out. The *Wahoo* then finished off the other two ships. Now out of torpedoes, the submarine turned for home. Once there, he and his crew became instant heroes. No one questioned his attack on the transport's survivors, a brutal symbol of the Pacific war. The war eventually claimed Mush when a Japanese patrol plane's depth charges straddled *Wahoo* on the surface on October 11, 1943. There were no survivors. Mush was credited with seventeen ships, making him one of the top three American aces.

Attacks like these increased the pressure on Japanese commerce. New and improved torpedoes, a surface search radar, and increasing numbers of sub-

Top: A shot taken inside the control room of the *Wahoo* (SS-238) on January 27, 1943. The submarine is rigged for silent running and is twisting and turning 300 feet (90m) down as a Japanese destroyer drops depth-charges nearby. Six charges had just gone off and the crew is waiting for more. *Wahoo* survived this depth-charging, described by "Mush" Morton as "Another running gun fight . . . destroyer gunning . . . *Wahoo* running." The shaved heads are due to a "crossing the line" ceremony three days before. Above: The *Harusame* lies smoking in the water with a broken keel near Wewak, New Guinea. The Japanese destroyer has just taken one of *Wahoo*'s torpedoes "down the throat." Despite the heavy damage, the destroyer was repaired and returned to service. *Harusame* participated in several battles in the southwest Pacific in early 1944 and, on June 8 of that year, was sunk by American bombers in Dampier Strait, West New Guinea.

marines began to take a toll on Japanese merchant ships. U.S. submarine patrols ranged from the waters off Japan to the trade routes of the East Indies. In seven hundred patrols during 1943, American submarines sank just over three hundred enemy merchant ships at a cost of fifteen submarines. Limited experiments with wolf packs were tried, usually involving no more than three fleet boats, but because the Japanese did not yet sail in convoy, the American submarines had more success working alone. Intelligence decoding continued: single U.S. submarines continued to intercept and sink enemy shipping.

Japanese antisubmarine efforts were similar to Britain's tactics from World War I. Unsure of how to combat the wide-ranging American submarine effort, especially since Japanese shipping sailed independently all across the Pacific, the Japanese did little for the first two years of the war. Air patrols were set up over the East and South China Seas, but a working convoy system, forced into existence by the growing losses, was not in place until January 1944. Called the "Grand Escort Fleet," it numbered roughly 150 escorts. Lacking effective sonar and radar gear (though both were being fitted by early 1944), the convoy escorts also proved vulnerable to American submarines.

WARSHIP KILLERS

Despite concentrating on enemy merchant ships, American submarines did attack major Japanese warships when the opportunity arose. During routine patrols in 1944, the Japanese cruiser *Tatsuta* was sunk March 13 by *Sandlance*; the cruiser *Yubari* followed on April 27, with help from *Bluegill*. *Flasher* sank the cruiser *Oi* on July 19. Two Japanese carriers were lost during the Battle of the Philippine Sea when *Albacore* torpedoed *Taiho*, which blew up because of inept damage control. *Shokaku* disintegrated when *Cavalla*'s torpedo found its magazine. Five more cruisers, a seaplane carrier, and three light carriers—the *Taiyo*, *Unyo*, and *Shinyo*—were also sunk by the middle of November. These losses were especially disconcerting because many of the warships sank in waters near Japan.

On November 21, for example, Commander Eli Reich and his *Sealion* were patrolling in the East China Sea. The moonless night was perfect for the American submarine, as few Japanese ships had sur-

Above, right: American World War II submarines were equipped with primitive air search radar (to spot enemy aircraft) and had radar warning receivers (to detect aircraft radar emissions), neither of which were fully trusted. The sailor standing on the periscope sheers with a pair of binoculars is keeping a lookout for aircraft and enemy shipping. He is using the oldest detection device ever put on a submarine, the eyeball. Left, top: This photo was taken by *Seadragon* (SS-194) as she approached a burning cargo ship. It may be the incident on May 17, 1944, when the submarine set an armed trawler on fire with 4-inch (10cm) gunfire and then approached in a failed attempt to take some prisoners. Left, bottom: : A periscope photo taken by *Seawolf* (SS-197) in November 1942. The Japanese ship is probably *Gifu Maru*, sunk November 2 in the Davao Gulf area off the Philippines.

Top: The *Silversides'* (SS-236) 3-inch (7.5cm) gun crew in action, probably October 14, 1942. The man in the chair is setting elevation and train while the others load a shell into the breech. The sailor on the left is lifting another shell from the stowage compartment. In a gun battle with a Japanese trawler on May 10, 1942, in which the trawler was sunk, an enemy machine gun bullet killed one of the deck gunners. Above: A Japanese picket boat near the Caroline Islands burns after being shelled by *Silversides'* deck gun. The range lines on the photo indicate it was taken through the periscope.

face search radar. *Sealion* detected seven targets on its radar, two of which seemed to be battleships. Reich first fired six torpedoes at extreme range and followed them with three more from a different angle. Reich saw three hit and blow up one target, the destroyer *Urakaze*, while a single torpedo struck the battleship *Kongo*.

The huge warship slowed to eleven knots, apparently damaged by the lone torpedo, and Reich maneuvered for another attack. Suddenly, a tremendous explosion lit up the horizon dead ahead. To Reich, ". . . it looked like a sunset at midnight." With a single shot that led to a catastrophic magazine explosion, Reich and the *Sealion* had accomplished what no other U.S. submarine has done before or since—they had sunk a battleship.

Sometimes, intelligence garnered from Magic intercepts gave the submarines an edge; other times it was just luck. Such was the case for *Archerfish* and its commanding officer, Commander Joseph F. Enright, on November 29. The Japanese aircraft carrier *Shinano*, a converted battleship, had sailed from Tokyo for the Japanese naval base at Kure for final conversions. The carrier, at the time the largest warship in the world, was still fitting out and many on board were workers, finishing the assignment. Unluckily for them, much of the damage control equipment and some important watertight doors had yet to be installed. The *Archerfish* chased *Shinano* and its four escorts for six and a half hours on the evening of November 29, before finally firing six torpedoes at the huge carrier. A glowing fireball marked four hits and the *Shinano* capsized and sank eight hours later. Another carrier, the *Unryu*, was done in by *Redfish* on December 19.

COMMERCE WAR WITH A VENGEANCE

By 1944, there were nearly ninety submarines operating from Pearl Harbor under the command of Vice Admiral Charles Lockwood, and forty operating from Australia under the command of Rear Admiral Ralph Christie. Advanced bases were set up in the Admiralty and Marshall Islands, decreasing transit time, and enabling the Americans to interdict Japanese oil convoys from Sumatra, Java, and Borneo.

With each boat equipped with radar, and the excellent TDC, the American submarines slaugh-

Above: A close-up of an XO at the periscope. The picture, taken off New London, Connecticut, is most likely of an officer undergoing attack training before being assigned to an active submarine.

tered Japanese convoys. Submarine commanders became so used to intelligence data that they were known to complain if a convoy did not appear exactly where their Magic intercepts indicated. Unlike the Atlantic, where U-boats had to deal with well-armed and radar-equipped escorts, the American submarines were technically superior to these escorts. The Japanese escorts, most without radar, could not contend with night surface attacks and were more likely to be sunk themselves if they challenged an American submarine. A total of fifty-six destroyers, escorts, and patrol craft were lost to American submarines that year. The Japanese sank only eight submarines in return.

American wolf packs also began to sink Japanese convoys. Generally consisting of three submarines, these packs found hunting easier than their German counterparts in the North Atlantic. In October 1944, while patrolling the Formosa Strait, two wolf packs, led by *Shark* and *Sawfish*, attacked several convoys carrying reinforcements and supplies to the Philippines. Seventeen Japanese ships went down in a three-day period. Two other packs operating in the

This photo of the drydocks at Kure Naval Base, Japan, circa February 1946, was taken by members of the United States Strategic Bombing Survey, who were investigating the effects of aerial bombardment on the Japanese war effort. The damage to the dock and the midget submarines shown, however, was done after American forces occupied Japan.

Yellow Sea, led by *Spadefish* and *Queenfish*, sank nineteen ships, including the troop transport *Mayasan Maru*, which was transporting much of the Japanese Army's Twenty-third Division to the Philippines. Another wolf pack, in a rare meeting between Americans and Germans, was vectored to attack the *U-537*, operating in the Indian Ocean. The *Flounder* fired four torpedoes, one of which hit. The *U-537* went down, with no survivors.

As in the Atlantic, these successes did not come without a price. The *Seawolf* disaster illustrated that, as in Europe, friendly fire could be deadly. On October 3, 1944, while on the surface near Moratai, in the Moluccas, two search planes from the carrier *Midway* bombed *Seawolf's* position. The boat submerged to escape, but was caught by the destroyer escort *Rowell*. The escort made a sound contact and destroyed the submarine with a well-aimed hedgehog attack, killing ninety-nine American submariners. Similar ill fortune befell *Dorado* in the Caribbean. It was misidentified as a U-boat by a patrol plane and depth-charged, at a cost of seventy-six, on October 12, 1943. Other tragedies, such as circular torpedo runs, caused by malfunctioning gyros, sank both *Tullibee* and *Tang* in 1944.

But by the end of 1944, the American *guerre de course* had decisively shattered the Japanese merchant marine, sinking more than five hundred merchant ships. The Japanese tanker fleet was ravaged, leading to acute oil shortages and warships stuck in port for lack of fuel. Raw materials shortages began to slow Japanese war production. In 1945, the overwhelming combination of submarine patrols, intensive minelaying by B-29 bombers operating out of the Marianas, and carrier-based fighter sweeps virtually shut down Japanese overseas trade.

The last Japanese oil shipment got through in March, and by the summer of 1945, surviving units of the once proud Imperial Japanese Navy swung at their anchors for lack of fuel oil. When the war ended, American submarines had accounted for 4.7 million tons (4.2 million t) of shipping, more than enough to stop Japanese trade.

OTHER SUBMARINE FORCES

Several smaller submarine forces, mentioned only briefly so far, took part in the war. The French, for example, had a difficult time. Although prepared to

Roballo (SS-273) splashes into a river at Manitowoc, Wisconsin, on May 9, 1943. Sailed down Lake Michigan, then down the Mississippi, the boat was commissioned on September 28, and joined the Pacific fleet soon afterwards. Over the next six months, the submarine conducted two war patrols in the western Pacific. *Roballo* departed Fremantle for her third war patrol on June 22, 1944 and, after reporting in while off Borneo, was never heard from again. Later sources indicated the submarine hit a mine near Palawan Island in the Philippines on July 26. Only four men survived the ensuing battery explosion and fire to swim ashore. The four were captured by the Japanese and subsequently died in captivity.

Top: This photo of the wreck of the *Antonio Sciesa* indicates the Italian submarine had seen better days. Following the second battle of El Alamein on October 23, 1942 and the ensuing retreat of the Axis forces from Egypt, British forces closed Tobruk. Royal Air Force planes caught the submarine on November 6, and severely damaged her with rockets and gunfire. Too crippled to escape Montgomery's troops, the submarine was scuttled in Tobruk harbor six days later. Above: Intelligence intercepts and HF/DF readings led a rocket-armed torpedo bomber from *Bogue* (CVE-9) onto the trail of *U-1229* south of Newfoundland on August 20, 1944. Caught on the surface, the Type IXC suffered heavy battery damage and after vainly trying to vent the chlorine gas through the snorkel (note the mast in a raised position), was taken under attack by no less than five Avengers. More rockets and depth bombs sank the U-boat shortly thereafter.

contest the Italians for the western Mediterranean, metropolitan France surrendered before much was accomplished. A very large portion of their force was scuttled at Toulon in November 1942, and then a dozen or so boats were lost to Allied ASW forces during the North African landings.

The Dutch, whose forces in the East Indies remained active after Germany occupied Holland in May 1940, operated about a dozen submarines against the Japanese until the end of the war.

The Italians operated 136 submarines at one time or another during the war (some of them, captured French boats), mainly in the Mediterranean. There, they tried to interdict Allied shipping, but without much success. Like the Japanese force, the Italians could not cope with modern escorts and accomplished little.

The Soviet Union operated submarines in the Black and Baltic Seas. Frustrated because most of their naval bases were taken by German ground forces at one time or another, the Soviets relied heavily on mines to protect these waters, using submarines to lay some fields. They were not in a position for offensive patrols until late in the war. German mining also took a very heavy toll on Russian boats. Some 104 Soviet submarines were lost to all causes.

In 1945, as German forces evacuated Baltic ports, Soviet submarines scored some successes sinking unarmed transports. Soviet submarines sank the refugee ships *Wilhelm Gustloff*, *General Steuban*, and *Goya* in January, with the loss of fifteen thousand lives. The *S-13*, which sank the *Wilhelm Gustloff* with three torpedoes, drowning 5,580, has the dubious distinction of being the submarine that has killed the most people with one salvo.

THE FINAL TALLY

The campaign in the Pacific illustrated that a *guerre de course* could succeed; indeed, it proved that a war against commerce can ultimately lead to victory. In the final count, U.S. submarines accounted for nearly fifty-five percent of Japanese shipping losses—an impressive figure considering that only two percent of U.S. Navy personnel served in the submarine forces. These two percent and their submarines sank 1,314 Japanese vessels and killed 16,200 merchant mariners.

The Imperial Japanese Navy lost one battleship, eight aircraft carriers, and eleven cruisers to U.S. submarines. The cost for the Americans may seem high: fifty-two submarines, with 3,506 officers and men, but compared to the submarine fleets of her enemies, U.S. losses paled.

The Japanese lost 130 submarines, and the Italians eighty-five. The Germans, however, took the heaviest losses. Of the roughly one thousand U-boats constructed, 781 were sunk by all causes, and with them 28,000 sailors were killed, many in the crushing darkness deep beneath the sea. In return, the U-boats sank 2,882 Allied merchant vessels of nearly 14.4 million tons, and destroyed 175 Allied warships. 30,132 British and 6,103 American merchant seaman died in these attacks, along with thousands more sailors, soldiers, and passengers. For their part in destroying Axis trade in the Baltic and the Mediterranean, the British lost forty-five submarines.

As a warship, the submarine significantly improved its reputation during World War II. More than in World War I, submarines had proved effective even where the enemy had air and surface superiority. Though too slow to be of much use on the defense, as all sides found out during the war, they functioned superbly when called upon to lay minefields, conduct reconnaissance, carry supplies, or land special forces behind enemy lines. But submarines functioned best when they waged a long war of attrition against enemy shipping. They had also proved more useful than the battle fleets in sinking enemy ships. Only carrier air power had been more important in this respect.

The submarine's wartime reputation carried through into the postwar period. Part of the submarine's success was due to the revolutionary changes in submarine technology developed by the Germans. Snorkels, streamlined shapes, and high underwater speed promised to make all current ASW forces obsolete. But part of the success also depended on the great disparity in resources needed to counter submarines. The U-boat, even though it had failed to bring Britain to its knees, had diverted many more resources into escorts, aircraft, bases, and ship construction than the Germans had put into the submarine campaign. If only for that equation alone, the submarine's place within the fleets of the world was secure.

Chapter 5

The Search for a Strategy

I N LATE 1945, GERMANY, JAPAN, AND ITALY LAY PROSTRATE BEFORE THE combined might of the Allies. The great U-boat fleet was neutralized—scuttled or captured—as were the Japanese and Italian submarines. The Allied submarine fleets remained sizable—not as large as in wartime, but vigorous. Postwar planners were not about to eliminate such a useful weapons system. Financial retrenchment, caused by declining defense budgets, forced the U.S. Navy to scrap or place in reserve 126 older boats, and to cancel another ninety-two under construction. About two hundred submarines remained in service. The British did the same, scrapping forty-five, canceling fifty, and leaving ninety-nine in service. The French, left with nothing after German occupation, put together a small but growing fleet of a few dozen ex-British and ex-German submarines.

The Soviet navy, meanwhile, adjusted only a little more easily to postwar conditions. The country's policy makers, concerned with absorbing Eastern Europe and recovering from the devastation of war, had little time for the navy. As the very junior partner in the Soviet defense hierarchy, the navy had only a limited role as coastal defense force and flank-supporter for the Red Army. Even so, and despite significant wartime damage to their shipyards, enough industrial base remained to operate a submarine fleet of about one hundred ocean-going and fifty coastal boats. A plan to modernize the surface fleet absorbed most new naval resources and the submarine arm grew slowly.

The immediate postwar period was a confusing time for the western countries. American foreign policy was hesitant, contradictory, and lacked cohesive purpose. The U.S. Navy, concerned about international commitments, pressed its case for a large peacetime Navy. But presidential and congressional domestic concerns forced the military to cope with relatively small budgets.

The U.S. Navy tried to keep much of its wartime fleet, especially the heavy surface warships, but it was a struggle contending with budget-conscious politicians and the new demands of the air force. With the Soviet Union the most likely future enemy, the Navy's arguments for seapower as a counterweight to land power seemed unsatisfactory; nuclear weapons seemed to make navies obsolete. The British navy, and to a lesser extent the French, suffered as their governments struggled with decolonization crises.

Perceptions began to change, however, as differences in economic and social outlook in general, and political disagreements over Europe in particular, led to growing distrust between the Soviet Union and the Western democracies. Fraudulent Polish and Balkan elections, wrangling over German reparations, and the Greek civil war created tension in the newly formed United Nations.

One of the last shots of the modernized *Cochino* (SS-345), taken while leaving Portsmouth, England, for an intelligence gathering mission to the Barents Sea, circa July 1949. On August 25, while *Cochino* was operating with *Tusk* (SS-426) off Norway, a violent polar gale caused a battery explosion and electrical fire. The following day, after a second battery explosion, the submarine sank at 71 35° N., 2335°E. The large streamlined sail, needed to house the snorkel, and the sonar box forward are only the most obvious changes that make the "guppy" boats different from their wartime predecessors.

The failure of the Eastern bloc to participate in the Marshall Plan, as well as world trade negotiations, isolated the communists. Growing Soviet military budgets, along with the establishment of the North Atlantic Treaty Organization (NATO) and the Warsaw Pact, heightened tension. Finally, the iron curtain, the Berlin blockades, and the outbreak of the Korean War in June 1950, led to outright hostility. The cold war was underway.

From a naval perspective, the clash between the West and the Soviet Union perfectly illustrates the contrast between maritime powers, which depend on the sea for international trade and communications, and the sealed borders of an insular continental power. Unlike the West, the Soviets did not need or even want to join the international community of nations. Able to mobilize Eurasian resources in a way Hitler could only have dreamed of, the Soviet armed forces embodied the same strategic threat posed by Germany during World War II.

For the third time in the twentieth century, the West faced an enemy that could threaten both Europe and the global shipping lanes. NATO interest in the waters off Europe grew, as navy planners grappled with possible Soviet moves against the eastern Mediterranean and the North Atlantic supply routes. Of special concern were the 150 submarines in the Soviet navy. But numbers alone were not what kept planners awake at night.

THE FAST SUBMARINE

The naval world in 1950 was very different from that of the war years. Naval warfare and the composition of fleets changed rapidly in the late 1940s. The aircraft carrier eclipsed the battleship, while new missile technology threatened to replace the shell and "dumb" iron-bomb. To top it off, atomic weapons threatened to make navies passé (a fervent desire of western air forces). But navies held fast; their forces survived budget threats, missile technology was gradually added to warships, and studies showed that nuclear weapons would be ineffective, even wasteful, against dispersed ships.

This argument was proven, to the immense relief of the American and British navies, during the Operation Crossroads atomic tests at Bikini and Eniwetok Atolls in 1947. Many target ships, even some close to ground zero, survived the blasts and

A close-up view of the conning tower of *U-3008*, an ex-German submarine in American service, taken at Key West Naval Station on July 25, 1947. The two vertical tubes shown behind the flag are the snorkel air shaft and exhaust vents, which allow the diesel engines to operate while the submarine is submerged. The submarine served with the Operational Development Force, which was tasked with designing new submarine and ASW tactics, into 1948. Although put out of service on June 18, she remained a Navy test hulk until sold for scrap in 1955.

remained operational. But there was another naval threat that promised a different kind of revolution— one that the NATO surface navies found very unpleasant to consider.

During the last few years of World War II, the German navy had redesigned the U-boat to foil Allied countermeasures. Realizing that most Allied attacks were directed against surfaced U-boats, the new designs stressed underwater operations over surface performance. The result was the Type XXI and XXIII U-boats. Luckily for the Allies, the war ended in Europe before more than a handful became operational.

After the war, most Allied navies acquired some of these U-boats, and their capabilities came as quite a shock. The streamlined outer hull and strengthened pressure hull reduced drag and allowed regular dives of more than five hundred feet (150m). New hydrophones and acoustic torpedoes allowed attacks from deep underwater. Most importantly, improved batteries enabled an underwater speed of seventeen knots—more than twice that of existing boats. Of all

Some of the 106 preserved, or "mothballed," American fleet submarines in the Mare Island Group, San Francisco, on July 26, 1946. They were unloaded, drained of fuel, and sealed against the elements before being put into reserve status following the end of World War II. In case of emergency, these submarines could be refitted far more quickly than new ones could be built. Some of these submarines were reactivated during and after the Korean War, others were lent to foreign navies, but most were eventually scrapped as obsolete.

the changes, it was this increase in underwater speed that most scared NATO planners.

High underwater speed would defeat the entire complement of western ASW escorts; moreover, a fast submarine made traditional search tactics useless. These tactics, called "box" pattern searches, were designed to examine the area that a four-knot submerged submarine could travel after firing a torpedo. A submerged speed of seventeen knots made the box far too large. But, even if the submarine could be found, that speed also made the submarine too fast

for sonar. Self-noise, the sound made by the escort's own hull and propellers striking the water, would drown out any sonar contacts.

Studies with captured Type XXIs also proved that high speeds and deep diving depth made traditional depth charges useless, since they sank too slowly. At full underwater speed, the submerged boats outran even fast-sinking weapons such as the hedgehog or the squid mortar. And radar-equipped patrol planes were neutralized, since the boats had snorkels to make extended, submerged cruises. To make matters worse, high-speed radio transmitters made radio intercepts very difficult.

THE SOVIET THREAT

NATO planners worried that the Russians would launch these fast boats and, in one fell swoop, completely disorganize western ASW forces. The Soviets had received ten Type XXIs after the German surrender and intelligence indicated that several more were captured in the Baltic. A number of prefabricated

sections and components also came under Soviet control with the seizure of the Schichau assembly yard at Danzig.

In 1948, a NATO intelligence estimate indicated at least 124 modern ocean patrol submarines were in Soviet service, with another ninety-nine obsolete or coastal types in reserve. It was unclear just how many of the ocean patrol Soviet boats had been modernized for high underwater speed. NATO lived in fear that the Russians, in time of war, would flood the Atlantic sea-lanes with hundreds of these fast submarines. Some admirals predicted the Soviets might have 1,200 such submarines within a decade.

As it turned out, Soviet postwar submarine construction was not that dramatic. The first fast production submarine was the medium-range *Whiskey*-class (a NATO code name that used letters to indicate different projects). Simple to build and operate, the snorkel-equipped submarine carried twelve torpedoes and had a submerged speed of 13.5 knots, more than enough to raid the merchant shipping lanes.

Reportedly, 236 *Whiskey*-class boats were constructed by 1957, when the program ended. The Soviets also built the larger *Zulu*-class boats, which clearly showed the influence of the German Type XXIs. With a submerged speed of sixteen knots, equipped with six torpedo tubes forward, four stern, and a load of twenty-two torpedoes, the *Zulu* was the NATO navies' nightmare. Twenty-one boats were constructed by 1955 and another five were modified to launch two ballistic missiles out of their conning towers by 1957.

HUNTER-KILLERS AND OTHER ASW DEVELOPMENTS

Given the secrecy surrounding the Soviet Union and the lack of intelligence about its activities, NATO planners estimated about 373 fast boats were in the Russian inventory by the mid-1950s. Although this was considerably more than the 292 actually in service, it supplied a dramatic sense of urgency to western antisubmarine research. After studying the German technical advances in the Type XXIs, British and American naval engineers implemented their own submarine upgrades.

Experiments with hastily modified fleet submarines, called "guppy" conversions in the U.S.

These are two Soviet submarines moored at Sudomekh shipyard, Leningrad, in 1946, possibly *M-90* (outboard) and *M-171* (inboard). American intelligence suspected the submarines were fitted with advanced propulsion technology and labelled them "experimental."

marines. Equipped with improved sonar gear and designed for ultraquiet submerged operations, these submarines seemed the best way to hunt Soviet boats that were too fast for the surface escorts. Improvements in acoustic homing and pattern-running torpedoes promptly followed.

The experiments with *Tusk* led to designs for the first two American "hunter-killer" boats, called *Tang* and *Trigger*. Commissioned in 1951 and 1952, respectively, they were designed to dive deep and operate in conjunction with surface forces. With a seven hundred-foot (210m) operating depth, and a 1,100 foot (330m) collapse depth, they served as test ASW platforms in both the Atlantic and Pacific fleets. Seven more were built before the U.S. Navy switched to nuclear powered submarines in the mid-1950s.

The British, meanwhile, designed their first fast diesel-electric submarine in 1954. Called *Porpoise*, this class incorporated both German and American improvements, allowing exceptionally quiet operations, a seventeen-knot submerged speed, and a range of nine thousand miles (16,679km). Equipped with six bow and two stern tubes, and thirty reloads, the *Porpoise* boat was a pure ASW design. Seven more *Porpoise*-class boats, plus thirteen *Oberon*-class diesel-electric boats, with similar characteristics, were built through 1967, before the Royal Navy also switched to nuclear power.

More research efforts to counter the fast submarines continued at a rapid pace. New weapons, such as air-dropped antisubmarine torpedoes, were designed to help the surface escorts. These acoustic torpedoes had a speed of thirty knots and could dive below five hundred feet (150m). Rocket-assisted magnetic mines and a nuclear depth charge also came into service. The principal problem, however, was still locating the submarine.

Short-wave radar, which had been so successful during World War II, did not work against snorkeling boats. Researchers concentrated on magnetic detection equipment, air-dropped sonobuoys, and a dipping sonar used by helicopters. Other work involved low-frequency radar, infra-red detection devices, and even attempts to detect the radioactive emissions from nuclear weapons stored in a submerged submarine.

Since submarines were really the best tool with which to find other submarines, the most important detection work involved sonar technology. Facing the same problem as the Soviets, Western streamlined

Navy, proved a submarine sonar was far superior to that of a surface ship. As a 1946 report stated, "Basic considerations of the ship vs. submarine problem seem to indicate that continued hunting of deep submarines by surface craft will become ridiculous and hence serious consideration of an antisubmarine submarine is in progress."

Tactical exercises with the snorkel-modified *Tusk* off Panama during 1948 showed that a submarine running silent, on batteries, could hear the bubbling noise of snorkel-boats at a range far greater than surface ships. And even if the enemy boat was using battery power, the submarine itself appeared to be the most effective ASW platform against enemy sub-

Above: A photograph, obtained from an official Soviet source, of a Soviet *Whiskey* diesel-electric submarine underway in November 1962. The cylinder forward the conning tower is a diver access chamber. The small "shark fin" near the bow is a sonar dome. At the time, the Soviets falsely claimed this submarine was nuclear powered. Left: *Sterlett* (SS-392) nested outboard of two other submarines at Yokosuka, Japan, on May 16, 1955. Their tender, *Florikan* (ASR-9), is in the background. Note the raked stem on *Sterlett*, and the rounded bows on the two inboard boats, indicating *Sterlett* received only a partial modification program—essentially a snorkel and a new conning tower.

Below: A famous photograph of two Soviet diesel-electric boats maneuvering in the North Pacific during 1957. The old L-class boat on the left may have been built before World War II. The far more streamlined *Zulu*-class boat on the right had the long range and 60-day endurance to attack the Atlantic or Pacific shipping routes. Right: The combination of fast streamlined submarines and long-range bombers capable of extensive mine-laying or missile attacks worried NATO planners from the late 1940s. Developing effective antisubmarine and antibomber defenses took up much of their energies throughout the Cold War. One answer was the radar picket submarine (SSR), ten of which were converted from attack submarines during and after the Korean War. Developed to avoid the losses suffered by the destroyer picket ships off Okinawa in 1945, the SSR would provide early warning of an enemy bomber attack and then submerge to avoid being attacked on the surface. Improvements in DEW-line (Distant Early Warning) radars made these submarines obsolete by the late 1950s. The scene shows the Combat Information Center (CIC) of *Pompon* (SSR-267), with the radar gang manning defense stations circa 1953.

submarines had difficulty maintaining sonar contacts during high-speed bursts. Self-noise, such as machinery and propeller cavitation, rendered even the most sensitive equipment useless. Dragging antennas and rattling equipment only made the noise worse.

But, slowly and surely, scientists began to understand the physics of underwater sound. By the late 1940s, American scientists had discovered how sound channels and convergence zones could allow passive sonars to detect underwater noise from great distances. Circular bow-mounted sonars, similar to the hydrophone systems used in late-war German U-boats, were developed by both sides to take advantage of underwater sound behavior. In 1951, an experimental sonar on *Guavina* (SS-362) detected another submarine and a fleet tug at a range of 9 miles (14.4km). The previous limit had been 1.4 miles (2.2km). In 1949, to support underwater detection efforts, underwater listening stations began the expansion of the modern Sound Surveillance System (SOSUS) that initially covered the North Atlantic. SOSUS was a series of sophisticated hydrophones embedded in the sea floor that listened for the sounds of enemy submarines.

STRATEGIC MISSILE SUBMARINES

In the face of these challenges, the Soviets responded with a new generation of attack submarines. In 1958, the *Romeo*- and *Foxtrot*-class boats, designed to replace the *Whiskey* and *Zulu*, began production. They were somewhat faster (15.5 knots submerged), had a greater range, more torpedoes, and they could dive deeper than earlier boats. Twenty *Romeos* were built through 1962, and sixty-two *Foxtrots* through 1967.

In the mid-1950s, however, new strategic and political considerations encouraged both the Soviet and U.S. navies to reevaluate their force structure. Computer and missile technology, combined with nuclear weapons, seemed to make old missions and warships obsolete. Submarines, as part of this equation, changed with the times. By the time missile technology became firmly established, a new kind of submarine had come into existence. The strategic missile submarine became one of the two types of modern submarines, the other remaining the traditional torpedo attack boat.

The missile, inaugurated during World War II, provided a long-range weapon for the submarine. The Soviets, who liked the idea of submarines having a long reach, equipped five *Zulu*-class boats with a vertical launch canister in 1955. The first submarine test firing occurred that September, when a liquid-fueled Scud missile was launched out of the boat. The era of ballistic missile boats had arrived. The Soviets also experimented with cruise missiles and converted seven *Whiskey*-class boats to carry flush-deck horizontal launchers for this purpose. These missiles were originally intended for an antishipping role, but later designs carried nuclear warheads for strikes against coastal cities.

The U.S. Navy, also seeking a nuclear strike capability, combined the range and speed of a rocket with the stealth and endurance of the submarine. Armed with missiles, submarines could secretly approach an enemy's coast and launch devastating surprise attacks. This idea was presented as an alternative, or at least a backup, to the carrier nuclear strike role.

In 1947, the submarines *Cusk* and *Carbonero* were converted to launch guided missiles. Stored in an airtight hangar, the single missile was pulled out and readied on a launch-rail while the submarine lay on the surface. The first tests, with an air-breathing cruise missile called *Loon*, were successful to a range of ninety-five miles (152km). By 1958, the next generation missile, called *Regulus I*, was fitted and test-fired from *Tunny*. Five years later, when *Grayback* launched the *Regulus II*, the missile had a range of one thousand miles (1,600km).

NUCLEAR POWER

Armed with nuclear-tipped ballistic or cruise missiles, the submarine became a lethal warship. But whether a torpedo attack submarine designed to hunt ships, or a missile submarine designed to strike targets from afar, the submarine still lacked the final piece of the puzzle. Simply put, no existing engine gave the submarine enough independence from the air to enable it to be the true scourge of the oceans. Experiments with hydrogen peroxide fuels proved too dangerous, and electric batteries did not last long enough.

Even the new streamlined submarines like *Tang*, or the British *Porpoise*, which carried more than one thousand battery-cells, could supply only enough

Above: *Growler* (SSG-577) cruising on the surface. This is a good view of the large hangar and the launch rail just forward of the conning tower. Before firing the missile, the crew had to pull the weapon from the hangar, set it up on the launch rack, and plug in the target coordinates—all of which took time and left the submarine on the surface and vulnerable. Right: A dramatic shot of the first *Regulus II* launch from *Grayback* (SSG-574) on September 17, 1958. The test took place in the Pacific with its target at Edwards Air Force Base, California. The missile carried a packet of mail—the first (and probably only) cruise missile mail run.

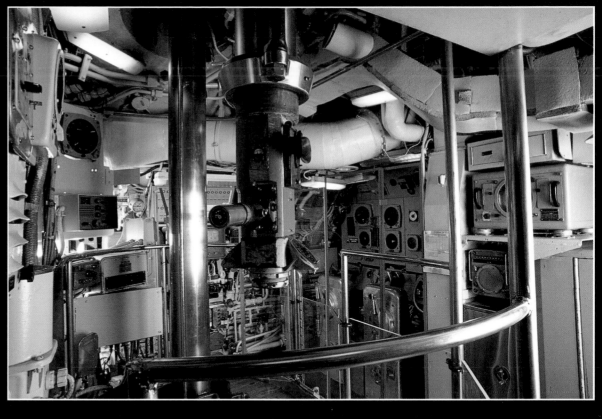

Above: A stern view of *Growler* (SSG-577). The bulging deck forward is the missile hangar, similiar to hangar shown top left. Right, top: An interior view of *Growler*'s control room. Right, bottom: The officers' wardroom aboard *Growler*. With space ever at a premium, these cramped quarters are familiar to generations of submariners.

power to last two or three days before running dry. Diesel-engines, meanwhile, required a submarine to "snort" by cruising just beneath the surface. Not only was this loud, as *Tusk's* Panama experiments showed, but it restricted speed and interfered with sonar readings. And diesel fuel tanks, no matter how large, still ran dry.

The breakthrough came with nuclear power. In the West, the prime force in this revolution was Captain Hyman G. Rickover, whose bronze bust now graces the foyer of the engineering building at the U.S. Naval Academy at Annapolis. Among the first to suggest that a nuclear reactor might be fitted into warships, he saw atomic power as liberating submarines from the twin restrictions of diesel-fuel and oxygen. With reactors, submarines could steam underwater for tens of thousands of miles without refueling. Nor would they be dependent on surfacing to obtain oxygen to run their diesels.

Like the engines of other ships at sea, a naval nuclear engine creates steam to turn turbine blades that then spin propellers. The steam is created by super-heating water in a series of metal tubes called a boiler. But, instead of using coal or fuel oil to heat the water, a nuclear reactor uses a controlled uranium fission reaction. Pressurized water, passing through the reactor, is heated into steam by neutrons spawned by the fission reaction. The hot steam passes through a turbine, providing impetus to the propeller shaft, and is then condensed back into water. The water is returned to the reactor and the process begins again. Unlike other fuels, uranium can last for years before being exhausted. This propulsion system, completely independent from the air, allowed the creation of the first true submarine.

Yet, ironically, the very independence of the nuclear plant from oxygen caused a new problem: how could the crew breathe if the submarine stayed

Left: Crew members ready *Skate* (SSN-578) to get underway from New London, Connecticut, on March 3, 1959. The nuclear submarine steamed north soon after this photo was taken, submerged under the Arctic ice pack, and surfaced through the ice at the North Pole on March 17—the second time she had done so. *Skate,* the third nuclear submarine built by the U.S. Navy, traveled more than 2,400 miles (3,840km) under the ice during this cruise. Right: A partially submerged Soviet *Zulu*-class diesel-electric submarine, photographed from an American patrol plane during July 1962. The heel at the after end of the tower is the snorkel exhaust vent.

underwater for two months? Unable to simply expel dangerous gases, submarines had to use a series of filters, scrubbers, and heaters to catch and incinerate carbon monoxide and other contaminants. Another idea was to use chemical "candles," which released oxygen when burned, to replace the air consumed by the crew. The eventual solution lay in a mechanical generator that separated oxygen out of seawater by electrolysis.

SSN Revolution

The first nuclear submarine, the *Nautilus*, was begun by the U.S. Navy in 1952 and finished in 1955. Like all new weapon systems, it was a combination of old and new: it had the blunt bow, sharp-angled hull, and the twin-screws of the guppy boats, and the German Type XXIs before them. Roughly 325 feet (97.5m) long and twenty-seven feet (8.1m) wide, it was just a little larger than the postwar diesel boats. But the nuclear reactor gave *Nautilus* the power to steam underwater at unprecedented speeds.

Though not immune to sonar, it could always hear surface ships at a greater range than they could the submarine. And since the nuclear submarine (called an SSN) needed no surface contact with air, it completely negated radar detection. Because of speed and operating depth, charges or even fast-sinking projectiles were unlikely to hit a nuclear submarine. *Nautilus*, even more so than the fast diesel-boats, was essentially immune to conventional ASW methods. One American submarine commander wrote in 1960, "After six years of operating nuclear submarines, we still do not have at sea a weapon system able to cope with even one of them. . . . The [nuclear submarine] can destroy our cities or our ships."

On the other hand, although SSNs can travel continuously at high speeds, that very speed can put them in jeopardy. In 1955, when *Nautilus* underwent its initial sound tests, comparatively little was known about reducing drag and limiting hull and machinery noise. In fact, *Nautilus*'s sharp-angled outer hull, combined with various vent openings and the shape of the sail, produced very loud vibrations. This self-noise was very easy for other submarines to detect and also interfered with *Nautilus*'s own sonars. The same problems were revealed in the propeller design and the reactor water-pumps. It took a long time

before engineers and scientists could understand why these sounds occurred and could take steps to correct them. Such corrective designs were included in the construction, and tested in the operations, of similarly shaped submarines, like the two *Skate*-class boats in 1958.

Working with the revolutionary nature of these new concepts in noise reduction, speed, and control, the U.S. Navy designed and built the experimental submarine *Albacore*. Launched in 1953 and placed in service two years later, its tear-drop shaped hull and single screw illustrated that the short, fat hull was the best form for operations underwater.

At high speeds, the vessel behaved like a submerged aircraft and, after some modifications to the control surfaces, it proved faster and quieter than all previous designs. The next generation submarine, a deep-diving, ultraquiet boat, combined nuclear power with the *Albacore*-type hull. Commissioned in 1959, *Skipjack*, like the French *Narwal* from so long before, became the precursor of all the submarines to follow. Four more *Skipjacks* and thirteen of the quieter *Permits* followed in the early 1960s.

The Soviet Union's first nuclear submarine was the *November*-class boat. Under the direction of Captain Vladimir Nikolayevich Peregudov, it was completed in 1958. Although loud, like *Nautilus*, it was fast (approaching thirty knots) and had a deep diving depth of around one thousand feet (300m). The Soviets also built the nuclear-powered, guided- or cruise-missile *Echo*-class submarine (called an SSGN). Like the earlier *Whiskey* variants, the *Echo* had to surface to fire its six land-attack nuclear cruise missiles. It also suffered from extremely loud self-noise. A third type, the *Hotel*-class SSGN, was an enlarged *Whiskey* configuration with three ballistic missiles housed in the sail.

By the late 1960s, the world's major navies all had well-established nuclear submarine programs. The boats' designs had evolved to the large, smooth hull familiar today and the production lines introduced new boats at a phenomenal rate. The United States built yet another class of deep-diving quiet boats, led by *Sturgeon*, with thirty-seven eventually in service. The British, following American developments, commissioned *Dreadnought* and *Valiant* by 1964. Both were nuclear-powered attack submarines, and these large boats were built with the *Albacore* hull improvements in mind.

An official photograph of a Soviet submarine sometime in 1962. The hull and sail shape indicates it is probably a second-generation diesel-electric Foxtrot submarine.

With both a smaller force and less money, the Royal Navy built just three more nuclear-powered boats by 1970. The Soviet Union, however, invested heavily in submarine construction. Their five major shipyards pumped out fifteen *November* attack boats, eight *Hotels*, thirty-four *Echos*, and twelve *Charlie*-class cruise-missile submarines by the end of the decade.

BUILDING AND SUPPORTING NUCLEAR SUBMARINES

These new submarines demanded very advanced construction techniques. Usually built with a single hull (although many designs have two or more inner cylinders), the modern submarine is composed of a streamlined hull, with ballast tanks and other equipment at the ends, and the interior pressure hull forming the middle.

The submarine hull has to be extremely strong, to withstand both intense water pressure and the shock of exploding enemy ordnance. Such a hull requires high-grade steel that is clean of contaminants, cracks, and other faults. The steel is welded in circular sections, followed by intensive quality control and testing, to form a cylinder with a cap at both ends. Hull openings are kept to a minimum but a few remain for hatches, sensors, propulsion, and weapons. Ever since the pioneering tear-drop shape of *Albacore*, the hull has been carefully designed to reduce drag and allow high underwater speed. Starting with a bulbous bow, with the boat's maximum width shortly behind that, the shape then tapers to a point with roughly an eight-to-one length-to-beam ratio. The resulting smooth water flow, save for a few breaks like the sail or steering fins, is similar to that experienced by whales and porpoises.

Ever since the 1960s, the most important lesson learned by any submariner is "heard first, dead first." An almost obsessive desire for silent operations, born out of the fear of discovery, has since become mandatory in the design and construction of new submarines. These requirements include the obvious: changing fin-designs, modifying propellers, and smoothing the hull-shape. In addition, though, a strict schedule of maintenance, upgrades, and inspection is necessary to keep the boat quiet. New propulsion gear, careful machinery installation, and

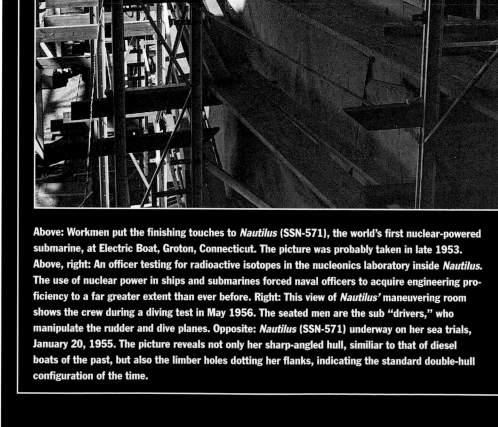

Above: Workmen put the finishing touches to *Nautilus* (SSN-571), the world's first nuclear-powered submarine, at Electric Boat, Groton, Connecticut. The picture was probably taken in late 1953. Above, right: An officer testing for radioactive isotopes in the nucleonics laboratory inside *Nautilus*. The use of nuclear power in ships and submarines forced naval officers to acquire engineering proficiency to a far greater extent than ever before. Right: This view of *Nautilus'* maneuvering room shows the crew during a diving test in May 1956. The seated men are the sub "drivers," who manipulate the rudder and dive planes. Opposite: *Nautilus* (SSN-571) underway on her sea trials, January 20, 1955. The picture reveals not only her sharp-angled hull, similiar to that of diesel boats of the past, but also the limber holes dotting her flanks, indicating the standard double-hull configuration of the time.

Above: Three views of *Nautilus* nuclear submarine construction techniques. On the left, heavy steel plates are rolled into a curved shape before being welded together to form the pressure hull. The middle shot shows a section of the wooden mock-up of *Nautilus,* used to figure out the best way to install various types of equipment. The photo on the right shows the hull receiving last-minute work before launching; presumably it has something to do with the steering planes. Opposite: The first of the ultra-quiet deep-diving attack boats, *Sturgeon* (SSN-637) is shown here during commissioning ceremonies at the New London Submarine Base in Groton, Connecticut, on March 4, 1967. Thirty years later, there are still a dozen of these fast submarines in service.

constant crew training are also prerequisites for silent operations.

Early SSNs were very loud because turbine gear vibration was transmitted directly to the hull. The accepted solution was to put all propulsion equipment on hydraulic jacks, a "machinery raft," that keeps noise levels down. Machinery and people are quieted through rubber padding under equipment, soundproof tiles covering the interior and exterior of the hull, and constant vigilance by the crew.

As might be surmised, such a warship is a very complex machine. And maintaining nuclear submarines takes a very large and skilled infrastructure. Eventually, as the Cold War navies adjusted to the nuclear era, they perfected a system of underway maintenance, naval base support, and dockyard modifications and repairs to support constant round-the-clock submarine patrols.

Onboard support is provided by trained engineers in the crew who carry out preventive maintenance and complete minor repairs while at sea. Base support comes from repair shops or, if afforded, mobile repair ships. Regular maintenance, crew training, and equipment upgrades are accomplished at naval bases.

Major overhauls, for equipment upgrades or when a reactor needs to be refueled, are performed in dockyards. This kind of care, not only for the nuclear plant, but every other system, illustrates the complexities and expense that have to be absorbed when building such boats. Because of these strict requirements, nuclear submarines are hugely expensive. Only a very few countries have the necessary industrial resources, the technical expertise, and the money to afford them.

LEVIATHAN

Nuclear submarines needed only one more addition to become the ultradeadly modern warships of today. Up to the late 1950s, only the torpedo attack submarines were true submarines, since they never surfaced while on patrol. The missile submarines, whether nuclear powered or not, all had to surface in order to fire their missiles.

The exposure was dangerous. And the threat could only be eliminated if a ballistic missile was launched from underwater. The U.S. Navy successfully experimented with a vertical missile launcher installed inside a submarine hull: this solution combined the stealth and surprise of underwater launching with the speed and endurance of a nuclear submarine.

Many technological problems still had to be solved, including solid-fuel ignition (liquid fuel

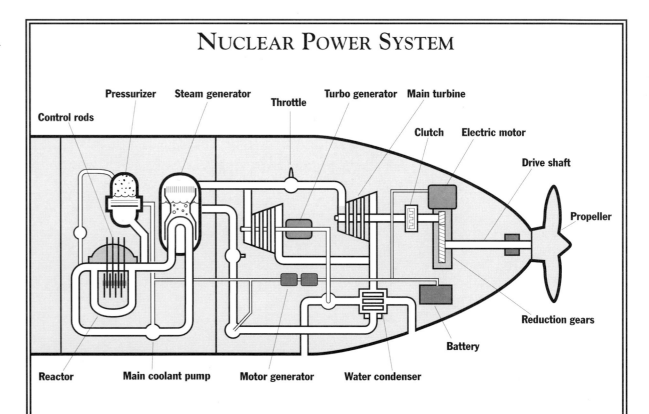

The component parts of a pressurized water reactor. Unlike the small diesel or electric engines found in SSKs, this is really an underwater steam engine driven by nuclear power. The fission reaction boils water into steam, which then drives turbines that generate power for electric motors and the propeller driveshaft. The high pressure and high temperatures provide enough power to drive much bigger submarines through the water at much higher speeds than either electric or diesel engines.

Above: A very famous photograph of the first firing of a Polaris missile from the submerged *George Washington* (SSBN-598) on July 20, 1960. In a demonstration of ingenuity and bureaucratic efficiency, Navy and civilian engineers had solved the problems of solid-fuel propellant, compact inertial guidance, tiny nuclear warheads, and submerged launch in a mere five years. Right: The *Sam Rayburn* (SSBN-635) at Newport News, Virginia, circa 1964-65. The sixteen Polaris missile tubes are exposed to view, with the hatch covers colored and numbered in billiard ball style. The missile tubes are fitted with internal "washers" that can be removed to widen the tube, thereby allowing missile upgrades in the future.

was too dangerous for a rocket engine inside a submarine), computer inertial guidance, the mechanics of a submerged launch, and miniaturizing a nuclear warhead to fit the small 1,500-mile (2,400km) range missile. But on July 20, 1960, the first Polaris missile was successfully launched from the SSBN *George Washington*. With the long box-like shape and the familiar hatches on top of the hull, the standard SSBN of the future had arrived. Over the next seven years, the U.S. Navy built forty-one of these submarines, each roughly 382 feet (114.6m) long, thirty-three feet (9.9m) wide, and carrying sixteen submarine-launched ballistic missiles (SLBM). Later models were built with extra-large tubes, to allow missile upgrades into the 1980s, and incorporated the newest in quieting technology.

The Soviet Union launched their own SSBN version in 1968. Called the *Leninist*, the boat was 426 feet (127.8m) long and also carried sixteen SLBMs. By 1974, they had built thirty-four of these "boomers." Unable to build adequate solid-fuel rockets for the SLBM, however, the Soviet designers

relied on the much more dangerous liquid-fuel rocket engine into the 1980s. The British, meanwhile, joined the SSBN club in 1967 with *Resolution*. Three more SSBNs, all carrying sixteen SLBMs, joined the Royal Navy by 1969. The French, not to be outdone, built four of their own *Redoutable* class by the mid-1970s.

Sailing on deterrent patrols, the huge submarine warships of today serve as weapons of last resort. Hiding deep in the oceans, they cannot be knocked out by surprise attack, and serve, by their mere existence, to prevent attacks against their countries.

The underwater launch of ballistic missiles from nuclear-propelled submarines signifies the last stage in the evolution of submarines. Capable of staying submerged for months at a time and carrying Armageddon within its vertical launch tubes, the once modest submersible has become the most lethal warship in existence. No longer the World War I weapon of a desperate, weaker power, the submarine has become an essential foundation of the superpower arsenal—it truly is Leviathan.

An impressive shot of the commissioning ceremony of *Ethan Allen* (SSBN-608) at Groton, Connecticut, on August 8, 1961. The wide angle gives a good impression of the 410-foot (123m) length and 33-foot (9.9m) beam of the submarine, larger than a World War II–era destroyer. The crew is standing on the hatch covers of the 1,500-mile (2,400km) range Polaris missiles.

Chapter 6

The Secret War

W E HAVE SEEN HOW SUBMARINE TECHNOLOGY EVOLVED, FROM DIESEL-
electric boats to nuclear-powered submarines. But technology does not drive why a weapon is
built or for what purpose it is used. It was the ideological conflict of the Cold War that built the
great fleets of nuclear submarines in the second half of the twentieth century. And it was the
Cold War that drove Soviet and NATO submarines to fight a secret but non-violent struggle deep in the
world's oceans. A tension-filled struggle of skill against skill, each side seeking an edge over its opponent
in case war did come. Information about this secret war is still mostly classified; what follows is a factual
timeline mixed with real events and several uncorroborated stories.

By the late 1940s, the U.S. Navy, with many overseas commitments, faced a growing threat from the
Soviet Union. With containment of communist expansion the guiding principle of U.S. foreign policy,
interest grew in supporting the democratic nations of Europe by sending naval forces for regular cruises in
the Mediterranean and the North Atlantic. The Americans helped create an anti-communist alliance in
Europe (NATO) and developed new roles and missions to meet their naval forces' new responsibilities.

The U.S. Navy trained with other western navies, especially the British Royal Navy, creating a multinational naval coalition in Europe. The United States and NATO also regularly deployed ships to the Far
East in response to the communist victory in China, and, later, the Korean War. These cruises illustrated
the West's commitment to protecting Western Europe, the Middle East, and the Far East from communist
encroachment, and also provided underway training in case another global war occurred.

The Soviet Union, on the other hand, anticipated a direct military conflict with the West. They
believed basic differences between communism and capitalism would provoke a war sooner rather than
later. Fear of American and British naval forces led the Soviets to begin a long-term shipbuilding plan.
Designed to prevent western amphibious and carrier operations in the Baltic, Arctic, the Black Sea, and
the Far East, the program was split equally between submarines and surface forces.

After World War II, Soviet naval yards were repaired and tremendous resources were funneled into
new naval construction. These naval forces were initially designed to guard the flanks of the Red Army, if
the order came to seize western Europe. Submarine and naval forces, including long-range aircraft, would
also sever the Atlantic sea lanes between Europe and North America. Operations against western naval

**A February 1960 nighttime photograph of *Sargo* (SSN-583) lying in the ice 25 feet (7.5m) from the North Pole. The subma-
rine had cruised under the pack ice for the previous 14 days, collecting oceanographic data and investigating operational
conditions in the cold waters of the Arctic ocean. The "bluenoses," a Navy nickname for sailors who travel above the Arctic
Circle, returned home to Pearl Harbor on March 3, 1960.**

forces, especially the carrier task groups, was given high priority. In the late 1940s, however, these plans were just taking shape and Soviet naval forces rarely sailed far from their coasts.

These two strategic visions, shaped by geography, diplomacy, and ideology, were very different. The West, led by the United States, sought to use global economic and military power to contain the expansion of communism. Mobilization of the resources of the Western Hemisphere, Europe, and the friendly nations of the Far East took place under the mantle of Western sea power. This long-term strategy, whose purpose was to prevent the collapse of democratic and liberal (and anti-revolutionary) governments in the face of communist ideology, was also designed to prevent a possible third world war.

The Soviet Union sought to use the resources of Eurasia and Eastern Europe to build a new communist society. Its leaders believed such a society, by its very existence, would eventually overwhelm western capitalism. But, assuming capitalist resistance, Soviet planners presumed an eventual war of annihilation with the West. Both of these strategic views were central to shaping the roles and missions of submarines during the cold war.

ROLES AND MISSIONS

Western submarine forces developed several different roles and missions during the first decades of the cold war. Although the great powers were technically at peace, most naval missions of the time were simply variations on well-known wartime missions, including intelligence gathering, covert or special operations, and tracking enemy submarines. Intelligence proved especially important in the early 1950s, because very little was known about the Eastern bloc or the Soviet Union.

NATO planners had little information about Soviet intentions or capabilities. As some intelligence analysts put it, the interior of the Soviet Union, a great big empty space on all the maps, might as well be labeled "Here be monsters." This ignorance became especially alarming in 1953, when the Soviet Union exploded several atomic bombs. Thereafter, a combination of spy aircraft flights, satellite missions (starting in 1959), signals intelligence, and submarine reconnaissance were used to uncover Soviet nuclear capabilities and assess the strength of their air, land, and naval forces.

For example, in order to effectively counter Soviet submarines if they tried to cut the Atlantic trade routes, NATO forces needed detailed intelligence on Soviet submarine technology, current operating procedures, and possible future developments. Like all intelligence, the best picture was developed through multiple sources. By 1954, photos from surface ships and signals intelligence indicated the Soviet submarine fleet was concentrated in the Baltic and the Arctic, was beginning to operate in the North Atlantic, and was conducting antishipping exercises with snorkel-equipped boats. In another case, a 1964 satellite photo revealed what was going on in the Severodvinsk shipyard, near Archangel in the Russian Far North. One of the largest Soviet shipyards, Severodvinsk had two buildings with a type of roof ventilator associated with industrial clean rooms. These are rooms kept free of dust and contaminants in order to manufacture stainless steel piping for nuclear reactors. This intelligence confirmed reports that the Soviet navy had embarked on a nuclear power program for submarine propulsion.

There still is, however, little better means of gathering intelligence than an "eye on the ground" or, in this case, an eye underwater. American and NATO submarines played a vital role in this sort of intelligence gathering, which was nothing new to submariners. They had played a significant part in intelligence operations during World War II. British submarines had landed commandos in occupied Europe, scouted out landing beaches, and watched enemy naval forces and bases. American submarines, in addition to waging a successful campaign against Japanese commerce, had shadowed enemy fleet movements, ferried special forces behind enemy lines, and photographed beaches and installations. They also conducted weather reporting, lifesaving, and mine laying missions.

Similar operations were conducted during the cold war. British and American diesel-electric submarines sailed in Arctic, North Atlantic, and Far Eastern waters to gather intelligence on Soviet intentions and capabilities. They photographed naval bases, shadowed the ever-growing surface fleet, and collected signals intelligence. They were able to closely monitor and gather crucial data on Soviet ICBM missile tests fired over the Pacific from the Kamchatka peninsula.

An undated photograph of three Soviet submarines firmly frozen in the ice of a northern port. Note the large bow-mounted sonar installations on the two *Foxtrot*-class submarines on the right, overshadowing the *Whiskey*-class boat on the left. An icebreaker lies in the background.

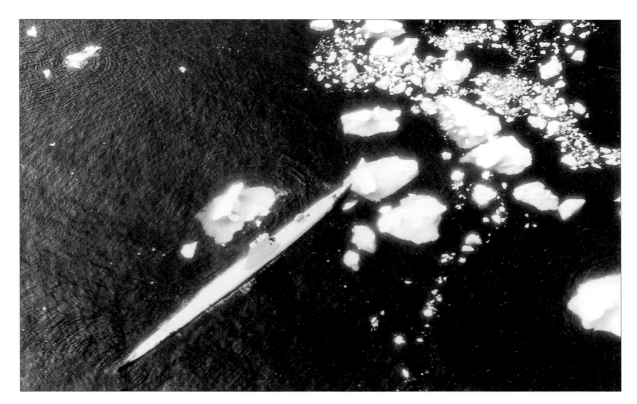

Halfbeak (SS-352), a wartime diesel-electric submarine, works her way through an Arctic ice field on August 19, 1958. The submarine, camouflaged with a coat of white paint, was conducting survey work and collecting hydrographic data in conjunction with the North Pole transit of *Skate* (SSN-578).

STRATEGIC POSITIONS DURING THE COLD WAR

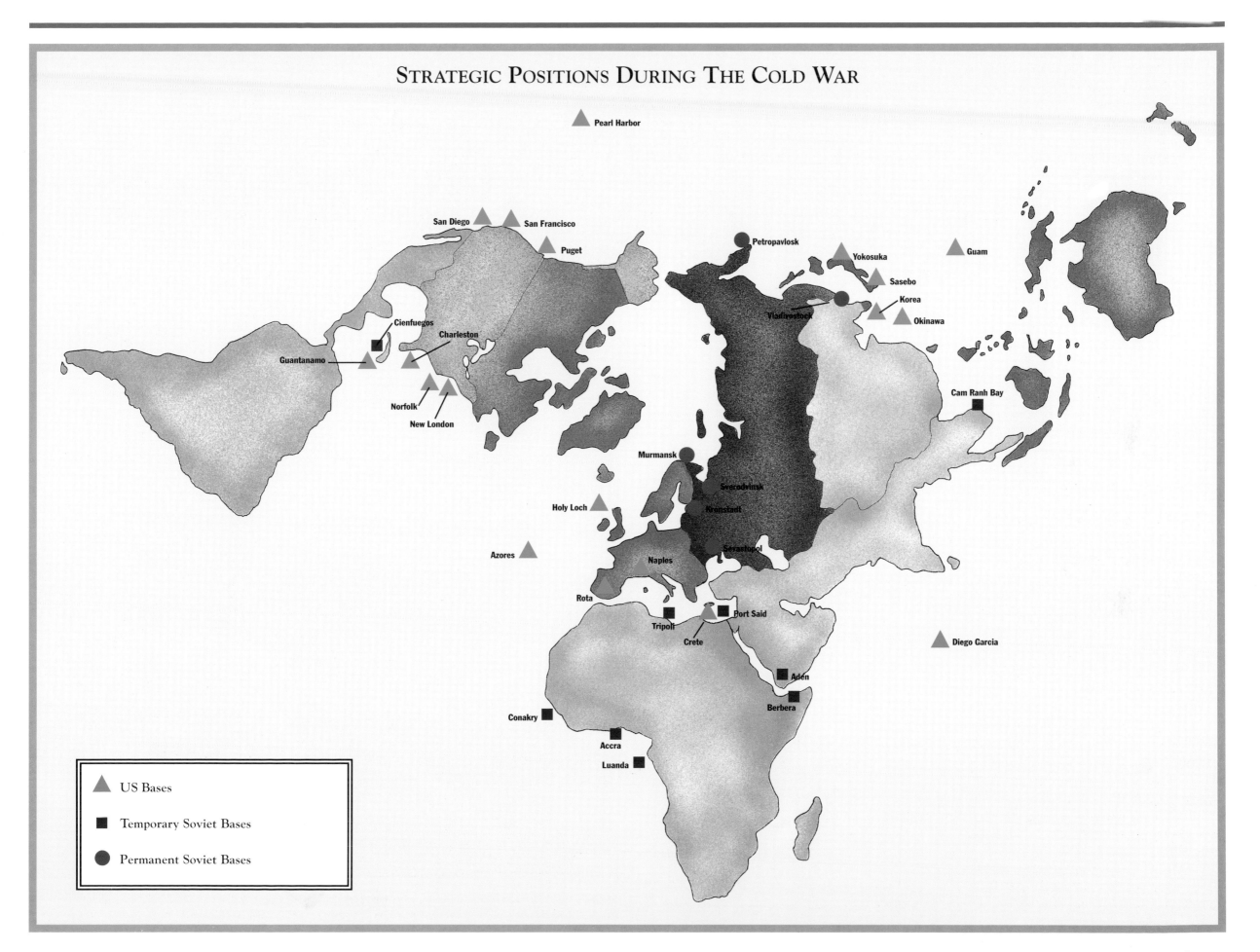

Pearl Harbor

San Diego · San Francisco · Puget

Petropavlosk · Yokosuka · Guam · Sasebo · Korea · Okinawa · Vladivostock

Cienfuegos · Charleston · Guantanamo · Norfolk · New London

Cam Ranh Bay

Murmansk · Severodvinsk · Kronstadt · Sevastopol

Holy Loch · Azores · Naples · Rota · Tripoli · Crete · Port Said · Aden · Berbera · Diego Garcia

Conakry · Accra · Luanda

US Bases

Temporary Soviet Bases

Permanent Soviet Bases

Joined later by SSNs, these missions widened to include the most critical mission of all—tracking Soviet attack and missile submarines. The missile boats tried to hide, keeping their deadly payloads safe until needed, and the elusive attack boats tried to protect their own SSBNs, while seeking out the enemy's boomers in a never-ending cat-and-mouse game beneath the ocean's surface.

Soviet submarines, not surprisingly, conducted the very same missions. They, too, gathered information on Western naval bases and surface forces, especially the NATO carrier battle groups, and collected other photographic and signals intelligence. The Soviets' job was made all the easier, since western naval forces regularly operated near the Soviet Union. As the Soviets became more experienced, they too sent submarines on long extended patrols, sending diesel submarines around Cape Horn to the Indian Ocean and through Arctic waters to patrol in Alaskan and Canadian waters. But, in contrast to NATO submarines, the Soviets spent the majority of their operations training for an attack on the North Atlantic supply line.

To this end, the Russian submarines focused on attacking surface ships with torpedoes, and in developing submarines (SSGs) to launch guided missiles against merchant ships and NATO task forces. By the late 1960s, when numerous SSBNs on both sides were in service, the Soviets, like the western powers, tried to defend their own missile boats with some attack boats, while ferreting out NATO boomers with others.

NATO SUBMARINE OPERATIONS

American and other NATO submarines during the late 1940s and 1950s concentrated on reconnaissance and intelligence gathering missions in the Arctic Ocean, North Atlantic, and Far East waters. The deepening cold war encouraged the American and British submarine forces to operate as if at war. In fact, the period is referred to by ex-submariners as "World War II Extended."

Active sonar was almost never used, stealth was emphasized, and submerged operations were preferred. Submarines ventured deep into Soviet waters to collect information, provide early warning in case of war, and, in the early postwar years, landed com-

Left: *Grayback* (SSG-574) and *Growler* (SSG-577), both cruise missile boats. Originally built as silent-running diesel attack submarines, the two boats had a 45-foot (15m) hull section inserted in front of the sail and the large Regulus missile hangars added forward. These bulbous hangars could hold four of the Regulus I missiles. Note that *Grayback*, built at Mare Island Naval Shipyard, had a noticeably larger sail. Top: The *Leninsky Komsomol*, a *November*-class nuclear submarine, lying in the ice near the North Pole in January 1963. The Russians had long operated on the edge of the pack ice and when the nuclear-powered boats came on line, the Russians expanded their range to conduct exercises deep under the Arctic ice. The Soviet Navy was especially concerned with preventing American submarines from launching missile attacks on Russia from under the ice. Above: Crewmembers of *Sea Dragon* (SSN-584) take a break during an Arctic cruise in September 1960. Note the many footprints in the snow. The lines on the periscope camera are range finding aids.

Thomas A. Edison (SSBN-610) **under the floodlights at General Dynamics Shipyard in Groton, Connecticut, on June 14, 1961. The small figures on top of the hull provide perspective and demonstrate the huge size of the Polaris missile submarine.**

mandos on the coast of the Soviet Union and some East European countries to gather intelligence on popular unrest. Reconaissance patrols in the Pacific investigated the Siberian coast, watched Soviet shipping, and, during the Korean War, conducted limited amphibious landing and raiding operations in North Korea. In 1952, for example, a team of four Russian emigrés was landed at Provideniya Bay in the Soviet Far East. There, they investigated a new airfield's runway to see if it was thick enough to bear the weight of a bomber large enough to carry an atom bomb. The team discovered that the runway was insufficiently thick, made it safely back to the waiting submarine, and reported the good news back to Washington. Operations like these helped the Pentagon with its never-ending contingency planning. By the end of the cold war, the number of such missions may have reached more than two thousand. They were not always successful.

In August 1957, the American diesel boat *Gudgeon* reportedly investigated the Russian naval base at Vladivostok. A sharp lookout spotted its periscope, however, and Soviet patrol craft closed on *Gudgeon's* position. Stuck underwater, and unable to snort, the U.S. boat faced the unenviable prospect of surfacing in the face of Russian guns when its batteries ran down. To make matters worse, the circling destroyers pinged it with sonar, holding it down for thirty-four hours, dropping practice depth charges all the while. The submarine was eventually forced to surface because of lack of oxygen, and to admit defeat before the Soviet destroyers let it go.

Other submarines, such as *Harder*, which crept into Severomorsk harbor to take pictures of ships and piers in 1961, were never detected. Later, as video cameras became available, submarines would glide under Soviet warships to take film of their hulls and propellers. U.S. submarines also investigated harbors in China, North Korea, North Vietnam, and Cuba. Cameras and recording equipment collected pictures and telemetry information on Soviet nuclear missile developments. Through these intelligence efforts, American submariners helped the United States stay on top of maritime technology and weapons development in these countries.

Submarines also conducted operations under the Arctic ice. Among the first warships to operate for any length of time in these waters, these boats were crucial investigators of peculiar Arctic weather and

hydrographic conditions. Submariners who weathered the icy conditions were nicknamed "bluenoses."

Submarines also assisted in global mapping efforts. Outfitted with research equipment, they helped map the sea floor and conducted acoustic experiments. The hazards of inadequate maps were illustrated in October 1967, when the nuclear submarine *Scamp* accidentally plowed into an underwater mountain off Guam. Luckily, only the hull buckled and the boat survived the heavy damage.

One of the most important missions for western submarines was the training of NATO antisubmarine forces. Many submarines sailed on overseas deployments specifically to operate with NATO hunterkiller task forces. Usually centered around a small aircraft carrier equipped with ASW planes and helicopters, these forces used the friendly submarines to practice their hunting operations. This exercise was particularly important, given the Soviet threat to shipping lanes. NATO had the advantage of fortuitous geography, since Soviet submarines had to pass through narrow land masses to reach the deep oceans. Defensive ASW exercises used these choke points—the Greenland-Iceland-UK gap, Gibraltar, and the Kurile Islands—to conduct barrier patrol exercises. In the event of war, air, sea, and submarine forces would attempt to intercept Soviet submarines in transit.

American submarines also tried to learn about Soviet ASW efforts by creeping into the Sea of Okhost and investigating nearby naval bases. In 1963, *Swordfish* was reportedly spotted by a Soviet patrol boat while on such a mission. For two days the American submarine endured random depth-charging as it maneuvered off the Kamchatka Peninsula. But, aided by American reconnaissance planes, *Swordfish* used the opportunity to collect intelligence on Soviet radars, communications antennas, and ASW efforts.

Although submarine technology and operations had advanced enough that the mistakes that plagued the first submarines no longer occurred, wear and tear on equipment and crews still caused losses. In August 1949, after a photographic mission in the Barents Sea, the American diesel submarine *Cochino* ran into severe weather off Norway. Eighty-foot (24m) waves damaged the snorkel, and flooding sparked a battery explosion and fire. Aided by another guppy boat, the *Tusk*, the two crews vainly battled the fire and flooding for fourteen hours.

returning home after a regular patrol in the Mediterranean. Underwater listening gear in the Atlantic registered a series of implosions. *Scorpion*, with ninety-nine on board, was never heard from again. An investigation of the wreckage, found southwest of the Azores, blamed the accident on an internal explosion—possibly a torpedo that ran "hot" in a tube or exploded while undergoing standard maintenance.

Yet another kind of accident, a collision with another ship, could be just as disastrous. In the total darkness of the oceans, submarines must navigate by sonar. Since they do not want to give their positions away by pinging with active sonar, the boats rely on passive listening and careful navigation. When another submarine is nearby, however, such navigation becomes quite hazardous. In June 1970, a Soviet missile boat on its way home from an overseas deployment was being shadowed by the American submarine *Tautog*. By hiding in the "dead zone" behind the Russian submarine's propellers, *Tautog* could follow the "boomer" without being detected.

The followed submarine has only a few solutions to this problem: it can pass by a friendly submarine, which can check out the "tail" in a maneuver called "delousing." Another is to swing from side to side, essentially "glancing back." A third solution, called a

The heavy seas finally overcame the crew and *Cochino* sank on August 26, taking seven men to the bottom. Accidental losses were not just an American phenomenon. The British snorkel submarine *Truculent* was rammed and sunk on January 12, 1950, by the Swedish tanker *Divina*. Only five crewmen were rescued. A similar accident three years later sank the Turkish submarine *Dumlupinar* in the Dardanelles, killing ninety-five. And a snorkel failure

doomed the Royal Navy's *Affray*, lost with all hands on April 16, 1961.

Nuclear technology, though kept under a strict regimen of safety inspections, also caused its share of accidents. According to unconfirmed reports, a valve on the *Thomas A. Edison* did not close when it submerged in December 1979. More than twenty thousand gallons (76,000L) of water flooded the SSBN and only careful damage control prevented the loss of

the boat. A more tragic accident, however, occurred on April 10, 1963, while *Thresher*, an ultra-quiet American SSN, was undergoing deep-diving exercises off Nantucket. About fifteen minutes after reaching test depth, the catastrophic failure of a pipe joint in the engineering spaces caused uncontrollable flooding and the boat was lost with all 129 people on board.

Another, very different, type of accident claimed the Skipjack-class boat *Scorpion* in 1968, while it was "crazy Ivan," from the tendency of Russian commanders to try this maneuver, is to conduct a quick U-turn. In *Tautog's* case, the Soviet submarine suddenly turned on the American and closed fast. The two collided, with the Russian boat's propellers slicing through *Tautog's* sail like butter, but causing no more serious damage. The crash heavily damaged the Soviet boat, however, probably opening up the engine room, and the boat flooded rapidly. Soon afterwards, stunned American sonar operators heard the ghastly sounds—like popcorn—of a submarine being crushed by the ocean depths. Much controversy still surrounds this incident.

SOVIET SUBMARINE OPERATIONS

In the late 1950s technological improvements in aircraft ranges and weapons capability, however the Soviet navy to operate farther away from their territory. Strategically, if the Red Fleet was to stop a NATO attack, then the Soviet surface fleet had to venture into the Atlantic, the Mediterranean, and the Indian Oceans.

After the Soviet surface fleet expanded its horizons in the early 1960s, their submarines soon followed. Emphasizing combined arms tactics, meaning close cooperation between air, surface, and submarine forces, Soviet submarines trained for attacks on NATO surface ships and submarines in the open oceans. Although some Soviet diesel-electric boats, such as the *Foxtrots*, had enough range to remain useful, the new nuclear-powered boats, like the *Novembers*, became the workhorses of such a global strategy. These boats were assisted by the nuclear-powered *Echo*-class cruise-missile submarines, and these, in turn, were supported by the diesel *Juliett* cruise missile boats, whose charter was to destroy American carrier task forces.

Early Soviet patrols were conducted only as far as the North Atlantic. But this range was far enough to bring the Soviet submarines into the NATO Iceland barrier patrol area, giving the Soviets practice against western ASW forces. Sometimes, the communists got the worst of it, as in 1958, when a diesel boat was pinned by a U.S. destroyer escort, and was forced to surface when its air ran out.

Expertise in long-range patrols improved with time, however, and five diesel boats were sent to the

The sail of a *Hotel* SSBN surfaced and disabled about 600 miles (960km) northeast of Newfoundland on February 29, 1972. Note the three missile hatches abaft the conning station and masts. The picture was taken from a U.S. Navy search plane.

West Atlantic-Caribbean area during the October 1962, Cuban missile crisis. Though both the Americans and Soviets learned about each other's operations, all five communist submarines were located, harassed, and forced to surface for identification by American ASW forces. During this period, other early Soviet nuclear boats sailed under the Arctic ice, and still others cruised to the Middle East, the Pacific, and even around the world.

One dramatic episode, known as the "Enterprise incident," occurred in January 1969. A *November* was discovered to be trailing the aircraft carrier *Enterprise* off California. Deciding to test the speed of the Soviet boat, *Enterprise* accelerated to thirty knots and waited for the submarine to fall behind. To the shock and dismay of the Americans, the *November* kept pace. This speed was particularly alarming, because intelligence analysts knew that second-generation

Soviet attack boats, such as the *Victors*, were just coming on line. They would certainly be as fast as the *November*, and probably a lot more quiet.

What the Americans did not know, however, was that Soviet nuclear submarines operated with minimal safety precautions and frequently suffered from mechanical troubles. The *November* could travel at such speeds because it had extremely limited (by western standards) radiation shielding. In 1961, for

A photograph of the doomed *Scorpion* (SSN-{tk}) underway in Long Island Sound in June 1960. Standing on the diving plane are Vice Admiral Hyman G. Rickover (left), the man most responsible for shaping the submarine force, and Commander James F. Calvert. The submarine would be lost at sea in May 1968.

example, a *Hotel* SSBN suffered a cooling pipe failure that contaminated large parts of the ship and much of the crew with radiation. Later, when this information was revealed, jokes abounded about how Black Sea Fleet sailors, stuck with the older and less safe submarines, glowed in the dark.

Equipment failures, such as that on *Thresher*, also killed Soviet submarines. The most spectacular loss, or gain from the U.S. Navy's perspective, was the fire and explosion of a *Golf*-class SSGN in 1968. The Soviet submarine, heading for a patrol zone off Hawaii, suddenly exploded and sank on the night of March 8. All ninety-seven crewmen were killed. American underwater hydrophones triangulated the location and a submarine was secretly dispatched. Six months later, the *Halibut* found the Soviet boat lying in twenty thousand feet (6,000m) of water.

Using special cables equipped with claws, cameras, and strobe lights, *Halibut's* crew recovered three cruise missiles with nuclear warheads. Even more important, in a coup reminiscent of Allied salvage efforts of U-boats during World War II, a cryptographic machine and missile-submarine codebooks were recovered. Not only did this allow a priceless look into Soviet missile technology, but it enabled cipher analysts to follow Soviet missile boat deployments for the next six years.

Another dramatic loss occurred on April 7, 1989, in the Norwegian Sea. The *Komsomolets*, a very large attack submarine with a titanium hull, suffered a break in a high-pressure air line while cruising at 1,250 feet (375m) below the surface. A fire broke out in the engineering room, spread out of control, and shut down the submarine's nuclear reactors.

Without power, the submarine surfaced and carbon monoxide gas forced the crew to abandon ship. Then, *Komsomolets* took on water and sank. Six men were trapped inside. Five climbed inside an escape capsule, but it jammed in the hatch. The men watched helplessly as the depth gauge went down past three hundred, five hundred, one thousand feet. At 1,300 feet (390m), they were off the scale, waiting helplessly for the explosive decompression that would crush them in an instant. Suddenly, an explosion rocked the doomed submarine and the capsule burst free, flying to the surface. The hatch popped off, but because of rough seas, only one man escaped before

the capsule slid down to the ocean floor, five thousand feet (1,500m) below. Help did not arrive until six hours later and much of the crew froze to death in the icy water. Of the sixty-nine crew members, forty-two died by fire, smoke inhalation, or drowning.

Similar accidents destroyed a *November* off the coast of Spain in April 1970, a *Charlie*-class SSGN off Kamchatka in 1983, and a *Yankee*-class SSBN in the western Atlantic during 1986. Many other examples of fires and radiation leaks have come to light, as well as the radiation poisoning of many Soviet submarine crewmen. Lack of skilled technicians, poor construction techniques, and inadequate crew training led to increased breakdowns and radiation accidents. In February 1989, the Soviet Union transferred a *Charlie*-class SSGN to India. But the radiation shielding and the construction of the power plant were so bad that it became derisively known as a "Chernobyl class" submarine.

THE NEXT GENERATION

By the 1970s and 1980s, both the Anglo-American navies and the Soviets had quiet, long-range ballistic missile submarines in service. These boats, unique in the world of naval operations, were designed to accomplish the single goal of nuclear deterrence. Unaffected by the storms of weather or politics, they seemingly ignored the Cuban missile crisis in late 1962, the entire Vietnam conflict, and the Arab-Israeli Wars. They simply waited for an order they hoped would never come.

A significant change over these decades, however, was the vast increase in range of ballistic missiles. The Soviets, aware that NATO ASW barriers, such as fixed hydrophones, patrol planes, and geographic choke points, blocked many of their transit routes into the open ocean, modified the *Yankee* hull to create a new class of boomer called the *Delta*. Equipped with twelve much larger vertical launch tubes, the *Delta's* new missile increased the range of Soviet SLBMs to 4,200 miles (6,720km). This range allowed the Soviets to set up "bastions" in the Barents Sea and the Sea of Okhost, where SSBNs were herded together in safe areas patrolled by friendly sea, air, and submarine forces. Thirty-eight of these long range SSBNs were built by 1982.

To succeed in this mission, the Soviets needed to redesign their attack submarines. Up to the late 1960s, these submarines had concentrated on the high speed needed to chase and sink American carrier task forces or western ballistic missile submarines. Now, like the Americans and British, the emphasis lay on deep-diving and silent operations. The first submarine to fit these requirements was the *Victor*.

The smooth tear-drop hull, low streamlined fin, and single propeller marked the *Victor* as an antisubmarine platform, though it took some time for western intelligence analysts to recognize this change. Covered with rubberized sound-absorbing (anechoic) tiles and equipped with a large low-frequency bow sonar, the *Victor* was designed to hunt enemy submarines if any attempted to enter the Arctic bastions. Twenty-three *Victors* were completed by 1978.

An improved version, with a towed sonar array and quieter machinery, was built in the 1980s and it approached the silence levels of the U.S. *Sturgeon* class. Twenty-three of these boats, which have the capabilities to conduct long-range sub-hunting missions, were built by 1987.

In an attempt to leap-frog American supremacy in nuclear power, the Soviets also experimented with a liquid-metal (lead-bismuth) cooled reactor. Although tried, and discarded, by the U.S. Navy in the 1950s, this reactor allowed much higher speeds with a smaller reactor. The resulting submarine, the *Alfa*, also employed a small-diameter titanium hull. This fast, very deep-diving submarine, better suited as an interceptor, was a step away from the bastion concept, but it did force NATO navies to develop fast, deep-diving ASW torpedoes. Only seven *Alfas*, including the prototype, were built.

The Soviet capabilities, including high speed and deep diving, plus the new emphasis on silent operations worried American planners. Higher Soviet performance abilities indicated the cutting-edge technology of the *Sturgeon* boats was crumbling rapidly. Meanwhile, current and future improvements in sensors, especially submarine passive sonars, dipping sonars on hovering helicopters, and the towed array—a series of microphones hung on a cable that could be strung out behind a submarine or a surface ship—meant it was all too easy to detect noisy submarines.

Left: A dramatic but undated view of a submarine hull-cylinder section at General Dynamics Shipyard in Groton, Connecticut.

The new American design, this time emphasizing high speed (to keep up with American carriers) and quietness (to combat the *Victors*), was the *Los Angeles* class. At 360 feet (108m) long and thirty-two feet (9.6m) wide, this new attack boat was larger than the SSBN *George Washington*. Improved sensors, a vertical launch system, and increased armament (up to fifty weapons) gave the *Los Angeles* boats the capability to conduct a wide range of new missions.

American missions included nuclear strikes, land attack, and antishipping strikes. And, like all American attack submarines, the boats remained suited for reconnaissance and sub-hunting missions. By 1991, more than fifty-eight had been ordered and forty-seven boats were in service. New British sub-marines, the three *Churchill*-, six *Swiftsure*-, and especially the seven *Trafalgar*-class boats, all incorporated new quieting technology, including rubber sound ane-choic coatings and special quiet propellers. The latter two classes also carry vertical-launch antiship missiles.

These new submarines can easily carry out sea-control and sea-denial operations. With their speed and armament, they can escort friendly ships into enemy waters, sinking enemy warships that get in the way. Or, the new boats can simply prevent an enemy from using the sea by blockading his ports. They can also provide underneath protection for friendly ships. Other tasks include beach reconnaissance before an invasion, landing special forces, and secretly and safely mining enemy harbors.

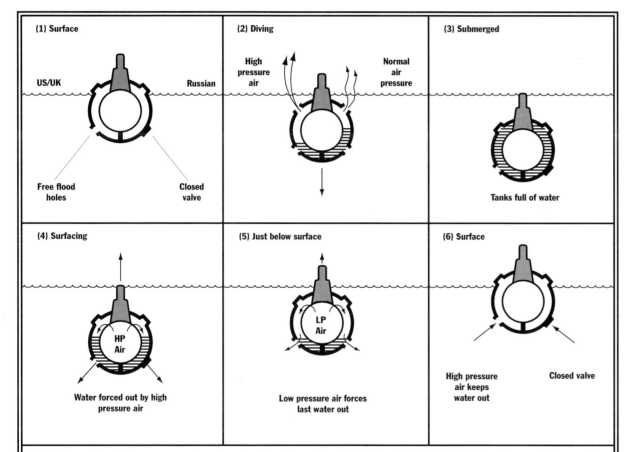

(1) Surface

US/UK — Russian

Free flood holes — Closed valve

(2) Diving

High pressure air — Normal air pressure

(3) Submerged

Tanks full of water

(4) Surfacing

HP Air

Water forced out by high pressure air

(5) Just below surface

LP Air

Low pressure air forces last water out

(6) Surface

High pressure air keeps water out — Closed valve

The diving and surfacing sequence for submarines has changed very little since the double-hull system became widespread in the early twentieth century. Just as the diesel-electric boats of the two world wars contained an inner pressure hull within a streamlined outer hull, so too do the modern submarines of the postwar world. The difference lies in the shape of the outer hull—the former were designed for surface speed while the latter evolved for underwater speed. The modern diving and sur-facing sequence is slightly different for American and British submarines versus Russian submarines. (1) On the surface with main vents shut, U.S./U.K. submarines use high air pressure to keep water out of the free flood holes, while Russian sub-marines use a valve system. (2) While diving, the high pressure air in U.S./U.K. boats roars out, with water creeping in after. Russian submarines rely on the higher density of water flowing through the valve to push air out the main vents. (3) When submerged, the main ballast tanks are full of water. (4) When surfacing, high pressure air is used to force water out of the main ballast tanks. (5) When on the surface in low buoyancy, low pressure air is used to force the last of the water out of the main ballast tanks. (6) On the surface, the ballast tanks are empty.

Above: A photograph of *Wyoming* (SSBN-742), probably taken just before her commissioning ceremony on July 13, 1996, at Groton. The white tent on the stern covers access to the nuclear propulsion plant on the 560-foot (186m) submarine. Note the other subma-rine on the surface in the background.

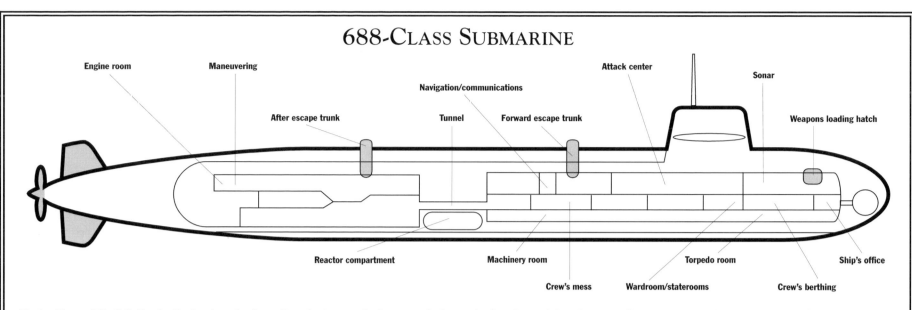

688-CLASS SUBMARINE

Engine room   Maneuvering   Navigation/communications   Attack center   Sonar

After escape trunk   Tunnel   Forward escape trunk   Weapons loading hatch

Reactor compartment   Machinery room   Torpedo room   Ship's office

Crew's mess   Wardroom/staterooms   Crew's berthing

The backbone of the U.S. Navy's attack submarine force, these boats are poised to carry the brunt of submarine work into the twenty first-century. Upgrades and design modifications have turned these boats into multipurpose platforms, capable of surveillance and intelligence-gathering missions as well as short-and-long range torpedo and missile strike missions.

A prime example of these missions was provided by the Falklands War in 1982. After Argentina invaded the Falkland Islands on April 2, the Royal Navy quickly deployed three attack submarines to the area. With their high sustained underwater speed—above twenty-eight knots—the three SSNs arrived in the battle zone later that month—long before a British surface task force could arrive from Portsmouth, England. The SSNs established a nautical exclusion zone in order to prevent Argentine reinforcements from reaching the islands.

Of particular British concern was the Argentine surface force of a heavy cruiser, the *General Belgrano*, and several destroyers. One of the British SSNs, *Conqueror*, spotted these ships on May 2, 1982. Ordered via satellite communication with London to eliminate the threat, *Conqueror* fired two Mk 8 torpedoes (a World War II design) from about two thousand yards (1,800m). One torpedo struck the

A Soviet *Tango*-class SSK slicing through the crystal blue waters of the Mayaguana Passage near the Bahamas. The diesel-electric boat was on its way to Havana, there to help celebrate the anniversary of the Cuban revolution. Visits like these, along with military and economic aid, were part of the Soviet Union's efforts to bolster their communist ally just 90 miles (144km) off the coast of Florida.

Designed to replace the original forty-one boomers, *Ohio*-class submarines are 560-feet (168m) in length, and come equipped with twenty-four 4,300-mile (6,880km) range Trident ballistic missiles. Since 1976, upgrades have increased the range. Twelve boats were in service by 1991; they have become the mainstay of the American nuclear deterrent arsenal. These submarines are so quiet that they emanate even less noise than the surrounding ocean, leading to the prideful American claim that an *Ohio*-class boat has never been tracked by a Russian submarine.

THE END OF THE COLD WAR

These new, ever-improving submarines continued the Cold War pattern of constant patrols, fencing with their counterparts. But following the failure of the August coup in 1991, the Soviet Union was officially dissolved on December 9. Much of the ideological conflict of the Cold War vanished along with the communist government. In theory, the transformation of Russia into a partial democracy, the loss of its Eastern European satellites, and the almost world-wide failure of communism ended the fifty years of tension between the West and Russia. But national security is a mission that never ends. And despite massive cutbacks, both the United States and Russia continue extensive submarine operations.

Argentine cruiser on the port bow and another hit the stern, destroying the ship's power and communications systems. It sank in little more than twenty minutes, drowning 368 of one thousand or so crew members. These two torpedoes persuaded the entire Argentine navy to spend the rest of the war in port.

Yet perhaps the primary mission for modern SSNs is to find and track enemy ballistic missile submarines. By the late 1960s, both NATO and the Soviets had SSBNs on deterrent patrols, sometimes just off the other's coast, and tracking these boats was given the highest priority. Supported by surveillance aircraft, surface escorts, and underwater hydrophones, U.S. attack submarines hunted down and followed the Soviet SSBNs—always keeping an eye on them in case of war. The *Lapon*, a new *Sturgeon* boat, actually trailed one of the first *Yankee* SSBNs for forty days while it cruised the Atlantic in 1969. And in 1973, during the Arab-Israeli war, ten U.S. attack boats kept track of twenty-three Soviet missile and attack submarines in the eastern Mediterranean.

Above: The Argentine cruiser *General Belgrano* listing heavily after being struck by two British torpedoes fired from the nuclear submarine *Conquerer*. Note the shattered bow forward and the many lifeboats in the water. The picture also reveals the cruiser's 8-inch (20cm) guns, the powerful armament that proved the warship's undoing. Fear of these guns attacking Royal Navy supply ships led to the decision to sink the cruiser on May 2. Right: A close-up shot of the conning tower of the *San Luis,* a German-built Argentine diesel submarine that saw action in the Falklands in 1982.

Soviet attack boats, meanwhile, found it difficult to track American or British SSBNs. Since the Russian boats were so noisy, the American SSBNs could easily fulfill their motto of "Hide with pride" by changing course. The Soviets, having a less extensive hydrophone system than NATO, tried to assist their submarines by deploying sonar-equipped trawlers. These helped to an extent, but the NATO missile boats were usually too quiet for detection by a Soviet submarine or trawler. In 1976, the NATO submarines were made even more silent with the introduction of the new *Ohio*-class SSBN program.

Ohio (SSBN-726) floats in her graving dock at Groton, Connecticut, on April 6, 1979, the day before her christening ceremony. The submarine hull in the background is the *Georgia* (SSBN-727), the second Trident submarine under construction.

Chapter 7

The World Outside the Cold War

THE COLD WAR, VIEWED AS A PREEMINENT STRUGGLE BETWEEN TWO LARGE and powerful alliance systems, diverted attention from the disagreements and conflicts of smaller countries. When the spotlight of world attention was on the global superpower confrontation, the desires, needs, and military capabilities of minor countries got lost in the shuffle. In some ways, small nations were like mice, sneaking an advantage when the coast was clear, trying to avoid the clumsy feet of the elephantine superpowers. This view does not mean that smaller nations' security concerns and violent disagreements are less dramatic than superpower conflict, only that the scale is smaller. The same is true for the many small navies, and their submarine forces, during the late twentieth century.

In the 1950s, when both Russia and the United States invested heavily in nuclear weapons and nuclear propulsion, the smaller navies of the world eyed those technological advances with worry. Clearly, only a few nations had the financial and industrial strength to build nuclear submarines, let alone atomic weapons. Through perseverance and sacrifice, Britain and France had joined this nuclear submarine club in the 1960s. The rest of the world, because of political restrictions, cost, or lack of skill, could only watch.

The SSNs and SSBNs, with their speed, quietness, and firepower, made the old diesel-electric boats seem quaint, even archaic. The great British, American, and Soviet fleets of wartime diesel submarines were decommissioned and most of the submarines scrapped. Old and slow, at least compared to nuclear boats, they could not keep pace with technological changes in weapons, sensors, and propulsion.

Given the dire threat posed to their security by the Soviet Union, many small nations leased these diesel submarines, which were certainly better than nothing. As demonstrated by Holland and Norway in the 1930s, a submarine, even an old one, provided good deterrent value. Some countries, with modern shipyards and a skilled labor force, could build their own diesel submarines. Sweden and Holland, with Soviet submarines lurking off their coasts, built modern (sixteen to seventeen knots underwater) diesel boats in the 1950s. They were joined by West Germany, which resumed U-boat construction in 1956.

With strategic positions on the shallow waters of the Baltic and the North Sea, these countries built small coastal boats similar to the German wartime Type XXIII. Building on advances since World War II, these submarines incorporated new sonars, snorkel technology, and quiet electric motors. Since many of these navies were small and short on manpower, widespread use of automation and hydraulic controls

The setting sun sharply outlines a "boomer" cruising on the surface. This picture was most likely taken just outside a naval base, as the secretive missile boats generally submerged once in deep waters, and remained undersea on deterrent patrols for up to six months at a time. Note the huge bow wave caused by the massive hull churning through the water.

Canadian Submarines

Faced with few external threats, Canada long maintained only a small coast guard, relying on the British Royal Navy for the strategic defense of her interests. A small naval force, including two coastal submarines bought by the province of British Columbia in 1914, was built up during World War I, but, owing to financial shortages, was reduced to a few destroyers by 1922. It was only during the German submarine campaign of 1939-45 that the Royal Canadian Navy (RCN) expanded into a permanent naval force, specializing in operating anti-submarine warfare frigates and escort vessels. ASW training and escort services were provided by the many French, Dutch, and British submarines that visited and operated out of the Canadian bases of Esquimalt and Halifax.

During the early years of the Cold War, training was provided by the British or the Americans, so no submarines were maintained in the Canadian naval inventory. In 1965-67, given the potential threat from the Soviet Navy, and Canada's role in protecting NATO's supply line from North America to Europe, The Royal Canadian Navy established a submarine squadron. Three *Oberon*-class boats purchased in England trained ASW frigates and conducted operations to support NATO forces in the Atlantic and Arctic oceans. In addition, the U.S. Navy lent Canada an old diesel boat, built in 1943, which served as an ASW training ship off British Columbia.

In the mid-1980s, Canada considered purchasing nuclear submarines as an answer to the problem of defending her long Arctic coastline from incursions by Soviet SSNs. A nuclear submarine could patrol under the ever-present ice-pack for long periods of time and would have the speed and mobility to reach any threatened region. The cost, however, was prohibitively high. To fulfill its current defense needs, the Canadian government is considering building four of the British *Upholder*-class boats or possibly four of the *Collins*-class boats to replace the older *Oberons*.

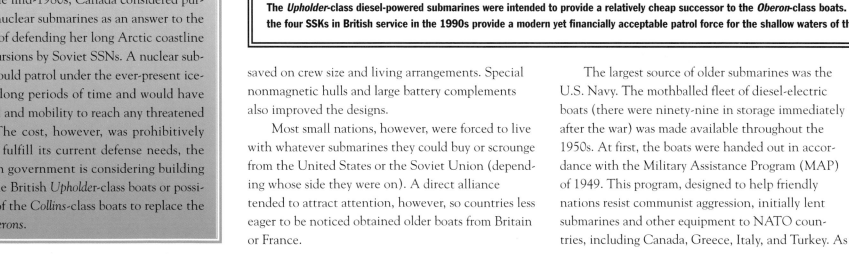

TYPE 2400 UPHOLDER-CLASS

The *Upholder*-class diesel-powered submarines were intended to provide a relatively cheap successor to the *Oberon*-class boats. Armed with 18 Spearfish torpedoes and/or Harpoon missiles, the four SSKs in British service in the 1990s provide a modern yet financially acceptable patrol force for the shallow waters of the North Sea and other coastal areas.

saved on crew size and living arrangements. Special nonmagnetic hulls and large battery complements also improved the designs.

Most small nations, however, were forced to live with whatever submarines they could buy or scrounge from the United States or the Soviet Union (depending whose side they were on). A direct alliance tended to attract attention, however, so countries less eager to be noticed obtained older boats from Britain or France.

The largest source of older submarines was the U.S. Navy. The mothballed fleet of diesel-electric boats (there were ninety-nine in storage immediately after the war) was made available throughout the 1950s. At first, the boats were handed out in accordance with the Military Assistance Program (MAP) of 1949. This program, designed to help friendly nations resist communist aggression, initially lent submarines and other equipment to NATO countries, including Canada, Greece, Italy, and Turkey. As

time went on and these countries obtained newer submarines, the program was extended to other allies.

Part of a long-term foreign aid policy to prevent communist expansion in the western hemisphere, the wartime boats were also given to Brazil, Chile, and Venezuela. These navies, many of which needed training and logistical support, slowly gained the skills needed to operate diesel-boat squadrons on their own. By the late 1960s, when the Asian economy began its expansion, South Korea and Taiwan obtained some wartime *Balao*-class boats as "hand-me-downs." Hopelessly out of date, these submarines were useful for training surface ASW forces. Spain and Israel also obtained American diesel boats.

The Soviet Union followed a similar policy for older submarines. Many of the World War II-era boats were handed out to Bulgaria, China, Egypt, Indonesia, Poland, and Rumania. As they fell out of Soviet service, forty of the *Whiskey*-class diesel submarines were exported. Another twenty-one were built at shipyards in communist China between 1956 and 1962. Yugoslavia, with shipyard facilities at Pola in Istria, built a few diesel boats, but these were obsolete even in the 1950s.

DIESEL-BOAT RENAISSANCE

In the mid-1960s, the wartime diesel boats owned by many NATO navies, particularly Norway and Greece, were out of date. They needed to be replaced by boats that were quiet enough to deal with Soviet

The *Hai Lung* (meaning "Sea Dragon") on the surface during February 1996 military exercises off Hualien, Taiwan. The Dutch-built modified *Zwaardis*-class SSK is framed in front of an unidentified destroyer, or frigate. Political pressure from mainland China has prevented Taiwan from purchasing more than a few modern submarines from European suppliers.

intrusions into their coastal waters. Since nuclear propulsion was out of the question—that superpower technology being both highly complex and very secret—the wartime submarines were replaced by new diesel boats equipped with sonar gear advanced enough to hunt Soviet SSNs. The United States helped finance the diesel-boat construction in European shipyards, and by the end of the decade fifteen boats had been delivered to Norway from West German firms alone.

In the 1970s, submarines were also built for Greece, Turkey, Argentina, Peru, Ecuador, and Venezuela. These first programs were the beginning of an export-oriented strategy, conducted by Italy, Sweden, and the Netherlands as well, that marks the diesel-electric submarine market to this day.

The British and the French, meanwhile, used their substantial maritime industries to support diesel submarine construction. These deep-diving boats were very quiet, particularly the British *Oberon* class, and they were exported to nations where friendly economic interests were well entrenched. The British

sold submarines to Canada, Australia, Brazil, and Chile; the French sold their postwar *Daphne* class to Pakistan, South Africa, Portugal, and Spain. Japan, allowed to build up a self-defense force in the face of growing Soviet strength in the Pacific, began its own diesel submarine construction program around the same time.

Over the next two decades, more developing nations saw the advantages of small diesel submarines. With new wire-guided torpedoes and up to eight torpedo tubes, the diesel boats packed a decisive armament punch. And, because of quick snorkel recharging and modern batteries, their underwater endurance had grown from hours to days. Cheap to build or purchase—about equal in cost to a frigate—and easy to operate, they were the perfect investment for a country without much money or manpower. These submarines were especially useful because, like submarines in both world wars, modern diesel boats deter enemy action by their mere presence. By hiding in secret places where it would be embarrassing to be caught on the surface, the boats can provide excellent warning alarms and introduce uncertainty into the naval plans of an enemy. These features gave the diesel-electric submarine (now called an SSK) an influence much greater than its cost.

South Africa, for example, bought a small squadron of the French *Daphne* submarines in the late 1960s because it was unsure of the intentions of India. Unwilling to match the Indians, who were building up an expensive surface navy at the time, South Africa's purchase sent a pointed message that it would accept no interference off its coast. It was a cheap deterrent.

A more active example of diesel-boat diplomacy occurred during the Arab-Israeli War in 1973. The Egyptian navy used a combination of cruise-missile boats and diesel submarines to declare the Red Sea, the Suez Canal, and the Israeli coast a war zone. Any merchant ships using these areas to enter Israeli ports would be sunk. The threat was taken seriously and few ships entered these waters. The United States used transport planes to supply Israel with ammunition and other urgently needed supplies.

Two other examples illustrate that submarines can, if modern or handled well, have an influence far greater than their size and cost, or, conversely, if the boats are obsolete or their enemies are willing to take risks, that they can be neutralized. During the

With a large coastline, limited manpower, and a relatively small defense budget, Australian defense planners found in the submarine a cheap deterrent. The Royal Australian Navy (RAN) acquired two diesel boats from Great Britain during the First World War. Although both were lost, one in an accident in the Bismarck Sea in 1914, and the second by a Turkish torpedo-boat in the Sea of Marmora in 1915, the RAN replaced these with six J-class boats received as a gift from Great Britain in 1919.

Tight finances led to the retirement of these boats in 1922. Under pressure from Britain to "pay her fair share" to defend the Empire, Australia built two new submarines, the *Oxley* and *Otway*, in 1926-27. In 1931, financial difficulties forced the Australians to hand over the submarines to the Royal Navy. After the Japanese declared war on Australia in 1941, the RAN took over an obsolete Dutch submarine in order to help the antisubmarine school in Sydney train ASDIC operators. The submarine was disposed of in late 1944.

For the next twenty years, the RAN relied on British and United States submarines to train antisubmarine forces. But between 1963 and 1971, as the Royal Navy reduced the number of conventional submarines in Far Eastern waters, the RAN purchased six *Oberon*-class boats from Britain as replacements. These continued the training of friendly surface ASW forces, participated in multinational naval exercises, and patrolled Australian waters.

In the 1980s, seeking more strategic reach, the RAN started a new generation of submarines to replace the aging *Oberon*-class boats. Equipped with 23 Harpoon SSM or Mk 48 torpedoes, able to patrol into the Pacific and Indian oceans, and incorporating modern quieting technology, these boats are designed to match any vessels they might encounter in their operational area. Built at Port Adelaide by a consortium of Australian, U.S., Dutch, and Swedish firms, the first of six *Collins*-class boats entered service in 1995.

Two *Ohio*-class SSBNs under construction at General Dynamic's Electric Boat Division in Groton, Connecticut. The overhead view gives a marvelous indication of the sheer size of the submarines, the intensity of detail, and the complexity involved in building one of these boats. It is no wonder that very few nations have the technical expertise and financial wealth to afford such expensive weapons systems.

Falklands War in 1982, only two Argentine submarines made significant patrols. One, a former American guppy, was caught on the surface by British ship-based helicopters. Heavily damaged by missiles and depth charges, the *Santa Fe* could not submerge and beached herself on a nearby island. The other, however, was a German-built submarine called the *San Luis*. Completed in 1974, it had the long endurance and silent-operation capability of a modern diesel submarine.

For thirty-six days the *San Luis* plagued the British Task Force, constantly worrying the Royal Navy's commanders in a deadly game of hide and seek. Though unable to damage any British ships because of fire-control and torpedo malfunctions, it did avoid all British ASW efforts. The unsuccessful hunt for the *San Luis* forced the British to expend ASW ordnance (torpedoes and depth charges) and sonobuoys (air-dropped detection devices) at extremely high rates.

Not all upgraded diesel-boat missions have been successful: for example, during the India-Pakistan conflict over Bangladesh in 1971, the much larger Indian Navy was able to blockade both Pakistani coasts, conduct carrier-based air strikes, and launch cruise missile attacks with little interference. Although the Pakistani submarine *Hangor*, a French *Daphne*-class boat built in 1970, torpedoed and sank the Indian frigate *Khukri* on December 9, 1971, the much weaker Pakistani navy was unable to deny sea control to India.

Despite such mixed success, however, SSKs were well established in the world's navies by the 1980s. While demand fluctuated, as old submarines retired and new countries entered the market (such as Indonesia and Thailand), the manufacture of diesel submarines remained constant. With the end of the Cold War, and the rapid expansion of small navies around the world, this trend will continue.

This expansion is especially likely because in many ways, at least in shallow waters, the modern diesel submarine has closed the technology gap with the nuclear submarine. To understand why, it is necessary to look at the dramatic changes that have taken place in the technology of electronics, computers, and weapons in the late twentieth century.

THE TECHNOLOGY REVOLUTION

Somewhat like the nuclear missile age before it, the digital revolution of the last twenty-five years has dramatically changed the capabilities of sensors, fire-control systems, and weapons. These improvements—including computers able to process information much faster than the old analog systems, and advances in power and efficiency via the microchip—produced significant changes in how submarines accomplished their missions.

Most of these advances are interrelated, with improvements in sensors calling forth new weapons, which, in turn, create a need for countermeasures or less propulsion noise. These technological developments can be broken down into five areas: sensors, electronic warfare, communications, weapons, and propulsion.

Since before World War II, active and passive sonars have been installed on submarines, enabling boats to hear enemy surface ships or submarines. All the active devices, including radar, were fitted in the bow, periscopes, or sometimes in the sail of submarines. Passive hydrophones were usually placed on the bow and flank, since propeller noise inhibited rear-facing receivers. Since self-noise interfered with all these receivers, one solution was the towed array.

Developed in the late 1950s, towed arrays are very long cables strung out behind the submarine. Dotted with hydrophones, they can listen for submerged submarines without interference from propeller noise. An additional advantage of a towed array is that it can listen for enemy submarines at different depths without the host submarine moving up or down. New arrays take advantage of computer processors to include torpedo warning sensors and decoy devices.

Other sensors, such as heading-, temperature-, and depth-finders, help solve the fire control problems. Short-range echo sounders help with navigation by detecting the sea floor when the submarine is close to the bottom, or surface ice when it is in Arctic waters. The big difference in modern sonars, however, is not in the device itself (hardware being much the same), but the computer software programs that interpret data. The better the algorithm, the better the sonar. And a software program can fit into any submarine, including a diesel.

Submarine electronic support measures (ESM) have also proved significant in helping diesel boats to

Columbia (SSN-771), which went into commission on October 9, 1995, is the sixtieth Los Angeles-class attack submarine built for the U.S. Navy. Technological upgrades and engineering improvements have changed virtually every piece of equipment since the first 688-class boats entered service twenty years earlier.

close the gap with nuclear submarines. They help the submarine with four critical tasks. The first is warning, specifically of patrol or surface forces using radar, through the use of radar detection devices. The second is target identification and tracking, which uses radar and communications signals to provide a fix on enemy warships. The third is passive targeting, by which enemy signals provide information necessary to fire long-range missiles or torpedoes at a target's general location. And the fourth is electronic intelligence, which collects data on enemy equipment by listening to it function.

Computers allow all this information to be collected via antenna or receiver, processed for combat, and recorded for later analysis. With miniaturization, this equipment can be installed on the smallest of submarines.

Communicating with and directing submarines from outside remains problematic. Submarine patrols need to be directed from a central command so they don't interfere with friendly forces and can find enemy forces. It is especially important to keep tabs on submarines actively cruising through a battle zone, so that no friendly-fire incidents occur. Two-way, high-frequency radio communications, though easy and convenient for directing submarines, proved deadly for the U-boats during World War II. In response, submariners have developed various communication systems: simple noise patterns to alert sea-floor listening devices; very high-speed burst transmissions to satellites; and slow low-frequency transmissions to listening stations. All these are difficult to intercept. Diesel boats, equipped with the same capabilities, can therefore have the same strategic "picture" as SSNs, making the diesels equally dangerous opponents.

Weapons have changed in both type and capability since World War II. There are now five main types: torpedoes, mines, cruise missiles, solid-fuel missiles, and SLBMs. The old familiar deck gun has disappeared, made obsolete by long-range patrol craft.

The tried and true torpedo remains—still the most versatile of submarine weapons. Starting with the World War II acoustic homing type, the torpedo has seen dramatic improvements in range, power, and

Left: The huge water displacement wave is plainly visible in this side view of *Rhode Island* (SSBN-740).

The World Outside the Cold War ⚓ 133

Laid down in 1989, launched in 1995, and in service in May 1996, *Seawolf* (SSN-21) is the U.S. Navy's next-generation attack-submarine. With improvements in speed, quietness, and weapons load over the *Los Angeles*-class, the *Seawolf* and two sister boats are meant to carry the submarine force into the next century. The small wedge at the base of the sail, a feature found on the Russian *Akula,* is meant to improve hydrodynamic flow, while a smaller length-beam ratio provides better maneuverability than the *Los Angeles* boats. The broom is the traditional symbol hoisted aloft when returning from a successful mission.

"intelligence" over the years. Current wire-guided torpedoes can be controlled from the firing submarine by miles of cable strung out behind the torpedo, providing direction and speed, and bypassing enemy decoys. Electric power for the early postwar torpedoes was adequate, but at the long ranges needed now, out to twenty miles (32km) or more, exotic fuels and special turbines are standard.

Submarine mines, now fired out of the torpedo tubes, can travel many miles before automatically deploying. The newest weapons are based on rocket technology. One is the familiar sea-launched ballistic missile (SLBM). These are not found in diesel submarines. The great equalizers, however, are the ASW and anti-ship rocket and the cruise missile, both of which can fit into small vertical launch tubes. The

ASW rocket fires underwater, bursts into the air, accelerates toward a programmed target (found through ESM or communications intelligence) and drops a homing torpedo in the water. The anti-ship missile, like the U.S Navy's Harpoon, works on the same principle.

The air-breathing cruise missile, on the other hand, has a much longer range, bigger payloads, and

can be controlled and directed in flight. The Tomahawks launched at Iraq during the Gulf War were sea-skimming cruise missiles. All these weapons have smart "brains" and can home-in on targets using radar, infra-red, television pictures, and other electronic "noise." Missiles are the favorites of diesel boats, because they can be fired at enemy targets from longer, and safer, distances.

Yet perhaps the greatest improvements in diesel boats are the tremendous advances made in propulsion technology. High-capacity batteries, with quick diesel recharges, make snorkeling less of a requirement—ultraquiet battery engines can propel boats underwater at twenty knots for short bursts. Long-term underwater endurance, meanwhile, has been increased from hours to several days. By snorkeling very infrequently, and with careful attention paid to radar receivers, diesel submarines can theoretically survive in areas even heavily patrolled by enemy aircraft. New propeller designs, with large, slow blades, or pump-jets, also make noisy water bubbles (called cavitation) less likely.

In the late 1970s, however, a dramatic improvement in ASW sensors, which limit snorkeling time, revived the push to develop air-independent propulsion (AIP) systems.

The idea, to eliminate the need to snorkel, has been around since Walter experimented with it in 1943-1945. The problem has always been how to get rid of harmful exhaust while retaining enough oxygen to run the diesel engines. The solution is to trap and expel the impurities in a filter leading to the sea, while the unburnt oxygen is recirculated. Enriched with small amounts of fresh oxygen, the cycle begins again. This system, and a similar fuel cell process, gives SSKs the air-independent capabilities of nuclear-powered submarines without the size, cost, or complexity.

OUT OF SIGHT, OUT OF MIND

All these improvements have made the SSK, as one analyst put it, the new "silent menace." During the cold war, diesel submarines played second-fiddle in the dramatic struggle between NATO and Soviet nuclear submarines. Most of the boats were old, as was the sonar technology inside, and the crews were

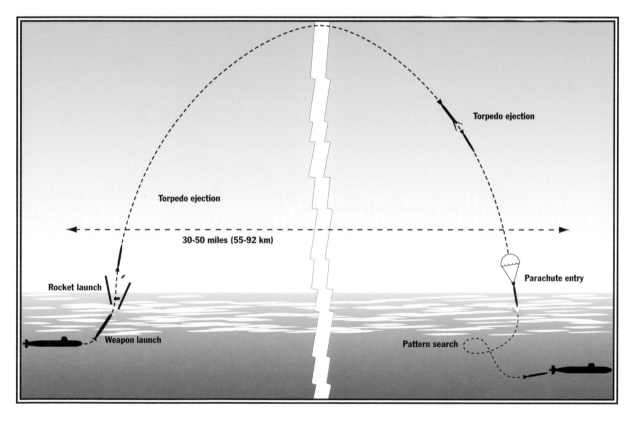

Torpedo ejection

Torpedo ejection

30-50 miles (55-92 km)

Rocket launch

Weapon launch

Parachute entry

Pattern search

This diagram illustrates the attack profile of an antisubmarine rocket. Launched from a submarine torpedo tube, a solid-fuel rocket lifts an antisubmarine homing torpedo out of the water. Provided with targeting information from the submarine's sonar or, ideally, from a closer platform, the rocket arcs over to the enemy's location and softly drops the torpedo in the water via a parachute. The torpedo sinks to a prescribed depth, turns on its homing sonar, and attacks any target detected during the search. The Soviet version of the weapon, the SS-N-16, has a range of 30 to 50 miles (55–92km). At the height of the Cold War the rocket was also fitted with a nuclear warhead for "area" strikes. Because of the dangers of a friendly-fire incident and the longer ranges of modern torpedoes, most Western navies no longer carry this weapons system.

The Submarine and Science

In addition to its obvious military implications, the submarine has many peacetime uses. One of the first such uses was experimental deep-diving. Unlike military submarines, which have a purpose other than diving, civilian submersibles were designed specifically to help oceanographers explore the ocean floor. Deep-diving bathyscaphes, like Auguste Piccard's *Trieste*, built in 1948, did no more than sink to the ocean floor before returning to the surface. In 1959, a second version of the *Trieste* departed for the Marianas Trench off Guam to descend to the deepest point on earth, some 36,000 feet (1,100 m) below sea level. On January 23, 1960, four hours and 43 minutes after leaving the surface, the submersible touched the muddy bottom. Once there, the crew saw strange phosphorescent fishes living in the abysmal deep.

Soon thereafter, other submersibles were built for research use. These vessels incorporated new devices to enable the submersibles to actually explore the ocean's depths. Equipped with scanning sonars, prehensile arms, collection baskets, and closed-circuit TV, these submersibles maneuver independently using small electric motors. Called Deep Submergence Vehicles (DSVs), they allow scientists to, among other things, explore wrecks, investigate deep sea life, and recover equipment—including a hydrogen bomb lost by the U.S. Air Force off the coast of Spain in 1966. Other submersibles were built by the oil industry to carry divers for pipeline observation or between underwater wellheads and drilling structures.

In the 1970s, when advanced computer technology became available, a new type of submersible was constructed. Known as Remotely Operated Vehicles (ROVs), these unmanned submersibles were loaded with lights and cameras, and could investigate where it was too costly—or too dangerous—for humans to venture. By 1983, there were over 500 of these unmanned robot vehicles in use around the world. Improvements in side-scanning sonars, imaging technology, motors, and computer software meant that a tiny robotic submersible could descend inside the wreck of the *Titanic* in 1986 and take pictures of a glittering chandelier. Today, scientific submersibles continue the tradition of underwater exploration—mapping the oceans' depths and examining the many new species of marine life to be found beneath the seas.

Submarine *NR-1* is a compact, deep diving, nuclear-powered, electric-drive undersea research and ocean engineering submarine. Placed in service in 1969, the submarine mainly conducts topographic, environmental, and geologic surveys of the oceans. It can also search for and identify objects lost at sea as well as place or repair objects on the ocean floor. Supported by submarine repair ship *Sunbird* (ASR-15), *NR-1* conducts missions for both the Navy and other government-supported researchers. Highlights of Submarine *NR-1*'s service include the 1976 retrieval of a Phoenix missile from an F-14 Tomcat lost at sea and the 1986 Space Shuttle *Challenger* search and salvage mission.

Two interior and an exterior view of *New York City* (SSN-696), a *Los Angeles*-class attack submarine put into service in 1979. Above: The helm and dive stations. Right: Three combat stations. Notice the many covers over some of the screens and instrument panels—a secret is still a secret in the submarine force. In a manner typical of all naval ships, the equipment shows a curious mix of modern and "ancient." The computer screens are contemporary but the standard government carpet, speckled linoleum, metal frames, duct work, copper piping, canvas fireproof wiring, and ubiquitous green "hospital" paint would seem familiar to most old Navy veterans. Far right: The *New York City* moored at an unidentified pier, probably somewhere on the Pacific coast.

not as well trained as the Americans or the British. An important submariner axiom states: "a submarine is only as quiet as the noisiest item on board." What that means is that all the quieting technology in the world—rubber pads, electric motors, sound absorbing tiles, machinery rafts—accomplishes nothing if a tool box falls out of place or a bolt comes loose. Crew training, and good maintenance, has a lot to do with keeping a boat quiet.

But in the 1990s, especially with advanced SSKs being exported by manufacturers in such disparate countries as Australia, Germany, China, Holland, Spain, and Russia, there is a growing emphasis on signature reduction. Small navies, like the major navies before them, are working to eliminate "leaks" that enable detection by prowling ASW forces. Like a mouse hiding from a cat, a modern diesel boat tries to close down the five ASW "senses": to prevent patrol planes from "smelling" diesel fumes, snorkeling time is strictly limited; radiant noise is avoided by machinery rafts and crew training; infra-red detection is prevented by moving deep and slow, thus eliminating thermal scars; radar reflections are limited by restricted use of periscopes and masts; and magnetism, the most difficult signature to reduce, is controlled by damping the magnetic field through electrical currents.

Particularly adept diesel boats include the Australian *Collins* class. Carrying twenty-three Sub-Harpoons or torpedoes, these Australian submarines are supposedly the quietest SSKs in the world. The Swedish Navy has three of the *Gotland*-class boats with an AIP installation, marking another new trend in diesel boats. Both illustrate the future of fast, powerful, and cost-effective diesel submarines.

Another diesel design is the larger Russian *Kilo*-class boat. First launched in 1980 to help defend Soviet SSBNs in the Arctic, the *Kilo* is an example of a simple but effective design. With a weapons load of eighteen torpedoes or twenty-four mines, adequate sensors, and a surface-to-air missile launcher for taking out ASW helicopters, the submarine has good combat capability. The *Kilo* has a diving depth of nine hundred feet (270m), an underwater speed of seventeen knots, and an endurance of forty-two days. Cheap and easy to maintain, and with a crew of fifty-two, it is a perfect submarine for navies without much money, such as India, Algeria, and Iran.

These SSKs are not only quieter, but deadlier as well. Fitted with vertical launch tubes, a large diesel boat can launch sea-skimming antiship and even land-attack missiles. This potential was demonstrated during the Gulf War by the U.S. *Los Angeles*-class SSNs, which fired Tomahawk cruise missiles at Iraq from submerged positions in the Red Sea. The ultra-quiet electric motors of an SSK also make it a perfect platform for shallow water operations such as photo reconnaissance and inserting special forces.

But perhaps the most important, and dangerous, mission for modern SSKs is blocking the principal maritime choke points of the world. An SSK, sitting quietly on the ocean floor off a shipping channel or a busy port, is a threat no navy can ignore. Most of the world's commodities and oil pass through narrow seas that channel merchant ships into shallow and easily blocked waters. The most important choke points are the Straits of Hormuz and the Red Sea in the Middle East, Gibraltar and the English Channel in Europe,

and the Straits of Malacca and the Tsushima Strait in Asia. Not surprisingly, twelve European nations own SSKs suitable for coastal work. Egypt, Israel, Iran, India, and Pakistan all have the capability to shut down Suez Canal or Persian Gulf traffic. And India, Indonesia, Thailand, China, Taiwan, Japan, and both Koreas can all reach strategic shipping lanes off Asia.

ASW REACTIONS

The threat posed by modern SSKs is substantial, even to sophisticated surface navies like the U.S. Navy. As stated by one American submarine commander in the early 1990s, "Everybody is jumping on the 'be quiet or you are dead' bandwagon." Some Third World nations can barely get a submarine to sea, and are easy to track, but others have become much more adept. And a well trained crew and good maintenance can make even an old submarine very dangerous. American SSNs train regularly with NATO diesel boats for precisely that reason.

Nuclear-powered submarines, meanwhile, have incorporated all the new weapons, sensors, and computer systems that are used in the SSKs. Because SSNs are larger, with more space for upgrades, nuclear submarines actually have a significant advantage over SSKs in adding new equipment and diverse weapons loads.

But just as submarine electronics, sonars, propulsion systems, and weapons have improved dramatically over the last two decades, so too have ASW forces. Maritime patrol aircraft (MPA), long used for searching the open oceans for nuclear submarines, now deal with the crowded coastal waters of the world.

New computers, with the capacity to handle sixty-four sonobuoys at one time, and new radar and magnetic sensors, have maintained the MPA's usefulness. With a range in the hundreds of miles, and a loitering time measured in half-days, these aircraft are several generations ahead of the Second World

War Liberators. They are, however, very expensive and limited to wealthy nations. The improving capability of SSKs in remaining submerged, the ever-present SSN threat, and the increasing range of sub-launched missiles have forced all navies to develop other ASW efforts.

The solution to long-range threats is to carry ASW aircraft onboard surface ships. And that means helicopters. By the mid-1990s, there were more than one thousand helicopters serving in more than forty navies. Depending on size and endurance, the helicopters can use sonobuoys, dipping sonars, radar, electronic sensors, and magnetic anomaly detectors (MAD) to find submarines. Then they can drop depth charges or homing torpedoes on a target. Fast, with a good range and the ability to land on small warships, helicopters provide excellent, and cheap, ASW coverage.

Formerly, because of weight restrictions, helicopters were little more than "delivery boys" that dropped a weapon where the parent ship directed it. Miniaturization of electronics and new software, better fuel efficiency (providing an endurance of four to five hours), and bigger payloads mean a helicopter is now a fully developed submarine hunter/killer. Going a step further than helicopters, unmanned drones, capable of dropping sonobuoys or weapons, are also coming into use.

Surface ships have also greatly improved their ASW capability. Vastly more sensitive sonars, both hull-mounted and towed arrays, have made hearing submarines easier. Rocket-launched homing torpedoes and ASW helicopters round out their defenses. Other solutions include expendable listening systems, similar to the old SOSUS network, that drift with the currents.

ROLES AND MISSIONS FOR THE TWENTY-FIRST CENTURY

Despite such increases in the capabilities of ASW forces, the submarine, whether nuclear, diesel, or otherwise, will always be too useful to be ignored. During the 1980s, for example, the United States, Britain, and the Soviet Union all launched new or at least upgraded nuclear submarines. While the two NATO navies upgraded their SSNs through internal modifications such as cruise missile launchers, the Soviet Union launched four new nuclear submarine designs.

Typhoon slowly moves on the surface in July 1995 near Murmansk on the Kola Peninsula. The tugboats are probably guiding the huge submarine into a berth. Note the heavy reinforced base around the sail. Because of the Soviet "bastion" strategy, which called for missile submarines to lurk near northern bases in range of friendly forces, the *Typhoon* needed the support to burst through the thick Arctic ice if it was to launch missiles during a nuclear war.

The *Oscar*, replacing the noisy *Echo*-class SSGNs, is designed to launch twenty-four very long range cruise missiles.

The massive *Typhoon*, the largest submarine ever built, carries twenty SLBMs and up to thirty-six torpedoes and antiship missiles. It is designed to operate under the Arctic ice and, when required to launch, punch a hole in thin ice areas. The *Sierra* and the

Left: Russian Navy sailors remove a 1.5 megaton RSM-40 nuclear ballistic missile from the submarine *Murena* at Severomorsk, Russia. It is almost certainly a *Delta*-class SSBN being prepared for scrapping (called "recycling") as part of the post–Cold War draw down. The photo, taken August 16, 1995, makes a fine contrast to that of the sailors lining the deck of *Nevada* (SSBN-733) on December 7, 1991, during ceremonies at Pearl Harbor. Although both superpowers have been scrapping old nuclear submarines as fast as money and technical skill allows, plenty of nuclear submarines remain in service.

Akula, both SSN attack boats, are perhaps the most alarming from the standpoint of Britain and the United States. Along with improved *Victor*-class submarines, these two SSN designs have incorporated all the quieting features introduced in western boats during the 1960s. Changes in turbines, pumps, and gears have made them almost silent in operation. Starting in the mid-1980s, sonar operators reported that it took much longer to find and target Soviet submarines. This difficulty led to the occasional embarrassing accident in which a hunting submarine, unsure where the target had gone, bumped into it. The world, it seemed, was poised on the edge of another great naval arms race.

But the end of the Cold War changed everything. As the communist threat crumbled, the great fleets of nuclear submarines were called into question. In a flurry of declining threats and budgets, many of the older submarines were recycled. The U.S. has been able to safely and efficiently scrap many of its older nuclear submarines. The Russians, owing to political and economic troubles, have been unable to clean up their nuclear mess. The region around Murmansk, the Kola Peninsula, is filled with dozens of inactive old submarines, many leaking radiation and other waste into the Barents Sea. Nuclear storage sites bulge with spent fuel and old reactor cores. The Vladisvostock naval bases are in no better shape.

Like the SSKs, the attack submarines have adjusted from a world in which global war was a real possibility to a world plagued by unpredictable, regional crises. Littoral warfare, as operation close to an enemy shore is called, promises to be the battlefield of the future. While this emphasis obviously makes SSKs more useful weapons, the nuclear submarines have made the shift as well. Most SSNs, and particularly the American submarines, have the speed, stealth, staying power, and independence to conduct operations anywhere in the world on a moment's notice.

Most recently, SSNs have guarded carrier battle groups engaged in U.N. operations, fired Tomahawk cruise missiles, and kept an eye on friend and foe alike. This power makes the submarine equal to, or greater than, most surface ships. It is this ability, to find and kill anything in the oceans, that allows submariners to declare, "There are only two types of warships: submarines and targets."

Suggested Readings

Blair, Clay. *Silent Victory: The U.S. Submarine War Against Japan*. New York: J.B. Lippincott Co.: 1975.

Calvert, James F. *Silent Running: My Years on a World War II Attack Submarine*. New York: John Wiley & Sons, 1995.

Clancy, Tom. *Submarine: A Guided Tour Inside a Nuclear Warship*. New York: Berkely Books, 1993.

Cocker, M.P. *Royal Navy Submarines, 1901-1982*. London: Frederick Warne, 1982.

Crane, Jonathan. *Submarine*. London: BBC, 1984.

Halpern, Paul. *A Naval History of World War One*. Annapolis: Naval Institute Press, 1994.

Hervey, John. *Submarines*. London: Brassey's, 1994.

Hezlet, Arthur. *The Submarine and Seapower*. London: Peter Davies, 1967.

Howarth, Stephen and Law, Derek. *The Battle of the Atlantic 1939-1945: The 50th Anniversary International Naval Conference*. Annapolis, MD: Naval Institute Press, 1994.

Marriott, John. *Submarine: The Capital Ship of Today*. London, Ian Allan Ltd., 1986

Polmar, Norman and Noot, Jurrien. *Submarines of the Russian and Soviet Navies, 1718-1990*. Annapolis: Naval Institute Press, 1990.

Price, Alfred. *Aircraft versus Submarine: The Evolution of the Anti-Submarine Aircraft 1912 to 1972*. London: Kimber, 1973.

Roskill, Stephen W. *The War At Sea, 1939-45*, 3 vols. in 4. London: HMSO, 1954-61.

Rossler, Eberhard. *The U-boat: The evolution and technical history of German submarines*. Annapolis: Naval Institute Press, 1981.

Syrett, David. *The Defeat of the German U-Boats: The Battle of the Atlantic*. Columbia, SC: University of South Carolina Press, 1994.

Terzibaschitsch, Stefan. *Submarines of the U.S. Navy*. London: Arms and Armour Press, 1991.

Photo Credits

AFP/CORBIS-BETTMANN: PP. 129, 138, 139 TOP

CORBIS-BETTMANN: PP. 16 ALL, 17 BOTTOM, 20 LEFT, 25 RIGHT, 27 BACKGROUND, 28 LEFT, 32-33, 35 BOTTOM, 36 RIGHT, 37 BOTTOM, 40-41, 42 TOP, 44, 47 BOTH, 78 LEFT, 104 LEFT, 104 TOP RIGHT, 106 RIGHT

© FRANK DeSISTO: PP. 101 RIGHT (BOTH), 136-137 ALL

ELECTRIC BOAT CORPORATION: BACK ENDPAPER; PP. 1, 6-7, 10-11, 120, 122 RIGHT, 126-127, 130, 131, 132-133, 134

FPG INTERNATIONAL: P. 38 INSET

BOB KEENE, MAP ILLUSTRATIONS: PP. 35 TOP, 113

© TOM W. FREEMAN, COURTESY OF SM&S NAVAL PRINTS, INC., FOREST HILL, MD: P. 70

NATIONAL ARCHIVES: PP. 18-19, 52 TOP, 66 BOTH, 71, 74, 76 BOTTOM, 78 TOP & BOTTOM RIGHT, 79, 80 LEFT, 80-81, 83 TOP, 86 BOTH, 87 ALL, 88 TOP & BOTTOM LEFT, 91 BOTTOM, 94 RIGHT, 96 BOTTOM, 97 TOP, 105

REUTERS/CORBIS-BETTMANN: P. 139 BOTTOM

COURTESY, BEVERLEY R. ROBINSON COLLECTION, UNITED STATES NAVAL ACADEMY MUSEUM: PP. 39 TOP RIGHT, 60 TOP LEFT, 68

© KEVIN ULLRICH: PP. 3, 84 BOTH, 85

UNDERWOOD & UNDERWOOD/CORBIS-BETTMANN: FRONT ENDPAPER; PP. 4-5, 12-13, 19, 54 ALL, 54-55, 56, 57 RIGHT, 58-59, 61 TOP LEFT & BOTTOM, 106 TOP LEFT & CENTER, 117 LEFT

UPI/CORBIS-BETTMANN: PP. 1 TOP LEFT, 37 TOP, 38, 42 BOTTOM, 45 BOTH, 48-49, 50, 53 RIGHT, 83 BOTTOM, 88 RIGHT, 94 LEFT, 96 TOP, 102 LEFT, 103, 104 BOTTOM RIGHT, 107, 109, 110-111, 115 TOP, 116, 117 RIGHT, 119, 123 BOTTOM, 124 BOTH, 125, 135

U.S. AIR FORCE: P. 89

U.S. ARMY: P. 64 TOP

U.S. COAST GUARD PUBLIC AFFAIRS STAFF: PP. 72-73 ALL, 75 BOTH

U.S. MARINE CORPS: P. 82 BOTH

U.S. NAVAL HISTORICAL CENTER: PP. 2, 8-9, 14-15, 17 TOP BOTH, 20-21, 21 BOTTOM (BOTH), 22 TOP, 23 ALL, 24, 25 LEFT, 27 INSET, 29, 30, 31, 39 LEFT & BOTTOM, 43, 46 LEFT, 51 BOTH, 52 BOTTOM LEFT & RIGHT, 52-53, 57 TOP & BOTTOM LEFT, 60 RIGHT & BOTTOM, 62-63, 64 BOTTOM, 67, 69 BOTH, 90, 91 TOP, 92-93, 95, 97 BOTTOM, 102 RIGHT, 108 BOTH; COURTESY OF THE INTERNATIONAL NAVAL RESEARCH ORGANIZATION, KARL GOGG COLLECTION: PP. 26 BOTTOM, 36 LEFT, 40 TOP, 40 BOTTOM & CENTER LEFT; COURTESY OF MR. F. M. LINDLEY: P. 21 TOP; PAINTING, FRANCIS MULLER: P. 46 RIGHT

U.S. NAVY: PP. 76 TOP, 77, 98-99, 100 BOTH, 101 LEFT, 112 BOTH, 114, 115 BOTTOM, 118

OLIVER YOURKE, ILLUSTRATIONS: PP. 22 BOTTOM, 26 TOP, 28 RIGHT, 34, 65, 84-85 BOTTOM, 106 BOTTOM, 122 LEFT, 123 TOP, 128, 134 LEFT

INDEX

A-1 (British), 26, 27, *27*
Aboukir (cruiser), *30*, 31, 35
Accumulators, 20
Aces
   Kretschmer, Otto, 67, 68
   Morton, Dudley Walker "Mush," 82, 86
   Schepke, Joachim, 68
   Walker, F.J., 68
Acheron, 32, 33
Adder (Submarine No.3), 20, *20*, 21, *21*, 28, *28*
Adriatic Sea, 26, *26*, 34, 39, 41
Affray, 117
AG-14 (Russian), 43
Agano (cruiser), 82
Aigrette, 22, 28, *28*
Aircraft, 67
   anti-submarine, 45, 67, 68, 77
   Avengers, 91
   B-24, 71
   bombers, 68, 70
   dive-bombers, 79
   helicopters, 138
   land-based, 69
   Liberators, 70, 138
   long-range, 71, 74
   maritime patrol, 138
   patrol, 46, 95
   seaplanes, 79
   spy, 112
   surveillance, 124
Akula, 27, *27*, 43, *43*
Albacore, 86, 103
Aleutian Islands, 77, 80
Allied Submarine Detection Investigation Committee, 50
Amalfi (cruiser), 39
Antisubmarine operations, 45—46, 50, 65, 74, 76, 95—97, 102, 116, 121, 134, 135, 138
Antitorpedo nets, 41, 42, *42*
Antonio Sciesa, 61, *61*, 91, *91*
Archerfish, 88
Argonaut (SF-7), 83
Ariel (destroyer), 33
Armando Diaz (cruiser), 66
Artic Circle, 65, 68
ASDIC. *See* Sonar
Athenia (liner), 64
Atlantic Ocean, 51, 70—74
Atrocities, 43

Australia, 79, 80, 88, 129
Austro-Hungarian Navy, 35, 39, 44

B-11 (British), 42
Ballast tanks, 19, *25*, 26, *26*, 28, 52, *52*, 61, *61*
Baltic Sea, 26, 29, 31, 35, 39, 42—43, 60, 68, 112
Baralong (Q-ship), 45
Barbarossa (battleship), 42
Barents Sea, 64, 121
Barham (battleship), 69
Bars, 43
Batfish (SS-310), 80
Bathyscaphes, 135
Batteries, 22, 94
   "accumulators," 20
   electric, 26
   explosions, 26, 116
   lead-acid, 20
   leaking, 26
   nickel-cadmium, 20
   safety of, 51
Battle of Dogger Bank, 36, *36*
Battle of Jutland, 44
Battle of the Philippine Sea, 86
Battle of the Santa Cruz Islands, 82
Bauer, Hermann, 37
Bauer, William, 16, 17
Belgium, 37, 47
Berwick Castle (liner), 26, 27
Birmingham (cruiser), 34
Black Sea, 39, 42, 60
Blockades, 17, 37, 38, 39, 43, 64, 65
"Bloody Winter," 71
Blucher (cruiser), 36, *36*
Bluegill, 86
Bluenoses, 111, 116
Boston (Massachusetts), 16
Boston Navy Yard, 54
Bremerton (Washington), 79
Brest (France), 67
British Admiralty, 31, 46
Brooklyn Navy Yard, 49, *49*
Buoyancy, 16, 26
   reserve, 22
Bushnell, David, 16
Buyo Maru (troopship), 86

C-24 (British), 45
C-44 (British), 35, *35*

Camp Nicholls, 19, *19*
Canada, 67, 115, 128, 129
Carbonero, 99
Cavalla, 86
Charles Martel (battleship), 25
Charleston (South Carolina), 19
Christie, Ralph, 88
City of Rome (steamer), 54
Civil War, 18—19
Cochino (SS-345), 92, 93, 116, 117
Codes, 67, 68, 69, 70, 71, 74, 79, 121
Cold War, 111—124
Columbia (SSN-771), *1*, 131, *131*
Commerce warfare, 37—39, 44—45, 50, 63, 64, 66—68, 80, 82, 88, 90
Communications
   equipment, 43
   HF/DF, 68, 71, 75, 91
   intelligence, 43
   long-range, 53
   radio, 68
   technology, 131
Communism, containment of, 111—124
Computers, 133
   fire control, 75
   tactical data, 77
   technology, 97
   torpedo data, 52
Conqueror, 123
Conte Rosse (transport), 66
Convoys, 45, 46, 64, 67, 68, 69, 70, 71, 74, 75, 82, 88
Coral Sea, 79
Cort, Henry, 15
Covington (transport), 44, *44*
Cressy (cruiser), 35
Crumbaugh, William, 72, *73*
Curie, 39
Cuttlefish (SS-171), 83, *83*
Cyclops (freighter), 69

D-1 (British), *30*, 31
Dardanelles, 41—42
David, 18, 19
Deep Submergence Vehicles, 135
"Delousing," 117
Denmark, 17, 29, 35, 37
Depth charges, 45, 68
   nuclear, 96
Depth gauges, *3*, 29
Der Brandtaucher, 16
Deschimag Shipyard, 69, *69*

Diesel, Rudolf, 20, 22
Disarmament conferences, 50
Disasters
   circular torpedo runs, 90
   collisions, 74, 117
   disappearances, 90
   explosions, 26, 116, 117, 121
   fires, 116, 121
   flooding, 116, 117
   friendly fire, 74, 90
   radiation, 121
   rammings, 26, 27, 54, 117
   sinkings, 26, 36, 61
   unsecured hatches, 26
   valve failure, 26, 117
Diving
   bells, 15
   mechanics, 25, 26, *26*, 122, *122*
Doenitz, Karl, 63, 64, 67, 69, 70, 71, 74, 75, 76
Dolphin, 52
Dorado, 90
Dover Barrage, 45
Dragon (cruiser), 66
Drebbel, Cornelius, 15
Drum (SS-228), 76
Duane (cutter), 72
Dublin (cruiser), 39
Dutch East Indies, 60, 77, 80

E-2 (British), 46, *46*
E-3 (British), 43
E-8 (British), 43
E-9 (British), 34
E-11 (British), 42
E-14 (British), 42
Engines
   combustion, 22, 29
   diesel, 22, 25, 49, 51, 52, 102, 129, 131
   diesel-electric, 22, 56, 61
   electric, 20, 49
   gasoline, 19, 22, 49
   kerosene, 20, 22, 29
   rocket, 108
   seizures, 28
   steam, 19, 23, 26, 30
   tests, 26
English Channel, 30, 45, 67
"Enigma," 68
Enright, Joseph, 88
Enterprise (carrier), 118
Ethan Allen (SSBN-608), 109, *109*

Falkenhayn, Erich von, 44
Falklands War, 123, 131
Farfadet, 26, 28, *28*
Fire control, 52, 56, 61, 75
Fisher, Sir John, 31, 36
Flanders Flotilla, 47
Flasher, 86
Flounder, 90
Foca, 28, *28*
Forelle, 29
Formidable, 36
Foucault, 45
France, 15, 29, 30, 31, 35, 39, 42, 43, 44, 49, 50, 51, 59, 63, 64
Friendly fire, 74, 90
Fulton, Robert, 16, 17

Garrett, George, 19
Gato (SS-212), 79, *79*
George V (King of England), 29
George Washington (SSBN-598), 108, *108*, 122
Georgia (SSBN-727), 125, *125*
German Imperial Navy, 31, 35, 47, 49
   Admiralstab, 37, 44
   High Seas Fleet, 36
   Kriegsmarine, 63, 66, 67, 68, 69, 76
   Germany, 29, 30, 31, 51, 63
   in World War I, 36, 39
   in World War II, 63—76
Gibralter-Suez trade routes, 44
Gifu Maru, 87, *87*
Gilbert Islands, 77, 83
Glitra (merchant), 37
Gneisenau, 69
Grampus (SS-207), 78, *78*
Grayback (SSG-574), 100, *100*, 101, *101*, 114, 115
Great Britain, 29, 30, 31, 49, 50
   in World War I, 35, 39, 42, 43, 44, 46
   in World War II, 63, 64
Great War. *See* World War I
Groton (Connecticut), 109, 125, *125*
Growler (SSG-577), 100, *100*, *114*, 115
Guadalcanal, 82
Gudgeon, 80, 116
Guerre de course. See Commerce wars
Guns
   breech-loading, 22
   deck, 52, 56, 57, *57*, 59, 60, 65, 65, 77, 84, 88, 88
   hydraulic recoil, 22

machine, 51, 52, 84, 88, 88
  machine cannons, 52
  quick-firing, 22
Gustave Zédé, 22, 22, 23, 23, 25
Gymnôte, 22, 23, 23, 25
Gyroscopes, 20

Halfbeak (SS-352), 112, 112
Hangor, 131
Hardegan, Reinhard, 69
Harder, 116
Hart, Thomas, 51
Hatches, 26, 54, 54
  escape, 61
Hawke (cruiser), 36
Hela (cruiser), 34
Helicopters, 138
Hermes (carrier), 36
Hersing, Otto, 41, 42, 43
Hitler, Adolf, 64, 68
H.L. Hunley (CSS), 19
Hogue (cruiser), 35
Holder (DE-401), 75
Holland, 37, 38, 60
Holland, John, 19, 20, 22, 26, 28
Holland Submarine Company, 20, 20
Holland (Submarine No.1), 20, 20, 22, 22,
  24, 24, 26
Hornet (carrier), 82
Hotel, 118, 121
Housatonic (USS), 19
Hulls
  airtight, 22
  circular, 28
  designs, 28, 28
  double, 22, 26
  interior, 22
  outer, 22, 102
  pressure, 22, 52, 94
  tear-drop, 103, 121
  Walter, 76
Hydrophones, 45, 50, 71, 77, 94, 97, 121,
  124, 131

I-6 (Japanese), 79
I-21 (Japanese), 82
I-173 (Japanese), 80
Indian Ocean, 50, 59, 74, 80, 90, 115
Intelligence, 68, 82
  communications, 43
  gathering, 51, 56, 112, 116, 123

German, 71
  signals, 112
Intelligent Whale, 19
Italy, 39, 50, 59, 66

Janckendorff, Heinrich von Nostitz und,
  46
Japan, 49, 50, 54, 56, 59, 76—91
Jean Bart (flagship), 39
Jellicoe, Sir John, 45
Juneau (cruiser), 82

Kaiser, Henry, 69
Karlsruhe, 69
Kinashi, Takaichi, 82
Kleinkrieg, 31, 37, 39, 59
Komatsu, Teruhisa, 80
Komsomolets, 121
Kongo (battleship), 88
Korean War, 94, 111, 116
Kretschmer, Otto, 64, 67, 68
Kriegsmarine, 63, 66, 67, 68, 69, 76

Laurenti, Caesare, 22, 26
Leipzig (cruiser), 65
Lemp, Fritz-Julius, 64
Lend-lease, 67
Leninist, 108
Leninsky Komsomol, 115, 115
Leon Gambetta (cruiser), 39, 40
Lethbridge, John, 15
Ling (SS-297), 3, 84, 84—85
Liscome Bay (carrier), 82
Lockwood, Charles, 51, 80, 88
London Naval Treaty, 50
Lusitania (liner), 38, 38
Lvica, 43

M-1 (British), 50
Madden, Sir Charles, 45
Majestic (battleship), 42
Mare Island Navy Yard, 31, 31, 79, 94, 94,
  115
Marshall Islands, 88
Marshall Plan, 94
Mayason (transport), 90
Mediterranean Sea, 30, 39, 41, 44, 59, 66,
  68, 69
Messudiyeh (dreadnought), 42

Midway, 79, 83
Midway (carrier), 90
Minefields, 45, 49
Mines, 42, 65
  automatic deployment, 134
  magnetic, 96
  mobile, 20
  rocket-assisted, 96
  self-propelled, 20
  underwater, 20
Missiles, 123
  air-breathing cruise, 134
  antiship, 139
  ballistic, 95, 99, 106
  Harpoon, 134
  intercontinental ballistic, 13
  launchers, 99, 106
  Polaris, 108, 108, 109, 116
  Regulus, 115
  Scud, 99
  sea-launched, 13, 134
  sea-skimming, 134
  submarine-launched ballistic, 108
  technology, 94, 97
  Tomahawk, 134, 138
Mizuho (carrier), 77
Moccasin (Submarine No.5)
Mohican (sloop-of-war), 25, 25
Mohr, Johann, 69
Moller, Paul, 72, 72
Momsen Lung, 54
Montgolfier, 57, 57
Morse, 22
Morton, Dudley Walker "Mush," 82, 86

Narval, 22, 26, 28, 28
Natsushio (destroyer), 77
Nautilus (SS-168), 16, 16, 58—59, 59, 77,
  77, 79, 102, 104, 104, 106, 106
Navies of
  Austria, 30, 34, 39, 44
  Canada, 128
  Denmark, 17, 29, 31
  France, 29, 30, 34, 39, 42, 90
  Germany, 20, 29, 31, 34, 37, 47, 49, 50,
    67, 68, 69, 91, 94, 127
  Great Britain, 22, 29, 30, 31, 34, 37, 39,
    42, 44, 45, 46, 50, 65, 66, 67, 68, 69,
    111, 127, 131
  Holland, 91
  Italy, 30, 39, 59, 66, 69, 91
  Japan, 54, 56, 59

Poland, 66
Russia, 17, 42
Sweden, 137
Turkey, 39
United States, 20, 20, 26, 47, 54, 56,
  69, 96, 99, 111, 127
Nereide, 39
New Ironsides (blockader), 19
New York City (SSN-696), 136, 136
Nicosian (merchant), 43
Nordenfelt, 23, 23
North Atlantic Treaty Organization, 111,
  112, 115—118, 121, 124, 128
North Carolina (battleship), 82
North Sea, 31, 34, 35, 36, 39, 41, 44, 69
Norway, 38, 65, 66, 68, 69, 76
Norworth, Leopold, 72, 73
Nurnberg (cruiser), 65

O-2 (SS-63), 52, 52
Oakville (corvette), 68, 68
O'Brien (destroyer), 82
Ohio, 28, 28
Oi (cruiser), 86
Okinoshima (cruiser), 77
Otway, 129
Oxley, 74, 129

Pacific Ocean, 50, 76—90
Palladia (cruiser), 42—43
Parkgate (steamer), 37, 37
Pathfinder (cruiser), 34
Paulding, 54
Pearl Harbor (Hawaii), 4—5, 59, 66, 68,
  76, 80
Peregudov, Vladimir Nikolayevich, 103
Periscopes, 25, 29, 33, 36, 36, 40, 40, 42,
  51, 88, 88
Permit (SS-178), 2
Philippines, 21, 25, 29, 29, 77, 80, 90
Phillips, Lodner, 17
Piccard, Auguste, 135
Pickerel (SS-177), 2
Plunger (Submarine No.2), 2, 20, 20, 26,
  29, 80
Pluviose, 28, 28
Poland, 51, 64, 66
Pollack, 80
Polyanthus (escort), 75
Pompon (SS-267), 97
Porpoise (Submarine No.7), 20, 20, 52, 96

Porter (destroyer), 82
Posen (dreadnought), 36
Prien, Kapitanleutnant, 64
Principe Umberto (transport), 40
Prinz Adalbert, 43
Prize Regulations, 37, 43, 44, 50, 64, 65
Propellers, 26
  cavitation, 97
  horizontal, 16, 16
  noise, 74
  nuclear, 106
  pump-jet, 135
  rear, 17
  slow-blade, 135
  treadmill-powered, 16
  vertical, 16, 16
Propulsion
  air-independent, 135
  battery, 22
  hydrogen peroxide, 75
  liquid-fuel, 108
  nuclear, 13, 99—109, 112
  solid-fuel, 108
  steam, 19
  surface, 16, 25
Provence (liner), 43

Q-ships, 45
Queen Elizabeth (battleship), 66
Queenfish, 90

Radar, 64, 68, 71, 74, 75, 82, 87, 88, 131,
  134, 138
  Distant Early Warning, 97
  short-wave, 96
Ramillies (battleship), 66, 79
Redfish, 88
Reich, Eli, 86
Remotely Operated Vehicles, 135
Resolution, 108
Retvizan (battleship), 24, 24
Rhode Island (SSBN-740), 12—13, 132—
  133, 133
Rickover, Hyman, 102
Roballo (SS-273), 90, 90
Robert E. Lee (SSBN-601), 10—11
Roosevelt, Theodore, 29, 38
Root, Elihu, 50
Rose, Hans, 39
"Rotterdam ship," 16, 16
Rowell (escort), 90

Royal Air Force, 91
Royal Australian Navy, 129
Royal Navy, 22, 29, 30, 31, 34, 36, 37, 39, 44, 45, 50, 65, 66, 67, 68, 69, 96, 111, 131
  Coastal Command, 67, 74
Rurik (cruiser), 27, *27*
Russia, 17, 31, 35, 42, 60. *See also* Soviet Union

S-4 (SS-109), 54, *54—55*
S-48 (SS-159), 52, *52*
St. Croix (escort), 75
St. Nazaire (France), 67
Salmon (SS-182), *2*, 52, 65
San Diego (cruiser), 46, *46*
Sandlance, 86
San Luis, 124, *124*, 131
Santay (transport), 40, *40*
Saratoga (carrier), 79, 82
Sargo (SSN-583), 52, *110*, 111
Sawfish, 88
Scamp, 116
Schepke, Joachim, 64, 68
Schleswig-Holstein War, 16
Schnee, Adalbert, 76
Scorpion (SS-278), 76, 116, 117, 119, *119*
Scotland, 36, 72, *73*
Screws, 16, *16*
Seadragon (SS-194), 87, *87*
Sea Dragon (SSN-584), 115, *115*
Sealion, 86, 88
Seal (SS-183), *2*, 56, *56*
Sea of Marmara, 42
Seawolf (SSN-21), 87, *87*, 90, 134, *134*
Self-noise, 97, 103, 106
Shark (Submarine No.8), 88
Shinano (carrier), 88
Shinyo (carrier), 86
Ships
  battleships, 24, *24*, 25, 41, 42, *42*, 50, 65, 66, 69, 79, 82, 88
  blockaders, 19
  capital, 47, 59
  carriers, 36, 71, 77, 80, 82, 88
  corvettes, 74
  cruisers, 30, 31, 34, 35, 36, 39, 42—43, 43, 46, *46*, 50, 65, 66, 77, 82, 86
  cutters, 72
  destroyers, 30, 33, 42, 46, 82, 88
  dreadnoughts, 31, 34, 36
  escort, 66, 67, 75

fishing, 65
freighters, 69
gunboats, 42
Liberty, 75
liners, 26, 38, *38*, 43, 64
merchant, 37—39, 42—43, *43*, 47, 49, 64, 65, 67, 68
mine-layers, 27, 31
patrol, 20, 29, 45, 67
Q-ships, 45
sloops-of-war, 19, 25, *25*
steamers, 42, 54
surface, 22
tankers, 66
torpedo boat destroyers, 22
torpedo boats, 19, *19*, 20, 22, 30, 31, 41
training, 79, 84
transports, 40, *40*, 42, 44, *44*, 66, 90
trawlers, 45
Shokaku, 86
Silversides (SS-236), 88, *88*
Sirène, 22
Skate, 82
Skate (SSN-578), 102, *102*, 112, *112*
Skipjack, 103
Snapper (SS-185), *2*
Sonar, 50, 51, 68, 71, 77, 82, 95, 103, 112, 116, 117, 124
  active, 50, 115
  buoys, 74
  circular, 97
  dipping, 96, 138
  passive, 50
  scanning, 135
Sonobuoys, 96, 138
Soryu (carrier), 79
Sound Surveillance System, 97
Soviet Union, 66
  Cold War submarine strategy, 111—115, 118, 121
Spadefish, 90
Speiss, Johann, 35
Spencer, 72
Spiegel, Adolf K.G.E. von, 43
Sturgeon (SSN-637), 106, *107*, 121
Submarines
  A-class, 20, *20*, 25, *25*, 27, *27*
  attack, 123, *123*
  coastal, 60
  Cold War strategies for, 111—124
  combustion engine, 22
  defensive uses, 34
  detection, 74, 75, 76

diesel-electric, 13, 25, 65, *65*, 96, 97, 112, 118, 129, 131
dual-drive, 26
early, *15—19*
E-class, 28, *28*
electric, 22
electrical systems, 52
experimental, 16, 54, 135
G-type, 28, *28*
high speed, 94—95
interiors, 21, *21*, 33, 84, *84—85*
long-range, 41, 44, 50, 51, 56, 60
mapping, 116
mercantile, 46
midget, 65, 66, *66*
"milch cows," 64, 69, 74
mine-layers, 42
minesweeping, 36
missile, 106
NATO, 115
nuclear, 13, 28, 99—109, 121
O-class, 8—9
patrol, 31, 35, 36, 52, 59, 67, 86, 108, 116
peacetime uses, 135
post-war strategy, 93—109
prewar strategies, 29—31
production, 69, 70
radar picket, 97
S-class, 4—5
  screening, 35
  sea trials, 26
  short-range, 42
  steam-driven, 19
  strategic missile, 97—99
  three-man, 16
  tracking, 115
  transport, 82
  two-man, 22
  X-craft, 66
Submarines, American, 99
  Adder, 20, *20*, 21, *21*, 28, *28*
  Albacore, 86, 103
  Archerfish, 88
  Argonaut (SF-7), 83, *83*
  Balao class, 84, *84—85*
  Batfish (SS-310), 80
  Bluegill, 86
  Carbonero, 99
  Charlie class, 121
  Cochino, 116, 117
  Cuttlefish, 83, *83*
  Dolphin, 52

Drum (SS-228), 76
Flasher, 86
Flounder, 90
George Washington, 122
Georgia (SSBN-727), 125, *125*
Grayback (SSG-574), 100, *100*
Growler (SSG-577), 100, *100*, 101, *101*
Gudgeon, 80, 116
Harder, 116
Holland, 20, *20*, 22, *22*, 24, *24*, 26
Hotel, 118, 121
Los Angeles class, 122, 136, 138
Moccasin, 20, *20*
Nautilus (SS-168), 77, *77*, 79, 102, 104, *104*, 106, *106*
New York City (SSN-696), 136, *136*
O-2 (SS-63), 52, *52*
Ohio class, 28, *28*, 124, 130, *130*
Plunger, 20, *20*, 29, 80
Pollack, 80
Pompon (SS-267), 97
Porpoise, 20, *20*, 52, 96
Redfish, 88
Rhode Island (SSBN-740), *132—133*, 133
S-4 (SS-109), 54, *54—55*
S-48 (SS-159), 52, *52*
Salmon, 52
Sandlance, 86
Sargo (SSN-583), 52, *110*, 111
Sawfish, 88
Scamp, 116
Scorpion (SS-278), 76, 116, 117, 119, *119*
Seadragon (SS-194), 87, *87*
Sea Dragon (SSN-584), 115, *115*
Sealion, 86, 88
Seawolf (SSN-21), 87, *87*, 90, 134, *134*
Shark, 20, *20*, 88
Silversides (SS-236), 88, *88*
Skate (SSN-578), 82, 102, *102*
Skipjack, 103
Sturgeon (SSN-637), 106, *107*, 121
Swordfish, 116
Tautog, 117
Thomas A. Edison, 117
Thrasher, *14—15*, 15, 26, 28
Thresher, 117
V-2 (SS-164), 53, *53*
Wahoo (SS-238), 82, 86, *86*
Wyoming (SSBN-742), 122, *122*
Yankee class, 121, 124
Submarines, Australian, 129, 137

Submarines, Austrian
  U-1, 40, *40*
  U-2, 39
  U-4, 39
  U-5, 39, 40, *40*
  U-25, 40, *40*
Submarines, British, 65—66
  A-1, 26, 27, *27*
  Affray, 117
  B-11, 42
  C-24, 45
  C-44, 35, *35*
  Churchill class, 122
  Conqueror, 123
  E-2, 46, *46*
  E-3, 43
  E-8, 43
  E-9, 34
  E-11, 42
  E-14, 42
  M-1, 50
  Oberon class, 74, 96, 129
  Oxley, 74
  Resolution, 108
  Salmon, 65
  Swiftsure class, 122
  Trafalgar class, 122
  Triton, 74
  Truculent, 117
  Upholder class, 128, *128*
Submarines, Dutch, 80
Submarines, French, 74, 90
  Aigrette, 28, *28*
  Curie, 39
  Daphne class, 129, 131
  Diane class, 57, *57*, 59
  Farfadet, 26, 28, *28*
  Foucault, 45
  Gustave Zédé, 22, *22*, 23, *23*, 25
  Gymnôte, 22, 23, *23*, 25
  Montgolfier, 57, *57*
  Narval, 22, 26, 28, *28*
  Pluviose, 28, *28*
  Redoubtable class, 59, 60, *60*, 108
  Surcouf, 59, 60, *60*, 74
  Turquoise, 43
Submarines, German
  Forelle, 29
  Type IIA, 51
  Type IX, 51, 63, 64, *64*, 68
  Type VII, 51, 63, 69, 76
  Type VIIC, 63, 65, *65*, 69, *69*
  Type XXI, 76, 95

Type XXIII, 76
U-1, 28, *28*
U-3, 26
U-9, 35, 36
U-15, 34
U-20, 38
U-21, 34, 41
U-24, 36
U-26, 42—43
U-27, 36, 45
U-28, 36, *36*
U-30, 64
U-35, 43
U-36, 45, 65
U-46, 67
U-48, 67
U-51, 61
U-53, 39, *39*
U-86, 44
U-110, 68
U-123, 69
U-124, 69
U-151, 46, 47
U-202, 43
U-331, 69
U-338, 75
U-384, 71
U-537, 90
U-549, 69
U-664, 71, *71*
UB-14, 39, 43
UB-57, 61
UB-88, 47, *47*
UC-5, 50, *50*
Submarines, Italian
  Antonio Sciesa, 61, *61*, 91, *91*
  Balilla class, 59, 61, *61*
  Foca, 28, *28*
  Marcello class, 59
  Nereide, 39
  Tricheco, 61, *61*
Submarines, Japanese, 77, 82
  I-6, 79
  I-21, 82
  I-173, 80
Submarines, Russian, 103, *103*
  AG-14, 43
  Akula, 43, *43*
  Bars, 43
  Delphin, 26
  Delta class, 121
  Foxtrot class, 112, *112*
  Komsomolets, 121

Leninist, 108
Leninsky Komsomol, 115, *115*
Livca, 43
November class, 115, *115*, 118
Typhoon, 138, *138*, 139
Victor class, 121
Whiskey class, 112, *112*
Zulu class, 95, 97, 99
Submarines, Swedish, 57, *57*
Submersibles, 13, 16, *16*, 17, *17*
Surcouf, 59, 60, *60*, 74
Surfacing mechanics, 25, 26, *26*, 122, *122*
Sweden, 38, 43, 137
Swieger, Walther, 38, *38*
Swordfish, 116

Taiyo (carrier), 86
Tanabe, Yahachi, 80
Taranak (trawler), 45
Tatsuta (cruiser), 86
Tautog, 117, 118
Technology, 13
  battery, 20
  communications, 131
  computer, 97, 131, 135
  digital, 131, 133—135
  electronic, 53, 131
  engines, 29
  limitations of, 15—31
  metal, 15
  missile, 94, 97
  sensors, 50
  sonar, 96
  weapons, 22, 29, 50
Thomas A. Edison (SSBN-610), 116, *116*, 117
Thresher (SSN-539), *14—15*, 15, 26, 28, 117, *117*
Tirpitz, Alfred von, 31
Tirpitz (battleship), 65, 66
Tobruk, 91
Torpedo boats, 19, *19*, 20, 22, 30, 31, 41
Torpedos, 16, *16*, 19, 20, 21, *21*, 30
  acoustic, 74, 75, 94, 133
  air-dropped, 96
  antisubmarine, 96
  detonators, 77
  exercise, 78, *78*
  failures, 65, 80
  firing solutions, 33, 34
  hedgehog, 75, *75*, 90, 95
  homing, 134, 138

"hot," 117
Long Lance, 56
long-range, 123
long-running, 82
Mark-14, 77
Mark-48, 129
  reliability, 77
  rocket-launched, 138
  shooting, 33—34
  short-range, 123
  Type 95, 82
  Whitehead, 29
  wire-guided, 134
  zaunkonig, 75
Trapp, Georg Ritter von, 39
Tricheco, 61, *61*
Triton, 74
Triumph (battleships), 41, 42, *42*
Trondheim (Norway), 69, *69*
Truculent, 117
Truk, 82
Turquoise (French), 43
Turtle, 16, *16*
Typhoon, 138, *138*, 139

U-1 (Austrian), 40, *40*
U-1 (German), 28, *28*
U-2 (Austrian), 39
U-3 (German Submarines,), 26
U-4 (Austrian), 39
U-5 (Austrian), 39, 40, *40*
U-9 (German), 34, 35, 36
U-12 (German), *32*, 33
U-15 (German), 34
U-20 (German), 38
U-21 (German), 34, 41
U-24 (German), 36
U-25 (Austrian), 40, *40*
U-26 (German), 42—43
U-27 (German), 36, 45
U-28 (German), 36, *36*
U-30 (German), 64
U-35 (German), 43
U-36 (German), 45, 65
U-46 (German), 67
U-48 (German), 67
U-51 (German), 61
U-53 (German), 39, *39*
U-86 (German), 44
U-110 (German), 68
U-123 (German), 69
U-124 (German), 69

U-151 (German), 46, 47
U-175 (German), 72, *72*, *73*
U-202 (German), 43
U-331 (German), 69
U-338 (German), 75
U-384 (German), 71
U-537 (German), 90
U-549 (German), 69
U-664 (German), 71, *71*
UB-14 (German), 39, 43
UB-57 (German), 61
UB-88 (German), 47, *47*
UC-5 (German), 50, *50*
Ultra, 68, 69, 75
Underhill (escort), 66
United Nations, 93
United States Naval Academy, 26, 102
United States Navy, 20, *20*, 22, 26, 44, 47, 54, 56, 69, 96, 99, 102, 111
  Bureau of Construction and Repair, 26
  Bureau of Ordnance, 77
  Operational Development Force, 94
  Pacific Fleet, 25, *25*, 79
  Pacific Fleet Submarine Force, 80
  Submarine Officers Conference, 51
Unryu (carrier), 88
Unyo (carrier), 86
Urakaze (destroyer), 88

V-2 (SS-164), 53, *53*
Valiant (battleship), 66
Versailles Treaty, 50, 64
Vittorio Veneto (battleship), 66
Von Arnauld de la Perière, Lothar, 43

Wahoo (SS-238), 82, 86, *86*
Wake Island, 77
Walker, F.J., 68, 74
Walter, Helmuth, 75
Wannamacher, Peter, 72, *72*
Wars
  American Civil, 18—19
  Arab-Israeli, 129
  Boer War, 31
  Falklands, 123—124, 131
  Napoleonic, 29, 31
  Schleswig-Holstein, 16
World War I, 33—47
World War II, 63—91
Wasp (carrier), 82
Weapons. *See also* Guns

anti-aircraft, 65, *65*, 75
anti-ship rockets, 134
antisubmarine, 45, 65, 135, *135*
atomic, 94
breech-loading guns, 22
depth charges, 45, 68
fast-sinking, 95
improvements, 61
mortars, 95
nuclear, 96, 99
quick-firing guns, 22
suicide, 66
Weddigen, Otto, 35, 36
Wehner, Frederick, 19, *19*
Weppelmann, Walter, 72, *72*
Whitehead, Alfred, 20
Wickes (DD-75), 47
Wilhelm Gustloff, 91
Wilkes, John, 80
Wilson, Woodrow, 38, 44, 45
Wolf, Dieter, 72, *72*
Wolf packs, 64, 67, 68, 71, 88
World War I, 33—47
World War II, 63—91
Wyoming (SSBN-742), 122, *122*

X-craft, 66

Yorktown (carrier), 80

Yubari (cruiser), 86
Zédé, Gustav, 22